D0426469

THE SMOKING PUZZLE

The Smoking Puzzle

Information, Risk Perception, and Choice

Frank A. Sloan

V. Kerry Smith

Donald H. Taylor, Jr.

HARVARD UNIVERSITY PRESS

Cambridge, Massachusetts

London, England 2003

Printed in the United States of America

Library of Congress Cataloging-in-Publication Data

Sloan, Frank A.
The smoking puzzle : information, risk perception, and choice /
Frank A. Sloan, V. Kerry Smith, Donald H. Taylor, Jr.
p. cm.
Includes bibliographical references and index.
ISBN 0-674-01039-6
1. Smoking—Health aspects. 2. Cigarette smokers—Attitudes.
3. Cigarette smokers—Health risk assessment. 4. Risk perception.
I. Smith, V. Kerry (Vincent Kerry), 1945– II. Taylor, Donald H. III. Title.

RA645.T62S58 2003
613.85—dc21 2002192185

Contents

Preface

To put it mildly, smoking is a major public health problem. It is also a personal health problem affecting nearly all of us in some way. The following quotation from an e-mail message sent by a colleague at another university is illustrative. The colleague was reacting to a recent conversation one of us had had with him about this book:

> I was taken by the topic. At age 50, my father, with about 80 pack years of smoking, stopped cold turkey on being diagnosed with lung cancer and stayed off until his death (from a pneumonia that would not have been fatal but for the long-term effects of his first and second primary lung cancers) 19 years later. He had long known of the bad health effects of smoking and had strongly (and persuasively, as it turned out) advised all three of his children never to smoke, but he had never even (as far as I can recall) tried to stop before his cancer (he had switched to low-tar cigarettes maybe 8 to 10 years before). An anecdote is not data, but his story seems consistent with your findings.

Some progress is being made, as reflected in the drop in the smoking rate for older persons, from 42 percent in 1965 to 25 percent in 1990. However, progress has been slow since then, primarily because the rate among young persons has failed to decline. Although smoking prevalence has fallen among older Americans, there is ample reason to question whether the rate of decline has been good enough, particularly in view of the high toll smoking takes in the forms of death, morbidity, and disability, as well as pain and suffering before death.

New policies are clearly needed. A two-part strategy—discouraging the young from picking up the habit and encouraging older persons to quit—

seems warranted. Although the vast majority of people start smoking when they are adolescents, quitting occurs at a much later age, often after the health impact of the habit has become noticeable to the individual.

This book begins with the premise that information must be relevant and understandable to the people who are intended to use it. Just because someone publishes a warning does not mean it will be read and understood by the target audience. If an employee of a major advertising agency were to propose that a successful campaign could be based on 2-by-½-inch ads, that person undoubtedly would be encouraged to seek his livelihood elsewhere.

Designing a successful information strategy should require no less work than designing a successful ad. To determine which information strategies are likely to be successful, we have studied the success of past public information policies in reducing demand for cigarettes. While the link between information about smoking and demand has been investigated in earlier research, a critical link in the causal chain between information and behavioral change has been ignored. That link is smokers' risk perceptions. For the public health objectives to be achieved, information programs must influence smokers' perceptions of the underlying risks of smoking. Our research provides evidence on this critical link.

Although this book is about smoking and public policies designed to reduce the prevalence of smoking, these issues are considered within the broader context of human behavior when choices call into question the merits of consumer sovereignty. Smoking as a topic of inquiry provides a window on a number of larger questions about personal decision making. Are people rational? Do they really take account of the future consequences of present actions? Why do some people engage in behaviors that are potentially harmful while others do not? How do people process information about their health? What are the bounds on people's cognitive abilities, and how do those limitations affect the design of risk messages? To the extent that constraints and cognition are important, how do they vary among individuals? How do people handle uncertainty that extends over very long time spans, when the threats of concern are likely to occur in the distant future?

Public information strategies can vary—from a laissez-faire approach of providing information on probabilities of harm and relying on consumers to make the ultimate decision about their behavior to a much more activist set of policies that seek to impose paternalistic constraints on choices. Although we are generally sympathetic to the notion of consumer sovereignty, our research clearly shows that not all information programs are created equal. A message removed from the relevant context and format has little hope of influencing individuals' risk perceptions or behavior. However, as we demonstrate, risk perceptions and behavior can be changed if the message is appropriately designed. Risk communication must be based on listening to people and then responding with relevant information.

For messages about the health risks of long-term addictive behaviors to be effective, people must consider the future consequences of decisions they make today. We find some evidence that people are forward looking, but regarding the ability to deal with probabilistic outcomes, people are very heterogeneous. The challenge for policy makers involved in health promotion is to recognize and incorporate responses to this heterogeneity as a part of policy design.

This book has several different audiences. Our primary conceptual framework is economic, but our analysis and results are also important for psychologists and specialists in public health and public policy. To our knowledge, our study is the first economic study to investigate information, risk perception, and choice together. Most of the book is nontechnical, and we provide explanatory material to assist readers when we use economic concepts. It is our hope that this research may encourage others to apply our general approach to studying other health behaviors as well.

Acknowledgments

This study was supported in part by a grant from the Robert Wood Johnson Foundation, administered through the Substance Abuse Research Program located at Wake Forest University. The Substance Abuse Research Program has funded numerous studies on the use of tobacco, alcohol, and illicit substances. The organization holds annual meetings of grantees and distributes a monthly newsletter. We benefited from participating in annual meetings held in Savannah, Georgia; Charleston, South Carolina; and Santa Fe, New Mexico.

A successful research project is the result of a team effort. Other members of our research team who are not listed as coauthors include William Desvousges, F. Reed Johnson, Hyun Kim, Tori Knight, Snehal Patel, Peter Rankin, Lynn Van Scoyoc, and Jonathan Yoder. L & E Research organized our focus group sessions and conducted our survey of smokers. We thank participants in the focus groups and the survey for their helpful insights.

Our primary data source was the Health and Retirement Study (HRS), a nationally representative survey of adults in late middle age, conducted by the Institute of Social Research (ISR) Survey Research Center at the University of Michigan. Funding for the HRS comes from the National Institute on Aging. We are very grateful for the survey data. In particular, Cathy Liebowitz of ISR was very helpful in processing our many requests. We also thank the HRS respondents for their help. It is a lengthy survey—one of us participated in a HRS pretest that lasted for two hours and nine minutes. The participants have been surveyed repeatedly.

The disaggregated tobacco price index was provided to us by William Cook of the U.S. Bureau of Labor Statistics. As our discussion in Chapter 8 suggests, these data played an essential role in our demand estimation. We are extremely grateful to him and the staff of the bureau for doing the extra work necessary to make these data available to us.

Portions of this research have been presented at various seminars, including the North Carolina State University Resource Economics Workgroup; the Marketing and Economics research workshop at the Fuqua School of Business at Duke University; the National Bureau of Economic Research; the Massachusetts Institute of Technology Public Finance Workshop; the International Health Economics Association meeting at Rotterdam, in the Netherlands; and the Taipei International Conference on Health Economics, held in Taipai, Taiwan.

We thank Blake Brown, Tom Capehart, Lee Craig, and Wally Thurman for their assistance in developing the annual cigarette price variable for our time series analysis and for explaining the role of the tobacco support program.

Several graduate and undergraduate students assisted in the data collection, telephone contacts, and data checking. Special thanks are due Melissa Brandt, Dimitrios Dadabas, and Michelle Holbrooke.

Several persons participated in preparing the indexes, bibliographic work, and drafts of the manuscript. We thank Alice Bowser, Jack Crawley, Kelly DeMarchis, Susan Hinton, Michelle Newman, Elizabeth Powell, Julia Smith, and Katherine Taylor for their help in turning raw material, in the form of data, handwritten pages, and preliminary typed drafts, into what is (we hope) a readable book.

Particular thanks go to Emily Streyer Carlisle, who edited several revisions of the manuscript, and to Khuwailah O. Beyah, who put it all together in the end.

THE SMOKING PUZZLE

CHAPTER

1

Linking Information, Risk Perception, and Choice: An Economic Approach

Today, no one debates the conclusion that smoking is harmful to one's health, not even smokers. After more than a century's experience with commercial cigarettes, the policy and legal debates have changed dramatically. As a society, we are prepared to question whether teenagers appreciate the consequences of a choice to smoke, and current public policy toward regulating access to cigarettes accepts the premise that a teenager's decision to start smoking must be controlled, because the choice does not appear to be based on a rational evaluation of its implications.

Older smokers, however, face a different context for their choices. The seemingly distant consequences of cigarette smoking at age sixteen are no longer speculative or distant at fifty. Yet heavy levels of cigarette consumption persist among persons in middle age. Is this purely a reflection of the addiction? It is hard to argue that it results from a lack of information. The past decade has seen a substantial change in public sentiment about smoking, as reflected in a dramatic reversal in court rulings—*against* tobacco companies—and an increase in advertisements of products designed to assist in smoking cessation.

Are today's adult smokers uninformed, irrational addicts, or is their behavior explained by something else? Older smokers have heard the health warnings. They do recognize cigarettes as addictive, and they acknowledge the personal hardship they will experience if they try to quit. However, they believe, based on what they have heard from well-intentioned—but misdirected—messages, that the harm they have done to themselves can be fixed shortly after they stop, *that it is all reversible.* Timing is everything for mature long-term smokers. These smokers' actions suggest a life's plan that includes continued cigarette smoking for "a while longer," slow or immediate cessation, and then restored health with no long-term impact on their survival prospects.

Within the groups providing the current warnings about smoking, no one really wants to give them a different message. After all, if we tell long-term smokers that what they have done is not reversible, they might never quit. Death, for the smoker who has not lost a parent or experienced a severe health shock such as lung cancer, a heart attack, or a stroke, is seen as a quick passage. One day a smoker is functioning in fairly good health, perhaps with a few warning signs, such as fatigue after climbing a flight of stairs, and the next he has a life-threatening health crisis. In this context, choices are easily reduced to how many remaining years of good health are put at risk with continued smoking. Reversibility implies it is just a matter of timing the pleasure-pain tradeoff in the short term.

In this study, we find that once smokers realize their perception of the path ahead is incorrect, *they do act.* Very often, this change in perception is the consequence of a personal health shock, such as a heart attack, stroke, or lung cancer. But for individuals in this situation, much of the harm is indeed no longer reversible, and such shocks frequently lead to death. Health shocks of the type that occur with increasing frequency in one's fifties and sixties are a major precipitator of smoking cessation.

Clearly it would be better for everyone if smokers heeded warnings of the dangers of smoking *before* these shocks occur. The sustained smoking habits of so many people in late middle age suggests that information about the harms of smoking is not getting through to a sizable portion of the population. In this book we argue, based in part on empirical evidence, that messages about smoking's harms have not been sufficiently salient to smokers. Although smokers have heard about the threat to longevity, they seem to think the threat applies to someone else, or that dying—presumably instantly and painlessly—does not seem that bad (at least, not before they have reached that point). By contrast, our discussions with smokers revealed that the prospect of years of disability and dependence on others as a result, for example, of lung disease or congestive heart failure, is quite unattractive.

We demonstrate that achieving a reduction in cigarette consumption of 11 to 15 percent is possible using a message informing smokers about the quality of their lives at the end. Based on our estimates of older smokers' cigarette demand, a 40 to 50 percent increase in cigarette prices would be required to accomplish the same size reduction.

Our bottom line is straightforward and optimistic. Offering a dose of reality about a smoker's life at the end of life is not a scare tactic. But it is information that some well-intentioned policy programs have been reluctant to provide.

Our story proceeds through five steps: we establish the context; describe the role of information in choice—information coming from both public sources and highly personalized sources, such as an individual's development of adverse health conditions; study factors that contribute to beliefs about risk and life expectancy; develop a new information message; and evaluate its performance through a policy experiment. These steps integrate the discussion in each of the chapters ahead.

The Context

Private and Public Roles and Responsibilities

Our society places a high value on personal choice. People should be free to allocate their resources in ways that yield the highest levels of personal satisfaction. Our society widely accepts that allowing individuals to make their own choices raises their sense of well-being, higher than it would be if such choices were made by a well-intentioned central planner. A central planner could not account for the heterogeneity of preferences underlying personal choices, and given such heterogeneity, the planner could not know what those preferences are. Also, no planner is immune to the scientific uncertainty inherent in any choice. All points speak for placing the onus of decision making at the most decentralized level possible, on the individual consumer.

The case for various public interventions in smoking decisions, however, is quite strong. However, much of the rationale for such interventions was invented after the fact by scholars and tobacco control advocates, and did not bring about the implementation of government antismoking initiatives, at least not initially.

The notion that the consumption of tobacco products is morally wrong explains the early history of tobacco control. To the extent that a moral society is a public good, a case exists to use government intervention to attain this goal. In the late nineteenth century, smoking was widely viewed as offensive, harmful to health, and contrary to the value of thrift. Even so, tobacco growers, manufacturers, merchants, and retailers did not bear the same social stigma as saloon keepers, prostitutes, and printers of pornographic material in the late nineteenth and early twentieth centuries (Burnham 1993, pp. 86–87; Kagan and Vogel 1993, p. 34). Concern over the immorality of smoking never reached the level of the movement against alcohol consumption. Correspondingly, the sanctions for tobacco use have been much milder than those for either alcohol or illicit drugs. The concept of smoking as an immoral act died with Prohibition, if not earlier. As with alcohol, the public decided to control the use of tobacco products rather than ban them outright.

Two other reasons for government intervention against smoking have emerged more recently. The first is the belief that people do not have sufficient knowledge to make an informed decision about tobacco use. The second concerns external effects of smoking. To understand the first argument, one must first understand that reliance on consumer sovereignty assumes that consumers are relatively well informed or could be informed at a relatively low cost. Good consumer knowledge is a precondition for the conclusion that we can rely on individuals' independent actions, based on their own preferences and beliefs, for a socially desirable outcome. The argument that people have inadequate knowledge for informed choices on tobacco use has at least two dimensions: (1) the ignorance of very young consumers and (2) the addictive properties of cigarettes.

The vast majority of smokers take up the habit at a very young age, well before they can be considered to be adequately informed about the long-run consequences such a personal choice. Initiation after the age of majority is relatively rare (Gruber and Zinman 2000). Young persons may not adequately consider adverse health effects that may occur many decades in their future. Forecasting the future is a difficult task, even for the well-informed, but it is likely to be more difficult for young persons. Thus, the state is assumed to have a role in restricting their access to products about which informed decisions cannot be made.

Also, as will be discussed much more fully in Chapter 3, tobacco manufacturers are alleged to have misinformed the public about the risks of smoking through their advertising campaigns (see, for example, Rabin 1993; Hanson and Logue 1998). Youths may be particularly vulnerable to such misinformation and therefore may underestimate their personal risk. To the extent that sellers of tobacco products deliberately misinform potential smokers about the risks of using their products, the public sector has a role in regulating the flow of such information. Government intervention can accomplish this objective in several ways, including advertising bans and regulations, direct provision of antismoking information or the requirement that the tobacco companies provide it, and tort litigation.

Bans on advertising, however, raise the constitutional issue of the right to free speech. For two decades, the U.S. Supreme Court has allowed governments to limit truthful and nonmisleading commercial speech if such limits directly advance some asserted government interest and are not more extensive than necessary, but as of 2001, tobacco companies have been contesting such limits as preventing their legal right to advertise their product to adults (*Greenhouse* 2001). Making noninformative statements about a product to promote consumer identification with it is not considered misleading.

An alternative response would be to ban sales of the product outright. In spite of all of the concerns about misleading information, tobacco continues to be marketed worldwide. As Rabin and Sugarman (1993) explained, "At first blush, the wonder may be that . . . cigarettes [have]) been allowed to remain in the marketplace at all. Yet, as a general matter, our society does not lightly impose bans on dangerous and deleterious products; witness the continuing controversy over cheap and easily concealed handguns, and consider the exception that might well be taken to underscore the rule—the disastrous experience with alcohol under Prohibition" (p. 6).

The government's ability to reduce addiction is limited. Because some people require personal evidence of health effects, general health messages about the harms of smoking may be an ineffective deterrent. Such people disregard a general message as applying to some "average" person but not to themselves. At one level, governments can strive to develop more effective health messages. At another, they can discourage initiation of smoking in the first place, for example by implementing and enforcing controls on sales of tobacco products to minors.

The second argument for government intervention is to correct the externalities of smoking. The externalities of smoking fall into three groups. The first comprises "pure consumption" externalities. Many members of society accept the notion of consumer sovereignty in general, but do not accept it in the context of health and medical care.

The second group comprises health externalities. Breathing secondhand smoke may have negative consequences for others. That is, the health of nonsmokers who live, work, and play with smokers may suffer as a result of their proximity to smokers.[1]

Third are financial externalities. For various reasons, private health insurers do not impose premium surcharges on smokers. Thus, to the extent that smoking increases one's medical expenses, the premiums of nonsmokers cross-subsidize the extra expenses incurred on behalf of smokers. Given the pay-as-you-go financing of Medicare and Medicaid, at any point in time smokers entitled to such public coverage benefit from cross subsidies from nonsmokers. Viewed in a life cycle context, the cross subsidies are more complex (see, for example, Viscusi 1992). Medical care of uninsured smokers is cross-subsidized as well.

One policy instrument that in principle compensates for financial externalities is the excise tax on tobacco products. Tobacco has been taxed since colonial times. Since the Civil War, tobacco taxes have been part of the U.S. federal tax system, rising in wartime and falling in peacetime. During the first half of the twentieth century, the primary rationale for imposing an excise tax was to raise revenue for the public sector. Today the tax is viewed as a policy instrument to discourage smoking, akin to the "green" taxes on polluting products that are designed to discourage their use.

Government intervention has not always aimed at reducing smoking rates. During the first half of the twentieth century, the overall thrust in the public sector was to promote tobacco, by subsidizing its consumption by military personnel and stabilizing tobacco farmer employment by means of price support programs. Only toward the latter part of the century did the government emerge as a major proponent of tobacco control.

Policy makers with an interest in tobacco control face many challenges. First are the tobacco growers' and cigarette manufacturers' interests. Given the number of growers and employees in the industry, opposition to tobacco control has been a potent force. Tobacco products are an important export for the United States, making them significant for a country facing a persistent balance-of-trade deficit. Sometimes industry interests have cast their opposition to tobacco control in terms of the rights of individuals. If nonsmokers have the right to exercise choice, so do smokers, they argue. They counter antismoking information with claims of new and allegedly safer products that allow smokers to avoid making the difficult choice of quitting. Another problem is the displacement effects that antismoking policies often have. For example, while advertising bans seem to have lowered the amount spent on ads for cigarettes and other tobacco products, companies have simply shifted their marketing efforts to direct promotions.

The Emergence of Smoking as a Public Health Issue

Consumption of tobacco products is the major source of preventable premature death in the United States. Of the 2.1 million persons who died in 1990, 49 percent died from preventable causes, and 19 percent of the total, or about 400,000 deaths, have been attributed to tobacco use (Bartecchi et al. 1994; Thun, Apicilla, and Henley 2000). Of the tobacco-related deaths, 180,000 involved cardiovascular diseases and 120,000 were attributable to lung cancer. About one-fifth of cardiovascular deaths in 1990 were attributable to smoking (Bartecchi et al. 1994). In addition, cigarette smoking is the leading cause of pulmonary disease and pulmonary disease–related death in the United States.

The most dramatic evidence is for lung cancer mortality. Smokers are twenty-four times more likely to die from lung cancer than are nonsmokers (Taylor et al. 2002). In addition to causing the vast majority of primary lung cancers, smoking has been associated with cancers of the mouth, pharynx, larynx, esophagus, stomach, pancreas, uterine cervix, kidney, urethra, and bladder (Bartecchi et al. 1994). For males in all age groups, cancers of the lung and related cancers were the leading cause of death from cancer in 1998, although death rates from such cancers declined during the 1990s. For females such cancers were the leading cause of death in women over age fifty-five. For younger women, the death rate from breast cancer exceeded that of lung and related cancers. For women age sixty-five and older, death rates from lung and related cancers increased dramatically during the 1990s. Even though women's rates were increasing, as of 1998, mortality rates from lung and related cancers for men were still about double those for women (U.S. Department of Commerce 2000, p. 96; *http://seer.cancer.gov/Publications/CSR1973_1998/lung.pdf*). The divergence in trends in mortality rates from such cancers reflects the fact that women started smoking cigarettes in greater numbers later than men.

Less easily documented are the morbidity, pain, and suffering losses attributable to smoking. Because of the long latency period involved, which may be thirty years and is often more, only relatively recently have we been able to observe some of the health consequences of decisions to smoke made many decades ago, such as the increase in smoking rates among women in the second half of the twentieth century.

Smoking emerged as a public health issue in the United States during the twentieth century, following the dramatic increase in tobacco consumption associated with the development and spread of machine-rolled cigarettes and safety matches and the adverse health effects that later became evident (Tate 1999, pp. 16–19). Most of the evidence on the adverse health effects of smoking has been accumulated since 1950, but public health concerns were first voiced much earlier. King James I of England opposed smoking for health reasons (Davidson 1996, p. 22). He wrote in 1604 that smoking tobacco was "a custom loathsome to the eyes, hateful to the nose, harmful to the brain, dangerous to the lungs and [that] the black stinking fume thereof, resembling the horrible Stygian smoke of the pit that is bottomless."[2] In 1857 the tobacco question was raised in several issues of *The Lancet,* a major medical journal published in London. Adverse health effects of smoking, based on, for example, observations of chronic smokers' hacking coughs and raspy voices, were discussed (*Lancet* 1857).

More recently, a few case reports linking tobacco to disease and at least one epidemiological study (Pearl 1938) appeared in peer-reviewed journals as early as the 1930s, but major numbers of such reports did not appear until the early 1950s.[3] The first studies published in the 1950s reported that the overwhelming percentage of lung cancer patients had smoked (Ochsner 1954). From 1950 on onward, results of randomized controlled experiments on animals were published. A report by the American Cancer Society and the British Medical Council, published in 1953 and receiving considerable publicity, claimed that death rates were significantly higher for smokers than nonsmokers (Schneider, Klein, and Murphy 1981). During the next four decades, statistical studies refined evidence on the increased probability of premature death (see, for example, Peto et al. 1994).[4]

For decades consumers received mixed signals. On the one hand, they were told that smoking was a bad habit and that the statistical evidence unambiguously demonstrated the substantial health harms. On the other, tobacco manufacturers criticized or belittled the evidence, until very recently. Cigarette companies disputed epidemiological findings as providing insufficient evidence that smoking causes adverse health outcomes. Instead, they made smoking seem cool. Thanks to advertising, smoking became a mechanism for identifying "with-it" people in much the same way that drinking Pepsi conferred membership in the "Pepsi generation" (Schuessler 2000).

Persistence of Smoking

Smoking activity can be measured in a number of ways. One measure is the per capita consumption of tobacco products, including cigarettes. The single most highly consumed tobacco product since the first two decades of the twentieth century is the cigarette (Bartecchi et al. 1994). For this reason, most policy emphasis has been on cigarettes rather than other tobacco products.

Information on per capita consumption of cigarettes is available for a long time period, so we can begin with a description of this trend. At the beginning of the twentieth century, per capita consumption of cigarettes in the United States was negligible (Figure 1.1). Demand grew rapidly during and after World War I, possibly because the U.S. government subsidized cigarette consumption for soldiers during the war (Tate 1999). Per capita demand declined during the Great Depression, but this was followed by other spurts in demand during World War II and the Korean conflict, again possibly on account of government-subsidized consumption. Demand rose until the mid-1960s, albeit at a slower rate, and plateaued, with some fluctuations, until the mid-1970s. Consumption began to decline rapidly after 1980 and continued to drop for the rest of the century. Nevertheless, per capita consumption of cigarettes at the end of the twentieth century was at about the same level as in the early 1940s and far above levels in 1900.

Smoking prevalence, the fraction of people smoking, also has fallen since the time it was initially measured in the mid-1960s. Warner (1989) analyzed changes in smoking prevalence by gender and age cohort between 1964 and 1985, using data from selected years of the National Health Interview Survey (NHIS). Data from his article, in five-year increments by gender and age cohort, are shown in Table 1.1. Since the NHIS includes only persons age eighteen and older, this analysis of smoking prevalence must be limited to adults. Current smokers were defined as persons who had smoked at least 100 cigarettes in their lifetime and smoked at the time of the survey.

In general, smoking prevalence declined between 1965 and 1985. It tended to decline with age, with a few exceptions. Smoking increased for both genders for the 1941–1950 birth cohort between 1965 and 1970. By the time males in the 1931–1940 birth cohort were age fifty or so, 35 per-

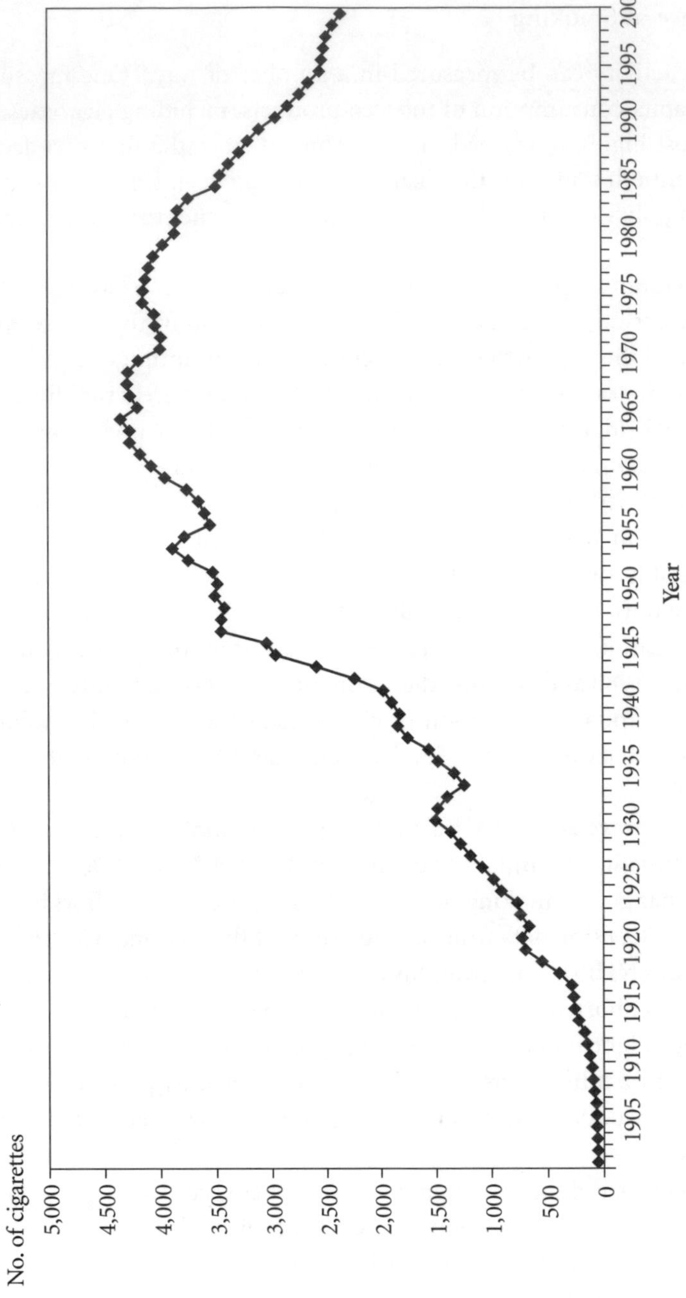

Figure 1.1 Per capita cigarette consumption

Table 1.1 Current cigarette smoking, 1965–1985

Birth cohort	Median age in 1965	Smoked in year (percent) 1965	1970	1975	1980	1985
Males						
1941–1950	20	46	58	53	44	38
1931–1940	30	59	53	46	44	35
1921–1930	40	62	55	47	41	32
1911–1920	50	60	53	46	30	22
1901–1910	60	45	39	30	18	16
Females						
1941–1950	20	30	41	40	34	32
1931–1940	30	44	43	42	35	32
1921–1930	40	43	40	38	31	27
1911–1920	50	36	33	28	26	18
1901–1910	60	21	18	15	15	8

Source: Warner (1989), p. 147.

cent smoked. By contrast, 60 percent of men from the 1911–1920 birth cohort smoked at this age. The decline was smaller for women. For women, 32 percent from the 1931–1940 birth cohort smoked at age fifty or so in contrast to 36 percent of persons at the same age from the 1911–1920 birth cohort. More recent smoking prevalence data, derived from the same source, shows a continued decrease in smoking prevalence over the decade from 1985 to 1995, but declines between 1990 and 1995 were minimal for both genders (Table 1.2).[5] Declines in smoking prevalence as people age reflect a combination of quitting and differential death rates between smokers and nonsmokers.

In recent years, the U.S. Substance Abuse and Mental Health Administration has conducted an annual National Household Survey on Drug Abuse. This survey collects information on a variety of substances, from people under age eighteen as well as adults. The data show declines in the prevalence of cigarette smoking for all age groups between 1985 and 1995. But use of other substances, such as alcohol and illicit drugs, generally declined as well, raising the question of whether declines in smoking preva-

Table 1.2 Current cigarette smoking, 1985–1995

	Percentage smoking, by year		
Age	1985	1990	1995
Total: 18+	30.1	25.5	24.7
Men	32.6	28.4	28.2
18–24	28.0	26.6	27.8
25–34	38.2	31.6	—
35–44	37.6	34.5	—
45–64	33.4	29.3	27.1
65+	19.6	14.6	14.3
Women	27.9	22.8	22.6
18–24	30.4	22.5	21.8
25–34	32.0	28.2	—
35–44	31.5	24.8	26.8
45–64	29.9	24.8	22.8
65+	13.5	11.5	11.5

Source: U.S. Department of Commerce (1999), table 239.

lence were the result of tobacco control policies or some more general trend toward healthier lifestyles or changes in social norms affecting use of a variety of substances.

Between 1974 and 1985, education replaced gender as a major demographic predictor of smoking status. Smoking prevalence declined for all education groups, but the decrease was much greater for more highly educated persons (Pierce et al. 1989). Education might be a surrogate for many underlying factors, including an individual's tendency to be present- or future-oriented (as reflected by the implicit rate at which one discounts future harms) and one's ability to process health information.

Although declines in per capita consumption and in smoking prevalence are essentially favorable developments, an appreciable share of the U.S. population still consumes tobacco products. Young people continue to start the smoking habit. In fact, during the 1990s, rates of initiation were constant for much of the decade. And many older smokers chose to continue smoking, at least until age sixty-five.

Information, Risk Perception, and Smoking Behavior

Scholars have no consensus on the appropriate analytical framework for studying behavioral decisions such as whether to smoke. At the risk of overgeneralizing, economics and psychology, the two disciplines offering explicit competing frameworks applicable to the study of individual behavior, have very different views. In psychology, behavior is seen as adaptive, learned through complex interactions of perceptions, motives, attitudes, and mood. In economics, the framework underlying this book's empirical analysis, consumers are assumed to behave according to a process in which information is used to form perceptions and beliefs about relationships that are inherently technical (for example, "If I place my hand on a hot stove, I will be burned," or "If I smoke, I might die of lung cancer"). An economic model of behavior assumes that each individual knows or can form subjective beliefs about risks that can affect his or her well-being. In this framework, the causal line of reasoning flows from information to risk perceptions and then ultimately to behavior.

Of course, some situations might also entail a "feedback loop." That is, when people recognize that a particular behavior exposes them to more risk, they might change. Walking at night on a street with heavy automobile traffic without wearing light-colored clothing or reflectors is dangerous. Once people appreciate the hazard, they might carry lights, wear reflectors, or avoid the walk. When risks are involuntarily imposed on people, they might undertake mitigating behaviors. Recognizing that contaminants in drinking water are hazardous might cause consumers to install home filtration systems or purchase bottled water.

When evaluating informed choice, this logic leads to a focus on how information is translated into risk perception. Perceptions and beliefs change as new information about the technical relationships change and are processed. There are a variety of ways of describing the process. One of the most formal labels is "Bayesian updating," after an approach to statistical analysis that envisions an individual as having prior beliefs, acquiring new information, and then using the two sources together. Each source is weighted by the individuals' confidence in the beliefs.

Consumer preferences are assumed to be given, consistent, and immutable. The consumer's decision process, which occupies a major place in cognitive psychology, is reduced to a relatively simple choice rule in economics. The individual is treated as making a choice based on what yields the greatest happiness or utility, given the constraints imposed by his or her available resources and the relative availability of goods and services. Other constraints, such as technical relationships underlying health production (McFadden 1999), can also be important to choice. As beliefs about the underlying technical relationships or subjective risk perceptions change, behavior is likely to change as well.

The concept of information as something valuable to individuals and often acquired at a cost is relatively new to economics. An anecdote is illustrative. A seminal contribution to the economics of information was George Akerlof's (1970) "The Market for 'Lemons': Quality, Uncertainty, and the Market Mechanism," in which he considered whether markets would exist if product quality were unobservable. Akerlof spent years trying to find a publisher. The article was eventually published in 1970, and Akerlof was awarded the Nobel Prize in Economics in 2001, in large part because of it. According to the authors of a recent discussion of rejected journal articles written by many of the most famous economists, "Akerlof believes that journal editors refused the article both because they feared the introduction into economics of informational considerations and because they disliked the article's readable style. 'They were afraid that if information was brought into economics, it would lose all rigor, since in that case almost anything could be said'" (Gans and Shepard 2000, pp. 32–33).

Today, students of information and risk recognize that the rigor is still present in economics, as in the traditional paradigm and as Akerlof recognized when he wrote his article. When a person takes action to acquire information, this is a behavioral choice related to the decision to change behavior. For example, changing one's diet based on new information about fiber and the risk of cancer is connected to the choice to pay attention to that information in the first place. Because of these connections, a person's efforts to enhance knowledge about risk should depend on the events at risk. This is the "feedback loop" to which we referred earlier.

Both economics and psychology have important roles in any effort to understand individual choice. The power of the economic theory is in generating testable hypotheses from a minimum number of underlying assumptions. Psychology does not have the same reductionist perspective. Puzzles are encouraged, and efforts to organize a unified treatment comparable to the constrained optimization in economics are not as highly valued. Nonetheless, psychology has much to contribute to understanding the effects of information and risk perceptions on behavior. Psychology is especially important to improving our understanding of how cognitive processes link different types of information to changes in people's risk perceptions.

The number of studies of personal choices, such as on the consumption of addictive goods, by psychologists vastly outnumbers the number of studies of such choices based on economic analysis. Ours is the first study to present a unified framework tracing individuals' smoking decisions from receipt of information messages through risk perceptions to the choices people actually make. Based on what we know about the adverse health effects of smoking, decisions to start and stop smoking are two of the most important personal decisions people make.

Challenge for This Book

We have presented rates of growth in cigarette consumption and in death rates for lung and bronchial cancer. The literature on tobacco has increased correspondingly. As of 2000, the main Duke University library (not including other branches) listed 678 books and other titles under the term *smoking*. Admittedly, Duke University is located in the historic heartland of tobacco production, North Carolina, but this means only that the collection is rather complete. Many books are historical accounts of the tobacco industry. Others deal with various aspects of smoking from the individual's perspective. Journal publication on the topic is voluminous as well. Then why is another book needed?

Economists like to divide the world into supply and demand sides of the market. Our book makes no contribution to understanding the supply side. Ours is a study of smoking demand and the environmental and personal factors affecting such demand. Thus, our comments on gaps in the literature refer to factors that influence demand and how they arise from individual choices under uncertainty.

Key public policies relate to price and information about the adverse health effects of smoking. Much is known about the effects of price on demand (see Chaloupka and Warner 2000). Less is known about tobacco pricing policy, but this refers to behavior of the suppliers. Although we, like others, must control for the effect of price, we make no contribution here.

The most fundamental issue with smoking from the economist's perspective is why knowledgeable people continue to do it. Most observers are willing to accept that young people may not fully appreciate the consequences of their initial decision to smoke. Adults are literally bombarded with negative smoking messages. If we believe these choices are being made by rational individuals, a basic hypothesis in most economic models, why does the information not influence these adults' choices? This is indeed a fundamental question. What do older smokers know about the harms of smoking? How do they acquire such information? How and to what extent are risk perceptions updated in the presence of new information? To what extent do changes in risk perception affect the decision to smoke and, conditional on this decision, how much to smoke?

Having answers to these questions is critical for the design of health policy in this field and for the development of effective antismoking messages. As will be discussed more fully in Chapter 3, previous research on effects of public antismoking information programs or advertising bans has used aggregate time series data or cross-sectional data on individuals. With time series data, one can look for changes in demand that coincide with the program's implementation. A lengthy time series has the advantage of allowing time for many different policies to be introduced and, in some cases, subsequently eliminated. However, such data also have important limitations. For one, with a limited number of observations, ability to obtain sufficiently precise measurement of the underlying parameters is also limited. Further, results are often quite sensitive to model specification.

With cross-sectional data on individuals, one correlates measures of smoking behavior with information treatments and other antismoking policies. Although messages necessarily operate through the sequence of treatment to changed risk perceptions to changed behavior, the intermediate step, risk perceptions, often is disregarded. Also, with single cross sections, how an individual's risk perceptions change following receipt of new information cannot be assessed. We must instead say that one person with new information would behave like a different individual who already was better informed. But as we already noted, the acquisition of information is itself a choice. It is entirely possible that the better-informed person is so because he is *different* from the individual receiving the new message.

Characterizing what smokers know and how they obtain information has been an important issue in litigation against the tobacco manufacturers. The manufacturers may be liable for damages, for example, if they concealed information they possessed about the health effects of smoking or deliberately misled individuals to disregard such harms. If as a result of those actions or inactions people smoked and suffered ill health, then the impacts are due in part to those actions or inactions. As the title implies, this book is about a piece of the puzzle, a critical piece: how information affects personal risk perceptions, which in turn affect behavior.

Much research on smoking behavior has focused on youths. This emphasis is sensible in that virtually all smokers begin their habit at a young age (see, for example, Douglas 1998; Gruber and Zinman 2000). However, an important aspect of smoking is the long latency period of its health effects. One can smoke for years without discernable effects. A doctoral student who analyzed data on a sample of persons with a maximum age of sixty at entry to the study remarked to one of us that he found few adverse health effects from smoking in his research. One reason is that the maximum harm occurs to persons at ages slightly below this age and older.

When people reach middle age, they are exposed to various types of information about smoking and health. Some of it is derived from analyzing personal outcomes as they are revealed through aggregates of outcomes for other individuals, such as the mortality rate from cancer of the lung and bronchus. On hearing an aggregate estimate of the probability of onset, perhaps age- and gender-adjusted, the recipient of the information either disregards the information as irrelevant to his personal circumstances or updates his belief about getting such a cancer himself. In addition, although smokers are exposed to such information over their life cycle, in middle and late life a smoker typically receives a larger number of personalized risk messages in the form of serious personal health events, or even the death of a parent or spouse. Ultimately, each of us at this age is subject to greater disability and disease. Such messages in the form of personal experience also influence our subjective risk perceptions. Smokers are likely to encounter more of these personalized shocks as they age.

Incorporating information in the form of personalized messages into the broader context of choice is a unique aspect of this study. Understanding how these messages affect people is especially important, because they are dramatic. A key goal of this book is to examine how risk perceptions are updated as individuals receive new personalized information and how risk perceptions affect smoking behavior. With those insights, we investigate whether it is possible to mimic the impact of personalized messages through an information treatment that does not require that a serious adverse health effect actually be experienced.

Although the focus of our empirical research is on information, risk perceptions, and smoking behavior measured at the level of the individual, examining why people engage in harmful acts raises larger questions about rationality of human decision making.

Main Data Sources

Our analysis is based on data collected in four waves of the Health and Retirement Study (HRS), a national panel survey conducted by the University of Michigan's Institute for Social Research (see Juster and Suzman 1995). Persons eligible for the survey were born between the years 1931 and 1941; they were between the ages of fifty-one and sixty-one in the year of the baseline survey, 1992. Spouses of sample persons are also included and can be of any age. They are administered survey questionnaires identical to those for the sample persons. Each respondent was surveyed in person for the baseline year and subsequently by telephone. The survey has been conducted every two years since 1992. By 2000, four waves of the HRS had been released at least in preliminary form: 1992, 1994, 1996, and 1998.

The HRS is uniquely suited for our study in several respects. First, the HRS asks individuals about their smoking behavior, including questions about smoking prior to the baseline interview and, in each wave, whether the person smokes currently and, conditional on smoking, the amount they smoke. The survey does not ask about the type or brand of cigarette smoked or about smoking habits, for example, extent to which the person inhales.

Second, the HRS asks several questions about the chance of a particular event's occurring (see Hurd and McGarry 1995). We focused on a question, asked in each wave, that elicited the person's perceptions about the probability of living to age seventy-five or older. The HRS also asks about the respondent's views of other uncertain outcomes, including the probability of living to age eighty-five, of being admitted into a nursing home, and of leaving an inheritance.

A third important feature is the panel structure of the survey. The same individuals are asked many of the same questions periodically over time. Having a panel of respondents allows the researcher to investigate the impact of events on subsequent beliefs and behavior. For example, in our research we could trace the effects of a person's heart attack. With a single cross section, such sequencing is largely precluded. Instead, analysts must rely on comparing different people, one who experienced the heart attack and another who did not. The analysis must in this case assume the observed differences in the two people's behavior are due to the heart attacks. Even with the most detailed effort to control for observable characteristics that differ across respondents, one must question the conclusions from such comparisons across cohorts. A panel structure allows individual-specific effects to be taken into account in measuring the effects of the heart attack. The HRS asked many questions about personal preferences, such as risk tolerance, that are likely to be relatively time-invariant over the period observed. Other, more standard time-invariant information, such as education level, was also obtained.

Fourth, the HRS is unique in eliciting detailed health and financial information. Most surveys offer detailed information on *either* health and health care *or* household finances. No panel offers as much information on both for a period as long as six years. The information on health is especially detailed. It includes specific diagnoses, such as cancer, heart attack, and stroke, the onset of which can be dated within a two-year time window, and numerous measures of disability. Dates of death are recorded, and deaths are distinguished from attrition from the survey. The collection of detailed financial information, including data on income, assets, and employment, was at least initially motivated by the objective to study retirement decisions (the "retirement" part of the HRS).

Because identical data are obtained from the sample person and the spouse, one can examine the effect of a life event—for example, the onset of a smoking-related illness—on the risk perceptions and smoking behavior of the spouse. Because the HRS collects some data on respondent cognition, we were able to account for cognitive status in our analysis of these subjective risk perceptions.

To supplement the data from the HRS, we organized focus group meetings with current and former smokers as well as interviews with current smokers in the same age range (50 to 64) in Raleigh, North Carolina. The focus group sessions served two main purposes. First, the sessions allowed us to observe how the smokers and former smokers interpreted questions that were patterned identically to those in the HRS. Because they framed their answers in terms of the same longevity expectations as the HRS, participation the focus groups helped us understand risk perceptions from a more in-depth perspective. Most important, the focus groups allowed us to probe the considerations people give to their behavior, parents' experiences, health events, and available information when they answer questions about their longevity expectations.[6] Second, we investigated which types of health messages were most salient to smokers. We designed and fielded our own survey in Raleigh. This was the experimental phase of our study. We used a computer-assisted interview method, and some respondents were resurveyed six months after the initial interview. Our interviews matched the HRS sample in terms of age, but were confined to current smokers. Because the smokers were surveyed three times (when they were first recruited, during the computer-assisted survey, and in the telephone follow-up), we were able to gauge the extent to which health information messages were retained over a six-month period. Questions included in our survey exactly matched some of the questions in the HRS, allowing us to combine data from the HRS and our survey in our analysis.

Overview

In Chapter 2 we present and evaluate a theoretical framework for analyzing individuals' decisions about their own smoking. We begin with a description of the expected utility model as applied to smoking decisions over the life cycle. Next we consider the definition of an informed choice and discuss how Individuals form perceptions about the probability that various events will occur in their life and about the influence of their own decisions on those probabilities.

In the expected utility framework we describe, individuals are forward-looking. At any point in time, they make the best use of the information at hand, recognizing that current choices have implications for future well-being. Consideration of future periods in an economic framework introduces concerns about time-consistent preferences and discounting. In contrast to the economic approach, the psychological perspective emphasizes limits on decision making and the tendency for people to make mistakes because they use "shortcuts" in their decision making. Although we adhere to an economic framework in our own analysis, we have not ignored the psychological perspective. In fact, we use it as a basis for recognizing people's cognitive limits.

Much of the rest of the book is organized around the three themes of the book—information in Chapters 3 and 4, risk perception in Chapters 5 and 7, and smoking decisions in Chapters 6 and 8. Information is hypothesized to affect risk perceptions, which might or might not be biased prior to the information's receipt by each person. Risk perceptions, in turn, affects decisions about health behaviors—smoking, in our context. Personal longevity expectations affect the life span over which a person anticipates incurring the costs and benefits of smoking. People may have overly optimistic, overly pessimistic, or realistic views about the effects of smoking on health, including survival. To the extent that people think smoking has a less important effect on health than it really does, they might be more prone to smoke or to smoke a greater amount. By helping to align subjective risk perceptions with objective reality, information about the adverse effects of smoking might reduce the amount smoked. Assessing how this causal chain works in practice is a central research question of this book.

In Chapter 3 we trace the public sector's role in information dissemination in the past 50 to 100 years. In contrast to other potentially addictive substances, with few exceptions there has not been an absolute ban on the sale of tobacco products. As already noted, government policy in this area has been mixed. Although the emphasis of policy in recent years has been on information control, and very recently on excise taxes on cigarettes, the federal government once served as a distributor of cigarettes to military personnel, especially during wartime. Even in the recent past, policy objectives have been mixed. Also, the tobacco companies have successfully encouraged the enactment of pro-tobacco legislation. In a democratic society, the public sector usually will not withstand focused pressure from vested interests without countervailing pressure from the public at large.

After describing the public policies, especially those that pertain to the government's provision of information and control of tobacco advertising, we summarize the empirical evidence on the effectiveness of public antismoking campaigns and on the effects of advertising on demand for cigarettes. We conclude that for much of the era since publication of the first U.S. Surgeon General's report in 1964 on the adverse health effects of smoking there has been a battle of the messages. Although the tobacco companies no longer touted smoking's benefits after 1964, their messages continued to imply that smoking a particular product is macho, good for keeping women slim (Virginia Slims), and otherwise cool (Kool cigarettes).

In Chapter 4 we focus on the personal health messages smokers are likely to receive as they age. We summarize existing knowledge about the effects of smoking on mortality and morbidity, and present new information from the first four waves of the HRS on these relationships. Our study's empirical contribution is in understanding the smoking behavior of persons over age fifty. We present new empirical evidence on the mortality and morbidity experience of current, former, and never smokers during their sixth and seventh decades of life. There is much literature on the adverse effects of smoking on survival, but there is comparatively little information from previous studies on the effect of smoking on morbidity and disability, a gap in evidence that we seek to fill in this chapter.

We find that smoking is particularly threatening to survival, but it has important impacts on morbidity and disability as well. During their fifties and sixties, many smokers receive personal health messages in the form of both minor changes in their physical abilities, such as the onset of difficulty climbing stairs, and major shocks, such as a heart attack—events that seemed like very distant prospects when they first started smoking.

Chapter 5 is the first of two chapters that examine how information influences risk perception. We focus on the respondent's own assessment of the probability that he would live to age seventy-five or more. The same basic question was asked in each wave of the Health and Retirement Study. We use it to consider the links between public policy, information, and risk perception. We evaluate individuals' responses to the risk perception question, addressing such important issues as how well individuals' own subjective longevity expectations predict actual survival. With the panel data, we were able to determine whether those persons who had thought their life expectancy was relatively poor were more likely to die earlier. Overall, people are remarkably good at predicting their own survival. Although smokers on average tend to be too optimistic about their longevity, nonsmokers tend to counterbalance that optimism with overly pessimistic estimates.

Further, we look at how people use new information about their own health to update their longevity expectations. We compare longevity expectation updating patterns among current, former, and never smokers, and find that people with different smoking statuses update their longevity expectations differently; in particular they process health information differently. One hypothesis advanced in the psychology literature as it pertains to smoking is that smokers are more optimistic about their chances of surviving to old age than are others of comparable age and gender (see Chapter 2). Presumably, being too optimistic is a deterrent to quitting. By contrast, some prior economic evidence suggests that smokers and others are too pessimistic about the adverse effects of smoking on survival. We find that, on average, smokers are more optimistic about their survival chances than others and give themselves too much credit in terms of added life extension when they quit.

In Chapter 6 we first review the extensive literature on cessation and present our own analysis based on four waves of the HRS. Although the literature is vast, no study before ours has been based on a panel as lengthy and nationally representative as the HRS, nor have other authors been able to link longevity expectations with smoking cessation. The empirical findings provide good as well as bad news. The good news is that many people in the HRS age cohort do quit, which is itself not a new finding. The bad news is that among the most important determinants of cessation are major adverse health events, such as heart attacks. We also find that the price of cigarettes is a determinant of quitting. Unfortunately, however, minor signals of an individual's deteriorating health, such as the onset of difficulty in walking up several flights of stairs, do not seem to provide a sufficient motivation to quit. We find that intensity of smoking predicts quitting. Rather than quit "cold turkey," many individuals quit gradually, suggesting that a policy of encouraging reductions in daily smoking frequency might be a more effective antismoking policy than encouraging everyday smokers to quit all at once. In spite of our focus group results, we find little empirical support for the optimism-bias hypothesis in its pure form—that is, that the people who have overly optimistic longevity expectations (relative to life table values) continue to smoke. But serious health events reduce longevity expectations, a finding reported in Chapter 5, and these events do lead to smoking cessation. It is regrettable that many of these adverse events could have been averted if the smokers had quit smoking at an earlier age.

Results from the focus group meetings and the survey of smokers we conducted in Raleigh, discussed in Chapter 7, revealed unanimous agreement that everyone hears and knows that smoking is bad for one's health. Many smokers had discussed smoking with their physicians. Current smokers were more likely than former smokers to state that they thought they had genes for long survival. On average, the smoker participants in our focus groups stated that health messages stressing the morbidity and disability effects of smoking were more salient than those emphasizing survival. The prospect of spending many years in a disabled and dependent state was one that participants wanted to avoid.

With the short-term follow-up feature of our survey, we could study the impact of health information messages on individuals' longevity expectations. Given the survey length, our experiments were limited, but our results do suggest clear evidence that a salient message can be designed about smoking that does affect smokers' longevity expectations and seems persistent based on our follow-ups after six months.

Chapter 8 is the second chapter that integrates our findings on longevity expectations of smokers and their responses to different types of information about the health risks of smoking with new estimates of the demand for cigarettes. The first part of the chapter provides an economic framework for assessing demand for cigarettes. It continues discussion of issues raised in Chapter 2 about basic assumptions underlying consumer behavior. Our demand analysis allows us to gauge the potential impact of information messages on an actual choice, the typical consumption of mature smokers, particularly the impact of the message we found most effective.

Chapter 8 focuses on daily cigarette consumption rates. With our parameter estimates, we evaluate the potential impact of a new information policy on daily cigarette consumption of smokers in the sixth and seventh decades of life. We gauge the effects on cigarette demand of the information treatment we found to be effective in changing smokers' longevity expectations (Chapter 7), and we find that this message reduces daily demand for cigarettes appreciably. A recent evaluation of California's aggressive antismoking policy also suggests that combinations of policies implemented simultaneously may achieve this goal (Fichtenberg and Glantz 2000).

Chapter 9 presents a review of our major findings, linking information, risk perception, and choice, both generally and in the causal chain applicable to smoking. We also step back from the blackboard to consider the implications of our research both for basic understanding of human behavior, especially in the context of addictive behaviors, and for public policy. We discuss unresolved scientific issues as they apply to smoking; they must be viewed with value questions, such as freedom of speech and choice. We also present our agenda for future research.

CHAPTER

2

Cognition, Perception, and Behavior: Are "Bad Choices" Allowed with Rational Choice?

Rational choice is central to the economic view of behavior, but the past two decades have seen an increasing array of contradictions to this key component of economics. Many mainstream economists dismiss these inconsistencies as irrelevant. Some, such as Nobel laureate Gary Becker, have seen the problems posed as opportunities to extend the traditional analyses of individual behavior. We agree with Becker's (1993) description of the economic view of people's behavior: They are not expected to be perfect optimizers, as evaluated by the analyst, or dispassionate external observers; rather, people do the best they can, given their information and their cognitive abilities to understand it. The choices we observe reflect these constraints along with people's abilities to pay and to devote time to making choices. People seek the highest level of individual well-being, and each person's conception of happiness or well-being can admit selfish, altruistic, spiteful, or even masochistic behavior.

Smoking is one of those subjects about which the challenges to the economic view of behavior seem especially great. Most people today believe smoking is an unambiguously bad choice. However, cigarette and other tobacco products do provide pleasure. Tate's (1999) description of her mother's attitudes toward smoking at the end of her life are especially telling: Recognizing she was dying of lung cancer, after a long period of illness, her mother nonetheless felt that cigarettes had "helped her through" many of her life's challenges. Even knowing the outcome, Tate's mother would not have changed her choice. Several smokers in the focus groups we organized for this study said the same thing (see Chapter 7). For some, cigarettes provide a "comfort," a "friend" in times of stress, and a benefit that outweighs all other consequences.

Does this imply that the economic paradigm has little to offer in explaining these behaviors? Should we, as some might argue (Lucas 1986), use economic analysis only in cases in which people have well-developed decision rules that "work" as the economic model would predict? In our view, this strategy would overlook most of what is interesting and important in people's behavior.

We instead develop various arguments to reconcile the conflicts in a smoker's behavior. These include informational, monetary, and cognitive constraints. Smoking choices take place in uncertain environments and require the consideration of forward-looking behavior; the addiction and the long latency of effects require that we consider how smokers view the future. This chapter draws its key elements from economic models of addictive behavior in the presence of uncertainty that evolves over time as a function of the consumption of the addictive good. Our objective is to identify a hypothesis that can be tested (1) to gauge the importance of forward-looking behavior for older smokers, (2) to examine how they use information about the risks and health effects of smoking, and (3) ultimately to evaluate whether information programs can alter the behavior of this group.

Uncertainty and Choice

At the most basic level, all choices are made under conditions of uncertainty, because life itself is uncertain. Regularity and consistency in outcomes have led modern societies and people to expect to have the ability to make some choices as if the outcomes were certain. Other choices are acknowledged to possess more uncertainty and to raise different expectations about the outcomes that will follow. This dichotomy stems, in part, from the universal confidence in science that has characterized modern society since the Enlightenment. We try to use science to increase our control. As this is not always possible, we encourage scientific exploration for most events outside human control.

Economists have described rational choice in the presence of uncertainty for much of the profession's modern history. Over the past fifty years, the expected utility model has been extensively used to try to describe behavior. It has served both a positive role, assessing decisions people *actually* make under uncertainty, and a normative role, describing the decisions individuals *should* make under uncertainty. The expected utility model augments a conventional, preference-based description of individual choice with the probabilities of events hypothesized to be important in an individual's decisions, yet unknown when these decisions are made. This expanded framework has required analysis of how people learn about probabilities and characterize uncertain outcomes.

The conventional approach in economics has been to leave questions of preference formation to sociologists and psychologists. Preferences generally have been taken by economists as a primitive concept. As we noted above, Becker led economists in changing this way of thinking. However, his approach is not comparable to that of psychologists, who hold that people must form preferences before making choices (see Payne, Bettman, and Schadke 1999). Rather, systematic factors enter a well-defined preference function and allow trade-offs underlying observed choice to be functions of past behavior (past consumption, educational decisions, or experience) or to be influenced by others' actions, such as charitable contributions, knowledge, or concern over having goods and services available to others through some form of altruism. In each case, the economist specifies arguments that link trade-offs of current consumption to past behavior, others' choices, or information.

We need not look far to see that many people who make these choices do not appear to appreciate the consequences of their actions. In other words, they do not appear to do things the way *we think* they should. To reconcile the different perspectives on choices under uncertainty, we need to consider the elements that contribute to the choice process itself. We should look at an important decision with serious consequences to reasonably ensure it is carefully weighed.

The elements are well established: information, perceptions of the probabilities or risks of outcomes relevant to the choice, the character and timing of the events at risk, and the other constraints to behavior. By probing deep into the role of these elements, using an empirical record of real choices, we can reconcile some of the existing controversies associated with informed and rational choices. Of course, an empirical study of smoking cannot be expected to resolve them all. Nonetheless, it can offer significant insight when a simple, direct, theoretical model is combined with data on individuals' choices and evidence of their responses to controlled information about the risks of smoking, as in the experiment we describe later in this book. This is our task.

We begin in this chapter with a discussion, at a general level, of the elements of the expected utility model most relevant to making choices. In Chapters 3 and 4 we will consider how "public" information on a topic like the health risks of smoking is formed as a composite of regulatory information programs, scientific findings, private firms' advertising messages, and each individual's experience with other people. This last source is a composite of private (personal) information and the combined experiences of family and friends. It is not public in the same sense as the government-mandated labels on cigarette packages. This information is spread through a variety of channels in a network of friends and acquaintances.

Private information as known best by each individual is discussed in Chapter 4. There we compare the health records of current smokers to nonsmokers, gauging whether smokers see their own experiences as different in ways that could reasonably be associated with smoking.

Our research in this book focuses on the personal smoking decisions of persons over age fifty. When the subjects of the analysis described in later chapters began to smoke, that is, during the 1940s and 1950s, relatively little was known to the public about the adverse health consequences of the smoking habit. Although such information was available to some experts, it did not begin to reach the general population until the early 1950s. From our own recollections, we know that many people suspected that the regular intake of a foreign substance into one's body would eventually impair health. But at the time, even many physicians—the presumed experts—smoked (Peto et al. 1994).

Understanding decisions to smoke requires a life cycle perspective. The smoking habit usually is acquired early in life (Gruber and Zinman 2000), many years before the age for which we begin our analysis. For this reason, our analysis focuses on decisions to reduce the amount smoked or to quit completely. Nonetheless, to understand behaviors at this later stage of smoking, we must start by asking, Why do people start smoking? What are their motivations? What risks of smoking do they perceive? How does the habit become established and then sustained? Only with these questions considered (largely based on the past literature) can we address the much less researched question of how to design effective strategies to encourage smokers to reduce their smoking or to quit outright.

As a first step, we outline a simple model of the smoking decision based on expected utility theory. This model provides a basic framework for assessing decisions about smoking, emphasizing the life cycle aspect of this decision and allowing for changes in smoking decisions as the person matures. We will modify this framework in several ways throughout the book, illustrating how each factor relevant to smoking behavior is observed in the information about smokers' choices.

A Simple Model of Smoking Decisions over the Life Cycle

We divide a person's life into four stages: (1) youth, when the decision is made to initiate smoking; (2) a discovery stage, at which the person does or does not have personal experiences that give "informational signals" about the adverse effects of his smoking behavior, such as an increased loss of workdays due to respiratory infections; (3) a day-of-reckoning phase, when the person either stays healthy or experiences a serious health shock, such as a heart attack or stroke; and (4) death, which occurs irrespective of the decision made about smoking.

To illustrate what we can learn about rational choice through people's choices, consider, for example, how forward-looking behavior, uncertainty, information, and addiction interact in a sequence of choices and outcomes designed to mimic the stages we introduced from discovery to death. We assume smokers are forward-looking, meaning they know there will be future opportunities to stop smoking. At such times they may reevaluate their smoking decision because "nature" sends a signal indicating the consequences of smoking. In the discovery stage there are small initial signals—a hoarse throat or an increased frequency of colds or respiratory infections. Later in life, the adverse health effects are larger and sometimes life threatening.

Expected utility, together with forward-looking behavior, implies that a person can anticipate potential outcomes, has expectations about what nature will reveal, and recognizes points at which to take action. A person makes a choice analytically by working backward, starting at the end of the time horizon and working back to the decision point. This framework assumes that a person makes as sound a decision as possible given what has already happened (for example, up to year t), and the logic is then repeated for one period earlier (for year $t-1$). The net result is an efficient string of choices leading back to the initial period (t_0), the initial condition that triggers the rest of the individual's personal choices. This analysis assumes a given information set; a surprise or a shock changes the sequence. While this process may seem tedious, we can use the logic to discuss how real-world complexities can change choices people make in the future.

Suppose the individual's utility is U_S (>0) if he smokes and zero if he does not. U_0 is the baseline level of well-being with no smoking. Because what is important about the problem is the differential level of well-being with smoking, we can normalize U_0 to equal 0. This is equivalent to measuring the utility of smoking as the gain in utility over the baseline due to smoking. Empirical implementation must recognize that the baseline utility, U_0, is not the same across all people, although the assumption of uniform utility at baseline is not important to the conceptual insights we can draw from the model.

In period two, nature determines whether or not the person receives bad news *(B)* or good news *(G)*. Based on the signal received, the individual can quit at a net utility cost of U_Q, which we assume is negative (<0). If he continues to smoke, he again receives utility U_S. In what we have labeled the day of reckoning, nature reveals to the smoker whether he will remain healthy and realize utility U_S or become permanently disabled, with utility $U_S(D)$.

The decision to initiate smoking is solved by backward induction, as illustrated in the game tree in Figure 2.1. The term *game tree* reflects the inherent uncertainty of downstream choices and reactions to choices as they unfold; the game is between the individual and nature. The person will start smoking only if the present discounted value of the utility stream at discount rate r is greater than or equal to zero. Thus, the description of the problem using foresight and expected utility leads to a path of choices, decided on in advance.

We now focus on the single optimal plan, to identify the elements in the decision process. Later we consider the issues posed by a more complex structure as we discuss the elements that address the decision process in the real world.

Ex ante, the probabilities of receiving good or bad news at the discovery stage are p_G and $1 - p_G$, respectively. If the person receives good news at discovery (no frequent respiratory infections, for example), the probability of receiving good news in period three, the day of reckoning, is p_{GG} for good and $1 - p_{GG}$ for bad news (that is, becoming disabled). If the person receives bad news at discovery, the probability that he or she will live out life in good health is p_{BG}; conversely, for those with bad news at discovery, the probability of disability in period three is p_{BB}. Bad news at discovery is a bad sign for period three, when life-disabling health shocks occur. Thus, p_{BB} is greater than p_{BG}.

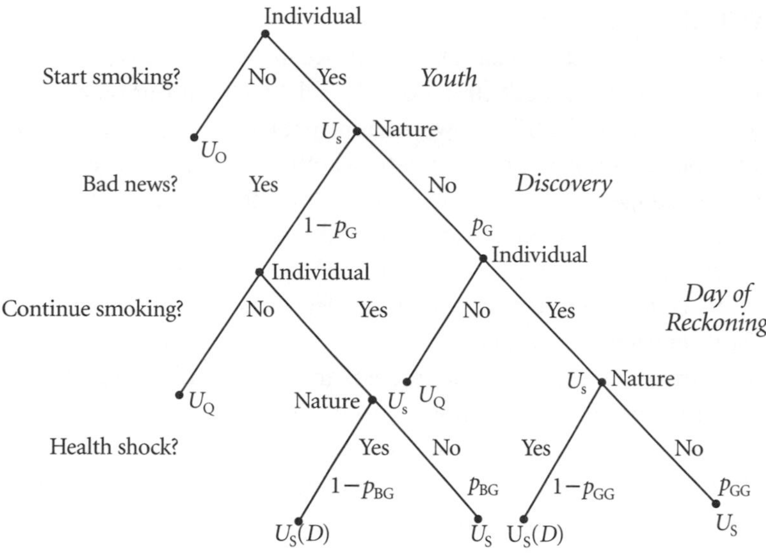

Figure 2.1 Decision to start smoking

The person who receives good (no) news at discovery quits if $U_Q > U_S + (p_{GG}U_S + (1 - p_{GG})U_S(D))/(1 + r)$ (and the comparable expression is true for persons who receive bad news at discovery); r is the person's discount rate, reflecting the person's rate of trade-off of future for present returns. Because p_{GG} exceeds p_{BG}, quitting is more likely following bad news at discovery.

Thus, in period one, expected utility (smoke)

$$U_S + p_G \max(U_S/(1 + r) + (p_{GG}U_S + (1 - p_{GG})U_S(D))/(1 + r)^2 = U_Q/(1 + r) + (1 - p_G)\max(U_S/(1 + r) + (p_{BG}U_S + (1 - p_{BG})U_S(D))/(1 + r)^2, U_Q/(1 + r)). \quad (2.1)$$

Eq. (2.1) illustrates how the composite of assumptions reduces the problem to appearing as if all is known by the beginning smoker. In fact, by treating the decision as a sequence of first steps at the beginning of each stage, we shift the focus to how a person revises the perceived probabilities of good and bad news (p_G, p_{BG}, and p_{GG}) and updates his beliefs about the utilities of the end states. Addiction enters the structure because we assume that U_S, U_Q, and $U_S(D)$ change with the amount smoked.

While the model certainly could be enriched with more analytical details about probability updating or assumed relationships connecting information and experience's effects on U_Q and $U_S(D)$, for our objectives it is most important to describe how different people actually respond to different types of information, evaluate whether those responses result in changes in longevity expectations, and attempt to link those expectations to smokers' decisions on cessation and the level of their smoking. The model characterizes periods two and three largely according to the empirical evidence for the role of information, decisions about use and quitting, and health effects of smoking.

The primary objective of this model is to partition the factors hypothesized to influence individual choice into distinct groups, allowing us to organize the discussion of each group in a context relevant to choice making. The first group is information and subjective beliefs about the future. Our framework assumes that information enters the choice process as a factor in gauging personal health and consequences of smoking through its influence on risk perception. This use of information reflects the cognitive limits people might have to understanding and using complex information about risk. Psychologists have found these limitations to be a key factor in determining how people simplify and adapt to complexity by using shortcuts to organize information. We will discuss these lessons in terms of understanding elicited risk perceptions and for designing information campaigns to communicate the risks and health effects of smoking.

Rationality and the Acquisition of Information

In the simple framework described above, a young person computes expected utilities from the decision to start smoking. The model assumes an ex ante calculation based on subjective probabilities of future events and the utilities of these events. The youth decides to smoke if the expected present value of utilities from smoking is greater than or equal to zero—recall that the zero utility condition represents the baseline situation each person experiences from deciding not to smoke. The ex ante probabilities taken as given in our model are, in reality, subjective beliefs—risk perceptions each person has formed at the time of the decision. Later in life, because of new scientific information available to the public, personal growth, and or other factors, the same individual may form quite different subjective beliefs for the same situation. The smoker may realize that if the youth stage could be revisited and the choice remade, the outcome might well be different. When new information is presented, the person can regret having started smoking. Regret, however, does not imply that the initial decision was irrational when it was made. Presumably if the individual experiences good news, there is no regret. Moreover, we do not tautologically argue that "what is done is rational, otherwise it would not have been done"; rather, our argument is an acknowledgment that choices are made in a constrained environment. They reflect each person's information set, preferences, and constraints. Only if the process were to be fully characterized could we determine whether a choice was constrained or irrational.

The process of acquiring and using information takes personal resources and effort. Making information "publicly" available does not necessarily ensure that an individual will receive and incorporate it into a decision. Psychological and other social science research on risk communication has established that people use a variety of processing rules or filters to interpret information according to its source, their own preconceptions and attitudes, and their cognitive abilities.

How does information enter the public domain? In our society, we often rely on the media. New scientific findings, government policies, others' experiences that are judged newsworthy, and even privately purchased advertisements contribute to public information that influences each individual's knowledge of an issue. Because of the increased complexity of public and private choices, the past three decades have seen increased efforts to present information about smoking and health in a way that ensures the recipients will understand what is intended, within the limits of the knowledge available. With better knowledge, the individual is empowered to make choices that are appropriate for his preferences. It is unlikely that smokers in their fifties and sixties in 1992, the year when our data began, had such knowledge when they first decided to smoke.

We do know that events that could have been used to characterize long-term health effects were relatively scarce in the 1940s and 1950s. And there were mixed messages—private advertisements for cigarettes contradicted early public warnings about smoking. In the early part of the twentieth century, many young persons started to smoke, but there were few elderly persons who had been lifelong smokers. The resulting lack of epidemiological evidence rendered impossible an accurate assessment of the long-term health consequences of smoking.

Also, paternalism reigned over health issues (see Starr 1982). Individuals were seen as largely ignorant of what affected their own health and safety. It was thought that giving people information on risk might make them too anxious, and it seemed doubtful that they could use such information very productively. Patients were thought to be better off not knowing they had a disease or a condition such as a terminal illness. The physician, or the expert, judged what was best. This notion has since been replaced by the doctrine of informed consent.[1]

Historically, it was the responsibility of various parties licensed by the state, such as physicians, to provide solutions to patients, rather than to contribute information to the patients' decision-making process. If doctors told patients anything at all about smoking (remember, many physicians themselves smoked), it was that smoking—and other health behaviors, such as excessive alcohol consumption—were bad for them. There was not much general knowledge about the probabilities of adverse health outcomes from smoking, and many of the "experts" were not familiar with the limited empirical evidence that did exist. Thus, rolling the clock back to the time when those individuals in our study began smoking, it seems highly unlikely that *anyone* had knowledge of the probabilities depicted in Figure 2.1, much less the potential smokers themselves.

Of the risks that people face, those of smoking are now among the more highly publicized. As early as in the 1970s people were substantially aware of the risks associated with smoking. Usually more than 90 percent of persons surveyed said they knew smoking causes lung cancer and heart disease. Most knew smoking could cause harm to a fetus (statistics cited in Schelling 1991, p. 132). Nonetheless, as Schelling (1991) noted, the scope of the information disseminated has been limited. It has focused on a few specific adverse health outcomes, or the messages have been cast in very general language, such as "smoking is bad for you."

Risk Perception

Our model suggests choice is influenced by both public and private information and assumes this information contributes to the formation of subjective probabilities, or risk perceptions.

Choices as described by our game tree are based on subjective beliefs about the probabilities of certain outcomes given particular actions. Subjective assessments of the probabilities may differ substantially from their objective counterparts. Experts organize the types of information available to the public differently from ordinary people. When samples of the lay public are asked to rank activities in which they engage (such as driving a car) or technologies (such as particular types of surgery) according to their "risk," the results frequently are different from experts' judgments or statistical estimates. An extensive program of research by cognitive psychologists (see Slovic, Fischoff, and Lichtenstein 1980; Slovic 1987) has established that people use a multiattribute perspective in judging risks. They assign higher probabilities to risks of events that are dreaded, those characterized by uncontrollability and catastrophic or fatal consequences, and lower probabilities to those risks that are more likely to be controlled by the individual or involve less severe outcomes.

In an early study comparing actual number of deaths per year to estimated number of deaths per year owing to various causes, lay persons tended to overestimate the probability of low-risk events and underestimate the probability of high-risk ones (Lichtenstein et al. 1978). Respondents overestimated the frequency of such rare causes of death as tornadoes, botulism, and floods, and underestimated probabilities of getting cancer, heart disease, and diabetes. Combs and Slovic (1979) found a strong relationship between newspaper coverage and the extent of overestimation, a conclusion supported by a subsequent study by Johnson and Tversky (1983). The estimates people produce also depend on the details of the elicitation process (Fischhoff and MacGregor 1983). Some changes in how the questions are asked will make an appreciable difference, and other scale-related factors might not be as important (Smith et al. 1987). Experimental research has suggested that some of the bias in lay persons' estimates might also be due to individuals' ability to recall past examples of the event in question or to relate the event to personal experiences. Tversky and Kahneman (1974) labeled this behavior as reflecting an "availability heuristic."

In a study of willingness to pay to avoid multiple sclerosis (MS), Sloan and coauthors (1998) found that survey respondents greatly overstated the probability that they would get MS. Based on responses to several questions, the authors were able to estimate the degree of overestimation. When smoking behavior has been considered as part of the risk questions in past research, probabilities of harm have been well within the zero-one interval. That is, they were neither minute, as is the probability of getting MS, nor virtually certain. The problem in individual perception of smoking hazards, which in part reflects cognitive limits, lies more with the delayed health response to smoking rather than with the underlying probabilities per se.

Several psychologists have conducted research on perceptions of smoking risk and the concept of optimistic bias, which refers to individuals' tendency to view risks of various behaviors as lower for themselves than for others engaging in similar behaviors (Weinstein 1989). Optimistic biases are said to be greatest when people have little experience with the hazard, the probability of the hazard's occurring is low, and when hazards are thought to be controllable by oneself (Weinstein 1989). In the context of smoking, youths, although not adults, have little experience with the hazard; the probability of the hazard's occurring (that is, addiction and health harms) is not low; and, at least before addiction sets in, the hazard is widely thought to be controllable by oneself.

Some psychologists as well as some economists have emphasized cognitive limits on individual rationality (see, for example, Kahneman and Tversky 1981). According to this view, people do not process information well because they lack the general intellectual skills, do not have specific substantive knowledge, and, for various reasons, do not devote sufficient effort to the cognitive task of evaluating risks.

Holding other factors constant, people should become more proficient at forming risk perceptions as they become older, to the extent that their cognitive skills and the general knowledge acquired from personal experience and other sources improve. However, at some time late in the life cycle cognitive capacity (the ability to focus attention, keep several facts in mind, and consider abstract and concrete issues) decreases. At the same time, the risky choices individuals face may become more complex, and they are less likely to be aided by others (such as parents and teachers) at a later stage of life (Fischhoff 1989).

Intriguingly, certain risky behaviors have been associated with measures of cognition. For example, adolescents with low grade-point averages are more likely to start smoking, holding a number of other background factors constant (Gruber and Zinman 2000). For persons in middle age, grades are no longer available; moreover, their past academic performance would not be an adequate indicator of cognitive capacity. Fortunately, surveys used in our study obtained age-appropriate measures of cognition (Herzog and Wallace 1997), allowing us to gauge directly the importance of cognition on risk perception (see Chapter 5).

Past research suggests that to understand effective information programs for current adult smokers one must consider both how people evaluate their personal risks as well as the types of information they find salient. This has been done in previous studies by comparing subjective probabilities of specific outcomes, as reported by individuals in household surveys, with objective probabilities that those same outcomes will occur. Research on the risk perceptions of current smokers, however, has been controversial. In several studies, W. Kip Viscusi (1990, 1991, 1992; Viscusi, Hakes, and Carlin 1997) has argued that current smokers perceive the risk of lung cancer to be too high, while others, such as Michael Schoenbaum (1997), have argued that Viscusi's conclusions are not warranted, especially in the case of heavy smokers. We enter this debate by reviewing the evidence and arguments and by presenting our own new results (Chapter 5). We find that the average smoker is reasonably accurate in assessing the mortality risks of smoking. The heavy smoker, however, is not so accurate; as Schoenbaum (1997) finds, they tend to understate their risk. Perhaps more important than the bases of their perception of their own risk, current smokers do not appear to update these perceptions in response to general risk information; they need the message to be *personalized.* We establish this result in Chapter 5 by considering how different health shocks affect both smokers and nonsmokers.

Endogenous Preferences

The expected utility framework depicted by Figure 2.1 assumes that preferences are exogenous. Utility changes with changes in behavior and depends on health outcomes. For example, utility is lower when the individual is disabled. But utility in the disabled state, conditional on its occurring, is set at the beginning. Economists have questioned the assumption of exogeneous preferences since the late 1980s. In an alternative framework, utility function parameters evolve over time as a function of consumption. Many economists, the vast majority of noneconomist scholars, and certainly the public would like an explanation for how people can rationally choose to engage in self-destructive behaviors. An easy answer (perhaps too easy) is that the benefits of the actions are assessed to be worth it, as in the game tree for youths deciding to smoke. An activity such as smoking yields personal benefits to the smoker, such as relief from stress and participation in a mutually enjoyable activity with one's peers.

A more sophisticated explanation describes a specific form of endogenous preferences linked through time by past consumption. With these endogenous preferences, the trade-offs between some goods change in response to the sequence of past consumption decisions, as a result, for example, of addiction. Sometimes these past choices can be described as if the sequence were a personal investment, such as (but not limited to) education or past consumption that yields valuable experiences. However, other types of consumption choices also affect the subsequent trade-offs a person makes. In these cases, as with addiction to an illicit substance, we recognize the complementarity but may not describe the process as an investment.

The foundation of Becker's rational addiction framework (see Becker and Murphy 1988 and other accounts of the rational addiction model, such as Becker 1992, 1996) is that people make current consumption choices that alter the trade-offs between some goods in the future. An example might be attending classical music concerts. Hearing an opera by Richard Wagner the first or even the second time might be not enjoyable or might even be boring, despite one's feeling that it would be nice to be able to enjoy Wagner. But over time one learns enough to actually enjoy it. Thus, someone who wanted to develop an appreciation for Wagner would need to be willing to endure a short-term sacrifice to acquire the understanding necessary for the long-term benefit of enjoying his work. Education also might increase a person's appreciation of history and the arts—and decrease his rate of time preference (that is, reduce his discount rate as in Eq. 2.1) in that he might learn to better anticipate the long-term benefits of his current actions. Through the social networks he develops, he might enjoy the act of going to the opera or just being seen at the opera, if not the performance itself.

A past consumption pattern may have a positive or negative effect on current and future consumption, but it is partly motivated by the change in future trade-offs it creates. With addiction, not all types of past consumption lead to positive future consequences. Some have harmful effects. In the cases of smoking, heavy alcohol consumption, use of illicit drugs, and compulsive gambling, past consumption has harmful complementarities with the future trade-offs a person faces.

In this framework, consumption over time leads to the accumulation of consumption capital stocks. This concept resembles the concept of physical capital in that it is durable and results from freely chosen actions. It is generally reversible, in the sense that it decays (depreciates) unless maintained. In the case of addictive goods, however, *reducing* the consumption stock takes effort. That distinction helps explain the difficulty of making a smoking cessation choice after many years of smoking (and accumulating a large consumption stock).

By consuming addictive goods, a person builds up his consumption capital, affecting the utility of present consumption of the good in two ways. First, current consumption might render it difficult for future consumption to increase the overall level of utility ("tolerance"). Second, current consumption nonetheless has positive marginal utility. Smokers act *as if* they are farsighted, in the sense that they anticipate the future consequences of present actions when deciding how much to smoke. Consumption of a good is termed an *addiction* if an increase in past consumption of the good leads to an increase in current consumption. This means an increase in the amount of current consumption is required before diminishing marginal utility occurs. Learning to appreciate classical music increases the marginal utility of listening to such music in the future, but, in contrast to cigarette addiction, acquiring music appreciation raises total utility in future periods.

During the 1980s and 1990s, a fairly large literature on addiction accumulated, providing empirical support for this basic rational addiction hypothesis as an explanation of addictive behavior. Chaloupka and Warner (2000) offer a detailed review of empirical research on rational addiction applied to smoking. The basic hypothesis of the rational addiction model is that individuals are aware of both costs and benefits of addictive consumption *before* they become addicted; individuals select an optimal consumption path after considering all current and future consequences of addictive consumption. The empirical evidence to date is consistent with the assumption underlying these models, that people are forward-looking, but there have been few direct tests.[2]

Discounting and Time-Consistent Preferences

Whenever we describe choice over time, the rate of time preference is implicit in the definition of the objective function that describes how consumption over time is aggregated. In our case, we are explicit and assume that future consumption is discounted, as seen in Eq. (2.1). Higher discount rates give greater weight to benefits and costs accruing early in the life cycle than do lower discount rates. The standard approach treats discount rates as exogenous.

An alternative approach is to consider discount rates as endogenous. Consumption of some goods might affect how a person values future versus current benefits, or time preference. Education may enlighten the person with regard to the value of deferred versus current consumption and might be undertaken, at least in part, for this reason. Addiction to some goods, such as drugs and alcohol, might also affect one's ability to judge the consequences of decisions that occur in the future—that is, addiction increase one's rate of time preference (Becker and Mulligan 1997). Accordingly, *awareness* of future consequences is not impaired by addiction—rather, the *weight given* to these consequences is influenced by it. Plausibly, many addictive substances might affect one's ability to think about the future, but this seems much less likely for tobacco products than for alcohol or illicit drugs.

Models underlying the game tree depicted by Figure 2.1 assume time-consistent preferences. In the Becker-type model, preferences evolve as consumption capital accumulates, but individuals' future behavior coincides with present desires for such behavior.

Two features distinguish time-consistent from time-inconsistent preferences. One is the use of self-control devices. In the time-inconsistent case, individuals have two selves (see, for example, Elster 1997 and 1999, also analyzed by Winston 1980 and Schelling 1984 in the context, among others, of smoking). For example, having peach ice cream in the freezer is likely to tempt one to eat it late at night. Therefore, to prevent this type of behavior, when one is in the grocery store, one might eschew purchases of such ice cream. If the consumer expects to have different preferences at different points of time, making welfare comparisons becomes exceedingly difficult. Time-consistent individuals presumably would not use such self-control devices (see Gruber and Köszegi 2001), although, in the context of an addictive good, we cannot rule this out. Smokers may use a quitting aid, as in the model in Figure 2.1 depicting the utility loss from quitting. In fact, willingness to pay for such aids is at least a partial measure of the cost of quitting.

To some scholars, the time-consistency model seems counterintuitive. For example, Elster (1997) finds Becker's argument to be rather circular. Taking steps to reduce the rate of time discounting in the future, such as by going to school, would seem to be motivated by a low rate of time preference in the first place. This is where Elster's notion of weakness of will comes in. Current actions are taken to reduce weakness of will in the future, such as would occur with peach ice cream in the freezer.

The second feature of time inconsistency is an inability to carry through on desired or planned activities. A smoker might plan to quit at a certain date but finds later that he cannot. Stated intentions to quit smoking and repeated but unsuccessful attempts to quit (see Chapter 6) are taken as evidence for this dimension of time inconsistency. However, statements of intentions are not fully conclusive evidence of time-inconsistent preferences. One might question the intensity or seriousness of intentions to quit. The remarks by a senior executive of a major tobacco company add some humor on this point (see Box 2.1).

Whether preferences are time consistent has important public policy implications. If preferences *are* time consistent, then government regulatory policy should reflect the external costs of individual behavior, such as the adverse health effects of secondary smoke and additional costs to private and public insurance pools (see Manning et al. 1991). However, with time-inconsistent preferences, internal costs (those borne by the smoker and his family) should also be considered in the formulation of regulatory interventions. We offer no solution for the time-consistent versus time-inconsistent question here.

Box 2.1 Testimony of Joseph F. Cullman III, former chairman of the board of Phillip Morris, in *Cipollone vs. Liggett Group, Inc.*

Q. But it is difficult [to quit]?
A. That's what it says here and I'm not disagreeing with it.
Q. They said it was very difficult. Do you agree with that?
A. I would say it's difficult.
Q. Let's see, most smokers have a tough time giving up cigarettes?
A. Well, if they didn't, there would be many fewer smokers than there are today.

Transcript proceedings, Feb. 29, 1988 at 3311–3314.

Peer Effects

In the above framework (Figure 2.1), people make decisions on their own, depending on the subjective probabilities and utilities assigned to particular states. There is no explicit rule for the influence of others on a person's preferences. However, peers are thought to have an important impact on some decisions to engage in risky behavior. For example, some of our study's subjects as teenagers might have raced hot rods to impress their girlfriends.[3] Similarly, smoking may be undertaken to impress one's friends. In principle, peer influences can be reflected in utility from smoking. As we noted earlier, Becker and Murphy (2000) have argued that some forms of these social interactions lead to simple modifications in preferences; what is rational is then derived from these modified preferences. Ignoring these modifications could lead observers to cite peer effects as a source of time-inconsistent preferences.

Peer effects change appreciably as people age. As people age, the peer group expands. Individuals learn what their society as a whole believes and make choices under that influence—that is, they become more responsive to what are termed social norms (Fischhoff et al. 1993).

Empirically, it seems difficult to separate aspects of behavioral change as attributable to peer pressure, biological change, or the acquisition of information about consequences of personal decisions. Overall, economic research on peer effects on behavior has been quite limited, although recently some interest has emerged among researchers studying effects of student peers on school quality (see Epple and Romano 1998).[4]

Except for observing that smoking is more common in certain groups than others, the influence of peer effects is not evidenced. Without presenting evidence, for example, Wynder and Orlandi (1991) concluded, "the social acceptance or non-acceptance of smoking within society's various population groups is the predominant factor that determines smoking habits for both men and women" (p. 112).

Whatever the peer effects are, it seems likely that peer influences to smoke should be less important than they once were. Smoking has disappeared from television except in old movies.[5] The diffusion of smoking bans (see Chapter 3) has greatly reduced public exposure to smoking and increased the inconvenience of smoking. At the same time, however, smoking by females in public was at one time widely viewed as something nice girls and proper ladies didn't do. Over time, in part abetted by advertising, peer sanctions against women who smoke have eroded.

Biological and Psychological Perspectives for Smoking Initiation

Smoking begins at an early age (Chapter 1 and Gruber and Zinman 2000). The smokers in our samples went through the initiation process many decades before they were surveyed by the Health and Retirement Study or by us. Fewer than 5 percent of smokers began smoking after age thirty. Indeed, a large fraction of current smokers began before age sixteen, and there exists a large literature on youth smoking. The expected utility model is silent about why the utility of smoking is positive. This is partly explained by evidence from biology and psychology.

Stress, anxiety, and pressure from peer groups are major reasons why adolescents begin to smoke. Stress is an important precursor to the initiation of smoking among adolescents as well as to the continued consumption of cigarettes as adults. Personality traits, particularly neuroticism among adolescents, has also been found to increase the likelihood of smoking initiation. This effect was independent of the role of external stress on smoking decisions, showing that forces both internal and external to adolescents play a role in smoking initiation (Byrne, Byrne, and Reinhart 1995).

Depression among adolescents is also a major predictor of experimental smoking. Experimental smoking, often among preteens, is how most adolescents begin smoking. Depression and anxiety appear to operate on smoking decisions by making it more difficult for adolescents to withstand peer pressure to smoke (Patton et al. 1998).

It has been postulated that nicotine itself causes depression. Until the 1980s, nicotine was not recognized as an addictive drug, but in recent years, there has been a virtual consensus on the important role of nicotine, although the mechanisms through which nicotine operates are not well understood. Nicotine might act on reward and punishment centers in the brain, or as a tranquilizer and a means of reducing anger, pain, and negative feelings (Ney and Gale 1989, p. 6). When smokers are depressed, electroencephalographic analysis shows a depressant effect (U.S. Food and Drug Administration 1995, p. 41488). Nicotine's rewarding or reinforcing effects occur via the release of dopamine, which plays a major role in regulating pleasurable sensations (ibid., p. 41535). Nicotine might also be a stimulant, releasing energy for motor routines, which in turn reduce stress and the effects of distracters, making it easier to concentrate. Smoking might protect the consolidation of memory, but the evidence is conflicting (Gale and Ney 1989, p. 13; U.S. Food and Drug Administration 1995, p. 41537).

Initially, the smoker might smoke for the reward of the positive feelings it allegedly induces. Later, after the smoker becomes addicted, smoking is driven in part by the avoidance of negative feelings, or the withdrawal symptoms, for nicotine is an addictive chemical substance that affects the central nervous system. Discomforts of withdrawal include cravings for cigarettes, weight gain, and a perceived loss of creativity.

It seems clear that adolescents do not make smoking decisions in a vacuum, in which they dispassionately judge the expected benefits of smoking against any expected harms. Instead, a variety of influences, including family, friends, and their own psychological well-being, play a role in determining whether kids experiment with smoking, initiate smoking, and become habitual smokers. Many of these influences, and the circumstances under which experimentation and initiation occur, suggest potential harms are not important in the decision to begin smoking and that benefits, including the types described here, are tantamount.

The Smoking Decision, Time, and Rationality in Decision Making under Uncertainty

Decisions about whether and how much to smoke are among the most important choices people make. The choices are complicated by the long period between the decision to smoke and the outcome of that choice. Over such a long time, a person can receive new information about smoking in general and about his own psychological and physiological responses in particular. Time also provides the opportunity for biological and developmental change, both as a result of and not directly attributable to smoking.

Time also might allow for changes in the person's decision-making process. Valid or not, many parents would agree with the proposition that children behave irrationally while we parents tend to make rational judgments. From a public health perspective, the idea that one could rationally decide to smoke seems an anathema. But in the end, knowledge of smoking benefits and harms are not static but are likely to vary over time.

This point has been explored by Elster (1997) in the context of addiction, a topic that, at least at first glance, seems particularly ill-suited to the assumption of rational decision making. He distinguishes two situations regarding the rationality of an addictive good. First is the situation of the decision maker in the discovery phase: Do full-blown addicts behave rationally? Second is that of the youth in period one: Is the choice of an addictive career rational? Even in the presence of quitting costs, the answer to the first question may be yes and to the second one, no. Thus, rationality is largely context specific. The rationality assumption may be tenable in some situations and not in others. Bad choices per se are not inconsistent with rationality.

Conclusions

Expected utility theory has been an important workhorse for the analysis of choices under uncertainty, but all scholars in the field, irrespective of discipline, recognize its shortcomings. At a minimum, it provides a useful framework for organizing ideas.

Although this chapter has explored sources for debate among the disciplines, we have argued that there is scope for cooperation and mutual learning across disciplinary boundaries. In part, the shortcomings can be addressed by adding complexity, such as by updating risk perceptions based on information, as will be explained in greater depth in Chapter 5. General information and person-specific information are discussed in Chapters 3 and 4, respectively. Framing and risk communication as research issues are part of the design of the survey we conducted for this study (Chapter 7). In Chapter 8, we will discuss the Becker-Murphy rational addiction model and findings based on this model, which will also provide a framework for our own empirical analysis of demand for cigarettes. In the end, a model should be assessed in terms of its ability to explain observed behavior.

Finally, although much research on risk has sought to be context-free, it seems that more progress can be made by explicitly focusing on important decisions (such as smoking) that individuals make over the life cycle in a process that includes new information and life experiences that affect risk perception and preferences.

CHAPTER

3

Government Policy and Advertising as Sources of Information for Smokers

In a free society we take for granted the availability of a wide array of information, but this luxury does not mean useful information is available without cost. Sorting the proverbial wheat from the chaff in the marketplace of ideas requires time, effort, and, often, direct monetary resources. As discussed in Chapter 2, the news media, government, the private sector (through paid advertising), and even friends and relatives contribute to the information available to each person. We can reasonably assume people will decide to devote more resources, directly or indirectly, to assembling information for important decisions than for those less consequential.

Information policy has become an increasingly important policy instrument over the past forty to fifty years, especially as related to the regulation of health and safety activities. Recently, some informational programs have been proposed and evaluated in the field of environmental policy as well.

Government action, in principle, sends signals to the individual. To the extent that these signals are understood as intended, a government program may expand the knowledge base used in decision making by providing new information or by reducing the cost to decision makers of understanding choices based on information previously available but not widely appreciated.

Our objective in this chapter is to summarize the current status of information on smoking as well as the evolution of that information as we can assume it was available to smokers in the Health and Retirement Study. The HRS was designed to sample persons born during the years 1931 to 1941 and their spouses (who could be any age). We consider government sources of information as well as the information that might have been available through the media and private advertising.

The history of information on smoking partly explains why the HRS respondents decided to smoke and not to quit. Given today's knowledge we might regard both choices as foolish, but the information available at the time the decisions were made was quite different. On a personal note, two of us fall in the age group corresponding to the HRS sample. One smoked cigars for nearly a decade, beginning in graduate school. The decision did not seem particularly risky to him at the time—public messages about cigars were nonexistent then, and those for cigarettes were, according to the detached account today, more mixed than we might think. Personal signals were, in fact, the most influential in convincing him to quit; a young son who thought the behavior was "dangerous" contributed as well. The other of us smoked a pipe on occasion, but never frequently enough to consider future health consequences.

In developing our story we take the full twentieth century as our setting. This was the century of the manufactured cigarette, which was introduced at the very end of the nineteenth century. While the most attention is given to federal regulation and information, we also discuss lawsuits, pricing policies, bans, and private advertising influencing the total information available to consumers.

The public sector can influence use of a harmful substance such as tobacco in several ways: by enforcing direct limits on supply, such as banning sales outright, restricting where the product can be used, and limiting its availability. Consumption can also be limited through excise taxes, which reduce use by raising the product's price and also raise revenue for the government. The public sector also can distribute its own information and control other information disseminated about a product. Excepting a complete ban, the government, at all levels, has tried all of these avenues to influence the use of tobacco products.

Economists generally classify a government's regulatory activity according to four strategies for influencing behavior: (1) direct information programs, (2) command and control policies, (3) performance standards, and (4) incentive-based policies. Government information programs are efforts to introduce information into the relevant segment of the population. The "Just Say No" campaign and descriptions of the effects of a mother's smoking on her unborn baby would be two examples. The command-and-control approach imposes specific requirements on a regulated business. Advertising control is one example. Performance-based regulations (for example, minimum miles-per-gallon requirements) set an objective but allow regulated businesses to achieve the objective using methods of their own choosing. The 1997 proposed settlement between state attorneys general and major tobacco companies required the tobacco companies to achieve specific reductions in youth smoking rates (although the final agreement reached in 1998 did not do so). Incentive strategies may be divided into ex ante and ex post approaches. An example of an ex ante incentive is a tax on cigarettes based on the anticipated external costs cigarette consumption impose. With ex post incentive-based policies, the penalty is imposed on the injurer after the injury has occurred, as is done by tort law.

Each approach has different advantages. Command-and-control regulation is especially attractive to many lawyers, who are often the primary authors of regulations, because it appears to have clear, direct effects. In many situations, however, regulators do not know how to meet the particular policy goal; performance-based regulation overcomes this shortcoming by prescribing the outcome rather than the method.

A regulator applying an ex ante incentive must set a surcharge or tax on the product that provides an incentive to reconsider the consumption choice. To set the charge at an efficient level, the regulation must be able to specify the marginal social cost (equivalently, the marginal damage) of the regulated activity. Ex ante charges are based on the assumption that an individual's behavior has external effects. If cigarettes become safer, the tax should be adjusted downward (Hanson and Logue 1998).

Ex post incentive-based regulation—imposing tort liability on any producer or seller—is intended to encourage an efficient level of precaution through the knowledge that any injury caused by a firm's action or inaction will result in a claim for damages, although tort's success depends on idealized conditions (which will be discussed later). Tort law is important for at least two reasons. First, it has become a major instrument of tobacco control during the past decade. Second, an important consideration under tort liability concerns what the buyers and sellers knew and when they knew it—tort is thus closely connected to information and risk perception. A necessary condition for damage to have occurred is that someone acted based on available information and risk perceptions and this caused a documented loss.

Overall, government policy has a mixed record. During the twentieth century, the tobacco lobby was successful in mitigating the public sector's efforts to deal with the health hazards of smoking, until at least the early

1990s. Of course, in the early part of the century, the tobacco industry had help from the government itself—public policy *promoted* smoking by subsidizing cigarette consumption by military personnel and by running an agricultural price-support system designed to stabilize employment in tobacco farming.

Evolution of Tobacco Regulation

Two federal agencies have had a role in the regulation of tobacco—the Food and Drug Administration (FDA) and the Federal Trade Commission (FTC). To understand how each agency developed its policies, we must begin with their earliest legislative mandates.

Early History

In the late 1800s and the early part of the twentieth century, a number of American states enacted restrictions on tobacco use (Kagan and Vogel 1993, p. 34). By 1909, under pressure from antismoking organizations, thirteen states had enacted restrictive legislation (Gottsegen 1940; Davidson 1996).[1] This legislation had two rationales: to reduce the risk of fires, and to improve public morality (Jacobson and Wasserman 1997, p. 3). Most of these restrictions vanished after the repeal of Prohibition, that is, by the mid-1930s. The Food and Drug Act of 1906 was the first federal food and drug law. This act contained no specific reference to tobacco products, and a 1914 interpretation of the law advised that tobacco should be included under the act only when it is used to cure, mitigate, or prevent disease (Pub. L. No. 59-384, 34 Stat. 768 [1906]).

The Federal Food, Drug and Cosmetic Act (FFDCA) of 1938 superseded the 1906 act. Under this law, the definition of a drug includes "articles intended for use in the diagnosis, cure, mitigation, treatment, or prevention of disease in man or other animals" and "articles (other than food) intended to affect the structure or any function of the body of man or other animals." The FDA has asserted jurisdiction under this act in cases where the manufacturer or vendor has made medical claims. Qualifying tobacco cases have included the Fairfax Cigarettes case in 1953, when the manufacturer claimed that the brand prevented respiratory and other diseases, and the 1959 case against Trim Reducing-Aid Cigarettes, containing the additive tartaric acid, which was claimed to aid in weight reduction (Centers for Disease Control and Prevention, 1999). In the 1950s, the FDA occasionally reprimanded tobacco manufacturers who attributed health value or medicinal properties to their products (Kagan and Vogel 1993).

In 1960, the federal Hazardous Substances Labeling Act authorized the FDA to regulate substances that are hazardous (either toxic, corrosive, irritant, strong sensitizers, flammable, or pressure generating). The rationale for labeling these substances was that they could cause substantial personal injury or illness during or as a result of customary use. In 1963, the FDA expressed its interpretation that tobacco did not fit the definition of "hazardous" and withheld further recommendations pending the release of the report of the Surgeon General's Advisory Committee on Smoking and Health (U.S. Centers for Disease Control and Prevention 1999).

The Federal Trade Commission Act of 1914, amended in 1938, empowered the FTC to prevent persons, partnerships, or corporations from using unfair or deceptive acts or practices in commerce. Between 1945 and 1960, the FTC completed seven formal cease-and-desist order proceedings for medical or health claims against cigarette companies. One of those complaints countered Brown and Williamson's claim that Kool cigarettes provided extra protection against or cured a cold.

Recently released documents have revealed a great deal of the thinking within tobacco companies during this period. The companies apparently possessed information about the harmful effects of smoking, which they concealed from the public. In fact, while suppressing this information, they publicized health benefits explicitly, as in the case of the Kool ads. In the 1990s a very different climate developed for the big tobacco companies.

In 1994, Representative Henry Waxman (a Democrat from California), then chairman of the House Subcommittee on Health and the Environment, held a series of congressional hearings on smoking and health. During the hearings, the chief executive officers of major tobacco companies all testified that they believed tobacco products that contained nicotine were *not* addictive. Waxman's subcommittee released a report entitled "The Hill and Knowlton Documents: How the Tobacco Industry Launched Its Disinformation Campaign" (Waxman 1994) (see Box 3.1). The report indicated that the Council on Tobacco Research was a public relations vehicle of the tobacco industry used to counter negative reports on the dangers of smoking. Within weeks of the hearings, copies of internal Brown and Williamson documents were sent anonymously to Waxman, FDA commissioner David Kessler, and several news organizations. The documents revealed that the tobacco industry had far greater knowledge of the addictive properties of tobacco products than was previously known. The documents also implied that tobacco companies knowingly and deliberately manipulated nicotine levels in tobacco products. This finding led to renewed interest in having the FDA regulate cigarettes as a drug.

The Surgeon General's Report

In the mid-1960s the FTC suggested placing restrictions on tobacco advertising, but tobacco industry resources were sufficient to block these plans in Congress. The Public Health Service argued in favor of interventionist government policies (Raffel and Raffel 1989). And most important, the surgeon general's 1964 report, by Luther L. Terry, summarized existing

---

Box 3.1 Information in confidential tobacco documents

The tobacco documents revealed the following:

- In 1946, H. B. Parmele, a research scientist at Lorillard, noted in an internal memo that studies of a cancer link were supported by just enough evidence to justify such a presumption, although this link had not been established absolutely.
- In 1957, a Liggett marketing firm conducted a motivation survey of smokers to assess smoker's attitudes toward potential health fears. The survey concluded that smokers said they wished they had never started to smoke, but once they had, they couldn't stop.
- On February 15, 1961, Arthur D. Little, a Liggett consultant, replicated results from a 1953 health study by Dr. Ernst Wynder (showing increased skin tumors in mice painted with smoke condensation including tar) and stated that biologically active materials are present in cigarette tobacco that are cancer causing; cancer promoting; poisonous; and stimulating, pleasurable, and flavorful.
- On November 15, 1961, Dr. Helmut Wakeham, research director at Phillip Morris, observed that carcinogens are found in practically every class of compounds in smoke and concluded that developing a medically acceptable, low-carcinogen cigarette might be possible but would require great expense and time.

medical research on the health hazards of smoking and pushed for federal action, associating cigarette smoking with increased rates of lung cancer, chronic bronchitis, emphysema, and heart disease (Department of Health, Education, and Welfare 1964). This report represented a watershed in the history of smoking control in general and in dissemination about the harms of smoking by a public agency in particular. The American Medical Association, the American Cancer Society, the American Heart Association, and the American Lung Association all endorsed the report, which added scientific weight and social respect to the antitobacco movement (Davidson 1996, chap. 2). The report was more noteworthy for its political significance than for the information it contained, which was largely already known.

The Regulatory Environment after 1964

On the heels of the surgeon general's report, several government initiatives were implemented to publicize the harms from smoking. Although some restrictions were imposed, the thrust of public policy throughout most of the latter part of the twentieth century was in providing information to allow adults to make more informed choices.

The federal Cigarette Labeling and Advertising Act of 1965 required cigarette packages to be labeled with the warning, "Caution: Cigarette Smoking May be Hazardous to Your Health." Other wordings were prohibited. This act required no labels on cigarette advertisements, and in fact prohibited labels or additional federal regulations on advertisements for three years. It required the FTC to report to Congress annually on the effectiveness of cigarette labeling, current cigarette advertising, and promotion practices, and to make recommendations for legislation. The act also required the Department of Health, Education and Welfare to report annually to Congress on the health consequences of smoking.

Tobacco lobbyists, however, managed to water down this law, in the end producing a vague statement that failed to fully describe the causal link between cigarettes and health hazards (Kagan and Vogel 1993, p. 34). Congressional tobacco industry supporters also succeeded in adding a provision to the 1965 act that preempted state governments from adopting more stringent advertising or warning label regulations.

In 1967 the Federal Communications Commission (FCC) ruled that the fairness doctrine applied to cigarette advertising; stations broadcasting cigarette commercials had to donate airtime for antismoking messages (Jacobson and Wasserman 1997). These antismoking public service announcements (PSAs) may have had some effect on consumer behavior, as the number of smokers who expressed concern about the harmful effects of cigarettes increased from 47 percent to 69 percent in the years 1966 to 1970 (Department of Health and Human Services 1989).

The Public Health Cigarette Smoking Act of 1969 required cigarette packages to carry the label, "Warning: The Surgeon General Has Determined That Cigarette Smoking Is Dangerous to Your Health" and prohibited cigarette advertising on television and radio, with enforcement authority given to the Department of Justice. The act also prevented states or localities from regulating or prohibiting cigarette advertising or promotion for health-related reasons.

The Controlled Substance Act of 1970, designed to prevent the abuse of drugs, narcotics, and other addictive substances, specifically excluded tobacco from the definition of "controlled substance." Also in 1970, Congress enacted a total ban on broadcast advertising for tobacco products (Jones 1997). Tobacco companies decided that no press would be preferable to the bad press presented in the PSAs and acquiesced to the 1970 prohibition of TV and radio ads for cigarettes (Pertschuk 1986). (The fairness doctrine's antismoking messages thus ended at the same time. In the next three years, from 1971 to 1973, per capita cigarette sales increased by 4.1 percent as tobacco companies put advertising dollars into print media and billboards. This record illustrates the interplay of regulation and the regulated companies. At least until recently, tobacco companies have had the political power to greatly influence the regulatory environment in which they operate.

Through this first phase of tobacco regulation, the federal government, which had taxed tobacco since the Civil War, did not consider raising excise taxes to discourage smoking (Department of Health and Human Services 1989). Nor did the federal legislature ever seriously consider restrictions on where cigarettes could be smoked.

The Consumer Product Safety Act of 1972 transferred authority to regulate hazardous substances as designated by the federal Hazardous Substances Labeling Act from the FDA to the Consumer Product Safety Commission. The term *consumer product,* however, did not include tobacco or tobacco products. The Little Cigar Act of 1973 banned little cigar advertising on television and radio, also with enforcement authority granted to the

Department of Justice. In 1975, the inclusion of cigarettes in the K-rations and C-rations given to soldiers and sailors was discontinued after nearly sixty years (from World War I).

A 1976 amendment to the Hazardous Substances Labeling Act of 1960 established that the term *hazardous substance* should not apply to tobacco and tobacco products (concurring with the FDA's 1963 interpretation of the term). The Toxic Substances Control Act of 1976 was designed to regulate chemical substances and mixtures that present an unreasonable risk of injury to health or the environment; the term *chemical substance* did not include tobacco or any tobacco products.

In 1983, the FTC determined that its testing procedures might have significantly underestimated the levels of tar, nicotine, and carbon monoxide that smokers received from smoking certain low-tar cigarettes (Centers for Disease Control and Prevention 1999). The FTC prohibited Brown and Williamson from using the tar rating in Barclay cigarette advertising, packaging, or promotion because of problems with the testing methodology and consumers' possible reliance on that information. In 1985, the FTC stopped R. J. Reynolds from running its advertisements that read, "Of Cigarettes and Science."

The Comprehensive Smoking Education Act of 1984 instituted four rotating health warning labels on cigarette packages and advertisements all of which were designated as "Surgeon General's Warnings." These labels were: Smoking Causes Lung Cancer, Heart Disease, Emphysema and May Complicate Pregnancy"; "Quitting Smoking Now Greatly Reduces Serious Risks to Your Health"; "Smoking by Pregnant Women May Result in Fetal Injury, Premature Birth, and Low Birth Weight"; and "Cigarette Smoke Contains Carbon Monoxide." These warnings replaced other package warnings. This law also required the Department of Health and Human Services to publish a biennial status report for Congress on smoking and health and created a Federal Interagency Committee on Smoking and Health. The act also required cigarette manufacturers to provide a confidential list of cigarette additives, although brand-specific quantity information was not required. The Cigarette Safety Act of 1984 was designed to determine the technical and commercial feasibility of developing cigarettes and little cigars that would be less likely to ignite upholstered furniture and mattresses.

The Comprehensive Smokeless Tobacco Health Education Act of 1986 applied many of the new cigarette regulations to smokeless tobacco. It instituted three rotating health warning labels on smokeless tobacco packages and advertisements: "This product may cause mouth cancer"; "This product may cause gum disease and tooth loss"; and "This product is not a safe alternative to cigarettes."

In 1987, a coalition of national health organizations, antitobacco lobbyists, and airline flight attendants pushed through Public Law 100-202, which banned smoking on all domestic airline flights scheduled for two hours or less (Kagan and Vogel 1993). Also in 1987, the Department of Health and Human Services established a smoke-free environment in its facilities. Public Law 101-164 in 1989 banned smoking on all domestic airline flights scheduled for six hours or less. In 1990 the Interstate Commerce Commission banned smoking on all regularly scheduled interstate buses.

The FDA asserted jurisdiction over alternative nicotine delivery products such as Nicotine Polacrilex gum in 1984, Favor Smokeless Cigarettes in 1985 (subsequently removed from the market), Masterpiece Tobacs in 1989 (a tobacco chewing gum that was ruled an adulterated food and removed from the market), and nicotine patches in 1991 (O'Reilly 1997).

The Sydar amendment to the Alcohol, Drug Abuse, and Mental Health Administration Reorganization Act of 1992 required all states to adopt and enforce restrictions on tobacco sales and distribution to minors (Jacobson and Wasserman 1997). In 1993, the Environmental Protection Agency (EPA) gave the antismoking movement another huge push when it officially recognized secondhand smoke as a cause of cancer in nonsmokers. The Pro-Children Act of 1994 required all federally funded children's service facilities to become smoke free, expanding on a 1993 law that banned smoking in Women, Infants, and Children (WIC) clinics.

In 1992, the FTC took its first enforcement action under the Comprehensive Smokeless Tobacco Health Education Act, alleging that Pinkerton Tobacco Company's Red Man brand name had appeared illegally during a televised event. In 1993, the EPA released a final risk assessment on environmental tobacco smoke (ETS) and classified it as a Group A (known human) carcinogen.

In 1994, the Occupational Safety and Health Administration (OSHA) announced proposed regulations to prohibit smoking in the workplace, except in separately ventilated smoking rooms. The Department of Defense banned smoking in its buildings in 1994. In 1995 the Department of Justice reached a settlement with Philip Morris to remove tobacco advertisements from the line of sight of television cameras in sports stadiums.

Also in 1995, President Clinton announced the publication of the FDA's proposed regulations that would restrict the sale, distribution, and marketing of cigarettes and smokeless tobacco products, to protect children and adolescents. On August 23, 1996, Clinton announced the nation's first comprehensive program to prevent children and adolescents from smoking cigarettes or using smokeless tobacco. With the August 1996 publication of a final rule on tobacco in the *Federal Register,* the FDA began to regulate the sale and distribution of cigarettes and smokeless tobacco to children (O'Reilly 1997). The provisions of the FDA rule were aimed at reducing youth access to tobacco products and the appeal of tobacco advertising to young people. Additionally, the FDA required the major tobacco companies to educate young people about the real health dangers of tobacco use through a multimedia campaign.

The Tobacco Industry Fights Back

Throughout the 1980s, tobacco companies enjoyed a huge and profitable market, which grew with increases in cigarette exports (Jones 1997). Tobacco companies began to expand by diversifying into other product markets. By 1991 Philip Morris was the fourth largest company in the world when measured by stock market value. Given their power and the prospect of further favorable returns, the companies were not willing to accept government antismoking information programs, restrictions on smoking, and higher excise taxes without a fight.

Like their clients, pro-tobacco lobbying groups were also powerful and financially successful. The industry's collective lobbying group, the Tobacco Institute, had an annual budget of more than $11 million and a staff of 100 in 1986 (Glantz et al. 1996), enabling it to carry out massive legislative and advertising efforts. In 1988, the Tobacco Institute gave more honoraria to members of Congress than did any other interest group. Congress failed to adopt any of the 160 anti-cigarette bills introduced in its 1985–86 session, and the smoking ban on two-hour flights represented the only legislative defeat for the tobacco lobby during the 100th Congress, in 1987–88 (Kagan and Vogel 1993).

At the time, cigarette companies were spending billions per year on advertising and promotion, which represented a vital source of revenue for magazine and newspaper publishers and the billboard industry. To defeat restrictions on print advertising, the tobacco industry created the Freedom to Advertise Coalition, which included the American Association of Advertising Agencies, the Outdoor Advertising Association of America, and the Association of National Advertisers (Warner et al. 1986). The tobacco industry's position was also supported by magazine and newspaper publishers and the American Civil Liberties Union (ACLU), which opposed advertising restrictions on First Amendment grounds (White 1988). A number of bills restricting cigarette advertising were introduced but never reached the floor of either house.

The hearings before the Waxman subcommittee, held over several years, revealed that the tobacco companies continued a strategy of combatting health measures following publication of the 1964 surgeon general's report. In 1968, one company official referred to a gentleman's agreement among tobacco companies not to perform internal health research. On May 1, 1972, the Tobacco Institute discussed its strategy of relying on creating doubt about the health hazard charge without actually urging anyone to take up smoking, and encouraging "objective" scientific research as the only way to resolve the question of health hazard. In 1974, a researcher at Phillip Morris, wrote that "a general premise in our model of the cigarette smoker is that the smoking habit is maintained by the reinforcing effect of the pharmacologically active components of smoke." In 1977, another tobacco company researcher embarked on a study of the "psychology of the smoker in search of information that can increase corporate profits." He concluded that a smoker's behavior was the result of "chemical compounds being introduced to the bloodstream. Without the chemical compound, the cigarette market would collapse, Philip Morris would collapse, and we'd all lose our jobs and consulting fees." This researcher observed that there was "understandable legal concern about any industry-endorsed reference to the pharmacological effects of smoke . . . The risk is great that cigarette smoke contains a dependency-producing drug classifiable with amphetamines and other opiates." In 1988, a former research scientist at Philip Morris who allegedly was familiar with some of the secret internal documents of Philip Morris, stated to the subcommittee that "the company began to realize that they could reduce the tar, but increase the nicotine, and still have the cigarette be acceptable to the smoker. After all their work, they realized that nicotine was not just calming or stimulating, but it was having its effect centrally, in the brain, and that people were smoking for brain effects."

Today, with the benefit of the information made available through the states' lawsuits in the 1990s, we now know that cigarette companies appear to have been aware they could control cigarettes' addictive effect and choose a path that allowed people's addictions to persist or even increase.

Success of Mass Torts Litigation in the 1990s

In theory, tort law should encourage parties to use the socially optimal level of precaution. This optimum states that precaution should be increased until the marginal social cost (cost to all parties) equals marginal social benefit. In this context, benefit is measured in terms of the value of injury losses averted. To the extent that expected litigation cost is reflected in the price of a product, demand for the product is reduced (see Shavell 1987). In the event that suboptimal care levels result in injury, compensation would cover the losses sustained. In the context of tobacco products, fear of lawsuits should cause manufacturers to develop safer, less addictive cigarettes and to mitigate damages by marketing to groups less susceptible to harm from tobacco use. Imposition of tort law is fair in that victims are adequately compensated and injurers are made to pay for their wrongdoings.

Another feature of tort law that may lead to deterrence of harm is the publicity aspect. Large judgments against tobacco companies carry an implication that the companies' product is harmful. Media accounts and congressional testimony publicize the harm done to the plaintiffs. Also, defendants' claims in court that company officials "didn't know" smoking was harmful or addictive, or that the evidence on smoking's effects is ambiguous, cast adverse light on the companies in particular and on smoking in general. In contrast to tort, public regulatory proceedings tend to be more secretive.

Prior to the 1992 decision of the Supreme Court in *Cipollone vs. Liggett Group, Inc.*, the tobacco industry had won virtually every case in which it was involved.[2] Juries were unsympathetic to habitual smokers, and the industry spent huge sums for their defense in smoking and health cases.

Current tobacco litigation can be divided into three general categories: (1) individual cases and class actions brought on behalf of past and present users of tobacco products who have allegedly been harmed from their use, (2) class actions brought on behalf of persons allegedly harmed through exposure to secondhand tobacco smoke and seeking compensation for damages based on strict liability for an unreasonably dangerous product, and (3) civil actions brought by governmental entities to recover the welfare and health care costs associated with illnesses arising from the use of tobacco products. In the third category, all fifty states filed lawsuits against tobacco manufacturers in the past decade. Of these, forty-six states collectively reached a settlement on November 13, 1998; the remaining four (Florida, Minnesota, Mississippi, and Texas) sought settlements independently. In 1999, the Department of Justice filed its own suit against the tobacco industry.

Tobacco Control at the State and Local Levels

Many state, county, and local governments have been successful in implementing antismoking legislation (Jacobson and Wasserman 1997). Such legislation has relevance to this study to the extent that it affects information and smoker risk perception about smoking's harms. It has been more difficult for the tobacco industry to lobby against legislation at these levels. State legislatures have been active in the period since the late 1980s, enacting smoking restrictions (such as bans on smoking in restaurants and workplaces) and restrictions on access to tobacco products by youths, including vending machine and point-of-sale restrictions. But state legislatures also have enacted nondiscrimination laws on smokers' behalf (for example, smokers' rights ordinances) and statutes preempting stronger local ordinances. The latter trend is noteworthy, as it reflects the political clout of tobacco companies, which have lobbied for "smokers' rights." Local ordinances have been similar, although sometimes stricter. In the private sector, one out of every three firms had banned smoking in the workplace by 1990, and 60 percent of companies had imposed some form of restriction.

State excise taxes vary widely, with the chief tobacco-growing states having the lowest tax rates on cigarettes. Local tobacco taxes are low, accounting for only about 1.5 percent of the excise taxes collected in the 1990s (Davidson 1996).

Litigation History

In the *Cipollone vs. Liggett Group, Inc.* trial, the initial jury in New Jersey returned a verdict in favor of the plaintiff for $400,000. The Third Circuit reversed the trial court on the basis of improper jury instructions and ordered a new trial (*Cipollone vs. Liggett Group, Inc.*, 893 F.2d 541 [3rd Cir. 1990]). When the case reached the Supreme Court, the Court held that the

Federal Labeling Act does not preempt common-law claims for the marketing of cigarettes with manufacturing defects, claims for the failure to use a demonstrably safer alternative design for cigarettes, claims that involve testing or research practices, and claims for breach of express warranties arising from the manufacturer's statements in its advertisements. The Court held that claims based on fraudulent misrepresentation of material also were not preempted by federal cigarette warning-label laws.

State tobacco litigation has occurred in three waves: the 1950s and 1960s, the 1980s through 1992, and after 1992. The early cases were brought under tort theories of breach of express and implied warranty, deceit, and negligence. All were unsuccessful, owing to the defense argument that plaintiffs had assumed the risks voluntarily (that is, that smokers had adequate information for making an informed choice) and that there was a lack of medical knowledge linking smoking to disease; the great deal of time and expense involved in such litigation also worked in favor of the defendants (Edell 1986). Admittedly, these arguments are somewhat contradictory. But tort law required that consumers have the relevant information that was currently available then for making informed choices.

The second wave of litigation was brought under the theories of strict liability and failure to warn (Edell 1986). These cases were also unsuccessful because the voluntary assumption of risk was still an effective defense.

In the post-1992 period, states were permitted to bring claims based on the theory that tobacco companies earn huge profits from tobacco sales, states have the burden of paying the medical bills for the harms caused by smoking. To the extent that public or private third parties pick up the tab, it was claimed, smokers have a reduced incentive to learn about the adverse effects of such health habits as tobacco consumption.

All plaintiffs now have available the claim that companies have a duty to disclose all knowledge about the harmful effects of smoking, and cases are allowed to proceed on the basis of a strict liability theory. Large state suits might limit opportunities for individual claimants, who still are burdened by the assumption-of-risk defense. But the disclosure of secret tobacco industry documents caused public outrage and resulted in the filing of many new smoking and health lawsuits with broader allegations and expanded numbers and categories of defendants.[3] For example, tobacco companies were sued for making cigarettes more addictive by manipulating nicotine levels (*Castano vs. American Tobacco Company,* No. 94–1044 [La. filed March 29, 1994]), and for targeting children through enticing marketing campaigns (Slade et al. 1995).

The States' Allegations against Tobacco Manufacturers

The state suits alleged that the cigarette manufacturers participated in a conspiracy of *deceit and misrepresentation* against the public designed to protect cigarette sales. Manufacturers joined in this conspiracy by agreeing to falsely represent that industry-sponsored research organizations would fairly and objectively answer questions about smoking and health. The suits allege that the companies misrepresented material facts of industry-sponsored research on the adverse effects of smoking, failing to disclose research results linking smoking and disease while simultaneously representing that such proof did not exist. Furthermore, the states contended, cigarette manufacturers manipulated the nicotine content of their products to create and sustain smokers' addiction to cigarettes, purposefully withholding this information from the public.

Most states also contended that cigarette manufacturers acted negligently, breached express or implied warranties, or should be held strictly liable in tort in connection with the development, design, manufacture, distribution, or sale of cigarettes, products highly addictive and unfit for human consumption. In their marketing practices, cigarette manufacturers also are alleged to have wrongfully targeted children and young teens, persons too young to legally purchase the products being pushed at them.

Most states sought injunctive relief, which included orders requiring the industry to cease and desist from activities that had the effect of marketing cigarettes to the underage population and to disclose all research results concerning smoking, health, and the addictiveness of nicotine. All states sought some form of compensation for damages.

Terms of the Master Settlement Agreement

The settlement reached in late 1998 between the six largest tobacco companies and the forty-six state attorneys general contained provisions on: financial terms, youth targeting, tobacco corporate culture, and attorneys' fees and enforcement. In return, the Master Settlement Agreement (MSA) settled all state, city, and county claims against participating tobacco companies as civil or statutory claims for past or future acts pertaining to exposure to tobacco products.

In principle, the MSA created a completely new information regime. The tobacco companies acknowledged directly (and presumably on a continuing basis) the harms caused by smoking. Resources are being made available with funds from participating companies to encourage those who do smoke to stop and to discourage initiation of the habit. The financial terms of the MSA provide that over the next twenty-five years states will receive $206 billion.

To ameliorate the smoking habits of young people, participating firms agreed to fund a foundation to carry out a national counteradvertising campaign directed at youth as well as to address other antismoking objectives.[4] The settlement banned the industry from targeting youth in advertising, promotions, and marketing, and limited but did not ban tobacco advertising outright.[5]

The corporate culture provisions of the MSA addressed limits on lobbying, establishing eight areas of state legislation and regulation that the industry is forbidden to lobby against.[6] The agreement prohibited tobacco manufacturers from conspiring to limit information about health hazards from the use of their products and limiting or suppressing research on smoking and health. The industry is required to operate a Web site giving the public access to internal documents obtained in tobacco litigation. The Council for Tobacco Research, the Tobacco Institute, and the Council for Indoor Air Research were disbanded.

The MSA is less burdensome on the tobacco companies than the agreement proposed in 1997 but never implemented. Nonetheless, it does serve as a major step in tobacco control, especially in its objectives on marketing to young people. The settlement provisions are not expected to have a direct effect on older smokers, except that the dramatic increases in cigarette prices should reduce their consumption of cigarettes. The litigation and the MSA also might have a subtle effect on near-elderly and elderly smokers. By their own admission in testimony and by their agreement to the MSA terms, industry leaders have for the first time effectively stated that it is stupid to consume their products—a far cry from the it's-cool-to-smoke assurance and the we-don't-know-if-smoking-is-dangerous-to-your-health story. Perhaps some mature smokers will resent having been duped and will quit, thereby withdrawing their financial support for the tobacco companies.[7]

Has Government Regulation of Information on Tobacco Products Been Effective?

Having surveyed the history of regulatory and information programs aimed at tobacco control in the twentieth century, we now turn to empirical assessments of the effectiveness of those controls. Several approaches have been used to evaluate the effectiveness of mechanisms other than price (see Chapter 8) on controlling tobacco use. First, one may gauge the extent to which information (positive or negative), bans, or limits to access actually affect the demand for tobacco products. Studies of effects of advertising on demand fall into this category. Alternatively, one can perform case studies to assess the stringency of regulations and the extent to which regulations are likely to be enforced. Absent enforcement, laws and regulations are unlikely to be effective, especially in the long run, when those regulated have learned about the lack of penalties for violations. A third approach directly assesses the effectiveness of particular types of tobacco control.

Prior Research on Advertising and Effects of Information Warnings

The past century witnessed a battle of the messages. Antismoking campaigns were countered by arguments from tobacco companies and affiliate organizations casting doubt on the evidence for harmful effects of smoking. Empirical studies of the effects of information messages have considered whether they reduced consumer demand for cigarettes. (And an older literature explored the effects on demand of messages extolling the benefits of the product.)

The economics literature generally has characterized advertising as an instrument for gaining competitive advantage (see Hamilton 1972); firms use advertising to gain market share. In the context of tobacco, before World War II the three market leaders—Camel, Lucky Strike, and Chesterfield—competed primarily by advertising. But in the early postwar period, competition through product differentiation became equally important (Telser 1962).

The popular view is that advertising affects not only the market share of individual firms but also aggregate demand for the product. This view is behind the rationale for limits or outright bans on advertising of tobacco products. Early studies, however, based on time-series analysis of demand for cigarettes, generally found little consumer sensitivity to advertising (Schoenberg 1933; Tennant 1950; Simon 1967; Schmalensee 1972). In contrast, Hamilton (1972) found that advertising increased demand, but that the public information spots emphasizing health impacts (required by the fairness doctrine) had an appreciably greater effect in decreasing demand.

Several recent studies have also failed to find a systematic relationship between cigarette advertising and demand. Chetwynd and colleagues

(1988) found in New Zealand that advertising did increase demand, but the elasticity of demand with respect to advertising expenditures was low (+0.07). The carryover effect of advertising lasted about a year. Duffy (1991) found no effect of advertising in the United Kingdom for the use of either alcohol or tobacco products.

While the bottom line in this research is that advertising has at best a small impact, this conclusion has not been fully accepted because the studies involved are subject to a number of criticisms, including lack of appropriate measures of advertising exposure, failure to distinguish between the influence of advertising and promotional activities, simultaneity between advertising expenditures and sales, the omission of key covariates, and a primary reliance on aggregate data for which multicolinearity among the explanatory variables is likely to be particularly problematic (Chaloupka and Warner 2000).

To our knowledge, only one econometric study of the effects of advertising on smoking has used data at the level of the individual. Lewit, Coate, and Grossman (1981) worked with data from the Health Examination Survey, conducted from 1966 to 1970. These data contained responses from 6,700 youths age twelve to seventeen. Based on measures of televised cigarette advertising, counteradvertising, and self-reported data on time spent watching television, the authors estimated the number of commercials targeting youth consumption choices. They found support for the hypothesis that tobacco company advertisements increase youth demand for cigarettes.

Overall, the effect of tobacco company advertising on aggregate demand for cigarettes is likely to be low, but research does not rule out the possibility that advertising can be an influential vehicle for increasing demand among certain groups, for example, young people. And advertising *has* had an important impact on firms' market share. A dramatic illustration of this is the experience with the "Joe Camel" ads for Camel cigarettes. During the Joe Camel campaign, the Camel brand share of the youth market rose from 0.5 percent to 32.8 percent (Centers for Disease Control and Prevention 1994). Econometric analysis hardly seems necessary to conclude that Joe Camel ads worked to switch young smokers to that brand.

Effects of Antismoking Campaigns on Cigarette Demand

Among the studies finding that information has a substantial impact on the demand for cigarettes, to our knowledge Hamilton (1972) provided the first published comparative evaluation of the effects of health information.[8] Using aggregate time-series data from 1926 to 1970, Hamilton measured effects of the onset of antismoking publicity in the 1950s, the 1964 surgeon general's report, and the FCC's fairness doctrine, which was in effect from mid-1967 through 1970. For the first two information events, the binary variables were set to one, starting with the date of introduction, and continued through the end of the observational period. Since the fairness doctrine was temporary, this policy was measured by dummy variables for the years in which it was in effect. Hamilton found that all three information programs reduced demand for cigarettes.

The FTC's technical report on health information programs (see Ippolito, Murphy, and Sant 1979) and as Warner's subsequent analyses (1981, 1989) offered stronger conclusions about the effectiveness of public information policies. Warner concluded that antismoking campaigns reduced tobacco consumption by one-third of what it would have been in 1978 (based on his 1981 analysis) and by 44 to 47 percent of what the level would have been in 1987. The FTC analysis suggested a decline of 34 percent from the projected per capita consumption of cigarettes for 1975. Warner's analysis included the state tax increases (and their subsequent effects on demand) accompanying antismoking campaigns. Enactment of such tax increases was considered part of the response to the antismoking campaigns, as the legislators who enacted the increases were considered to have been influenced by the campaigns. The FTC analysis limited its description of effects to qualitative variables linked by their time profiles to specific public warnings.[9]

In addition to his analysis of aggregate demand for cigarettes, Warner (1989) analyzed changes in smoking prevalence based on several cross sections from the National Health Interview Survey. Since the NHIS did not collect data on smoking behavior before 1964, Warner used 1964 as a baseline and determined effects of antismoking messages from changes in prevalence of smoking for selected age-gender cohorts. Prevalence declined on a demographically adjusted basis. He thus inferred that antismoking information programs had reduced demand. Perhaps so, but a substantial amount of unexplained variation warrants caution in the interpretation of his findings.

Two other approaches have led to the conclusion that antismoking messages might have been effective (perhaps even too effective), in the sense that the message might have caused people to overestimate the risks of smoking. Viscusi (1990, 1992) used elicited risk perceptions associated with the effects of smoking on lung cancer to evaluate the implicit effectiveness of antismoking information. Viscusi's analysis was based on a national sample of individuals sixteen years of age or older, interviewed in 1985 by a private research firm to elicit attitudes toward smoking and risk perception. The question, intended to estimate each respondent's belief about lung cancer risk among smokers, was: "Among 100 cigarette smokers, how many of them do you think will get lung cancer because they smoke?" He found that smokers overestimated the risk.[10] Of course, this type of third-person risk assessment might not indicate smokers' *individual* assessment of their own risk of getting lung cancer. In a different context, Smith et al. (1987) elicited subjective risk perceptions regarding death from radon exposure, finding substantial differences between perceived risk for the general public and the individual's personal risk perception. This is a potentially important distinction because smokers' interpretation of information about the effects of smoking is central to our objective. It provides part of the answer to which risk perception is the "right" one. Moreover, it underlies any answer to questions about whether an information program can be "too effective." Ideally, we want to encourage informed choices, not decisions based on scare tactics. We explore comparative risk perception more thoroughly in Chapter 5.

Schneider, Klein, and Murphy (1981) used still another analytical approach, arguing that prior analysis of effects of information used the wrong dependent variable. They argued that the focus should be per capita tobacco consumption, measured in pounds per year, rather than cigarette consumption per capita, measured in number of cigarettes consumed per year. These authors suggested that the main effect of antismoking messages was to change the composition of demand—that is, to shift demand toward filtered and low-tar cigarettes. In fact, tobacco consumption per capita peaked around the time of the health scares of the 1950s and declined thereafter. Schneider, Klein, and Murphy found that by 1964, demand had decreased by 15 percent as a consequence of the health scares of the early 1950s. The 1964 surgeon general's report decreased demand further. These authors demonstrated that tobacco use per capita declined steadily from 1954 until the end of their sample, 1978. The antismoking commercials required by the FCC's fairness doctrine further reduced per capita tobacco consumption by 5 percent, for a total reduction of 30 percent. By contrast, the ban on broadcast advertising introduced in 1970 increased per capita tobacco demand by making it more difficult for cigarette manufacturers to introduce new products containing less tar. Cigarette prices fell as a consequence, which also stimulated demand.

Although compelling at first glance, this study seems to claim too much. First, tobacco content per cigarette fell with the introduction of filters (Kluger 1996, p. 261). Although increased demand for filters may have been a consequence of antismoking messages, neither the messages nor the underlying scientific evidence claimed that smoking filtered cigarettes had a beneficial health effect. According to Kluger (p. 261), who analyzed the 1964 surgeon general's report and accompanying documents, "the committee [which reported to the surgeon general] felt that developing better filters or more selective filters is a promising avenue for further development . . . Nobody knew with certainty whether the product had been modified sufficiently by manufacturers to negate the whole thrust of the advisory committee's report. Cigarettes with a filter that was more than cosmetic simply had not been on the market long enough for epidemiologists to conduct a meaningful population study." In fact, to this day there is no conclusive evidence on the effects of specific cigarette characteristics on health. Thus, if smokers responded to antismoking messages by changing the mix of cigarettes they smoked, as the evidence indeed suggests they did, they responded to the wrong message.

Second, reductions in tobacco content per cigarette may have reflected changes in cigarette manufacturing.[11] Third, health effects of smoking depend on both product characteristics and the habits of smokers. For example, people may smoke lower-tar cigarettes or fewer cigarettes but inhale more deeply (Evans and Farrelly 1998). This latter point is a deficiency of virtually all the previous studies.

Some research concluded that antismoking campaigns are ineffective or are less effective than other policies. Baltagi and Levin (1986) updated the Hamilton (1972) analysis, applying a Zellner-Geisel search procedure for estimating the distributed lag of information messages from advertising. They reached a more conservative conclusion, finding "mild" support for the effectiveness of subsidized antismoking messages in reducing cigarette consumption and no support for the notion that the ban on cigarette advertising increased per capita cigarette consumption.

The analysis of Lewit, Coate, and Grossman (1981), using microdata on teenagers' smoking, criticized the use of a binary variable for measuring the impact of restrictions. They developed a time-series analysis for the number of antismoking messages during the time the fairness doctrine was in effect and found that they had little impact on the quantity of cigarettes smoked per teenager. While the fairness doctrine did reduce teenagers' smoking participation during the first year it was in effect, by the second and third years this effect had diminished. The persistence of smoking among teenagers through the 1990s, in the face of decades of antismoking messages, is a failure of past and current efforts. As Lewit and coauthors acknowledged, the impact of antismoking messages on adults may have been quite different. One would plausibly expect the effect of an individual information campaign to have a smaller effect for adults, because adults would place less weight on new information, given that they have experienced a wider set of information and as a result place greater weight on their own prior beliefs formed from this past information.

Several studies have examined before-and-after effects of various antismoking interventions. One approach is to look for dips in demand for cigarettes following major antismoking events. For example, Warner (1985) found that each of the three decreases in per capita consumption that occurred in the four decades following the end of World War II happened in the same year as a major antismoking event: (1) in 1953–54, after the first public smoking-and-health "scare" (his quotation marks); (2) in 1964, following the publication of the surgeon general's report; and (3) over a four-year period from 1967 to 1970, the precise years that the fairness doctrine antismoking messages were broadcast on television and radio. In each case, there was an increase in per capita demand after the event ended.

By contrast, in analyzing the per capita demand for cigarettes over the entire twentieth century, we found that such events as the publication of the surgeon general's report were effective when the time series was limited the second half of the century; the effect disappeared when data from the entire time period were used (Sloan, Smith, and Taylor 2002).

Today, twenty years after the FTC report, there is broad consensus among specialists in tobacco control that the information on the health effects of cigarette smoking has contributed to the decline in demand. Despite important exceptions, economists tend to be more pessimistic.[12]

Case Studies of Effects of State Tobacco Control Policies

Jacobson and Wasserman (1997) conducted case studies in seven states to determine how tobacco control policies in those states were been implemented and enforced. One theme that emerged from their interviews was that the relative salience of the smoking issue was low compared with other public policy questions. Public officials at state and local government levels were reluctant to commit the effort and resources to enact, implement, and enforce increasingly stringent antitobacco measures. Enforcement was inadequate, with relatively few initiatives for enforcing statutes and regulations, and largely complaint driven.

Several cases are before-and-after investigations of policies implemented in individual states. In 1988, California passed Proposition 99, the California Tobacco Tax and Health Promotion Act, increasing the tax on each package of cigarettes from 10 cents to 35 cents, beginning January 1989, and earmarking 20 percent of the revenue raised by the new tax for health education programs designed to reduce tobacco use. Hu, Sung, and Keeler (1995a) assessed the impact of both the tax increase and the media expenditures on the antismoking campaign, using eleven quarters of media expenditure data. Based on an estimate of the effect of media expenditures, the authors computed an elasticity of per capita demand of −0.05 in response to the information, which was appreciably smaller in absolute value than the elasticity of per capita demand of −0.30 with respect to the sales tax.

In another study of the California antismoking campaign, Hu, Sung, and Keeler (1995b) used a time series autoregressive integrated moving-average (ARIMA) model to investigate the effects of positive (pro-smoking) and negative advertising and other factors on per capita demand for cigarettes. Both types of advertising had statistically significant effects, and coefficients for both types of advertising had plausible signs. Although the coefficients were similar, the authors did not present elasticities or present sufficient data to permit an assessment of the magnitude of response. More recently, Fichtenberg and Glantz (2000) evaluated the success of tobacco control efforts in California. They found substantial decreases in tobacco consumption and in deaths from heart disease in California relative to the rest of the United States, and concluded that "a large and aggressive tobacco control program is associated with a reduction in deaths from heart disease in the short run" (p. 1772). Their definition of "aggressive" includes a strategy that combines a price increase with a major media campaign stressing clean indoor air quality and other community interventions to promote a smoke-free society.

Overall, a case can be made that the policies and the litigation serve a larger role than simply controlling amounts smoked per smoker; they educate the public about the ill effects of tobacco (see, for example, Jacobson and Warner 1999). Public debate about laws, and the litigation itself, attracts media attention and raises public awareness. These composite effects are difficult to capture with a rigorous statistical design.

Conclusions

Public policy in the twentieth century as it pertains to smoking was dynamic. If the emphasis since 1964 has been on control of tobacco use, policies implemented earlier in the century had the opposite effect. Inexpensive or free cigarettes were provided to soldiers during the two World Wars, and price supports for tobacco growers kept many people employed in the industry and voting for pro–tobacco industry causes. Even now, given the political strength of this constituency, part of the tobacco Master Settlement Agreement is going to tobacco growers.

Even the post-1964 era has been one of policy zigzags. As states passed antismoking laws, the industry successfully encouraged state legislatures to pass laws guaranteeing rights to smokers and overriding local antismoking ordinances. During 2000, the Supreme Court ruled against the FDA's role in tobacco control, stating the Court's view that regulatory oversight of tobacco production does not fall within the jurisdiction of the FDA, based on the Court's interpretation of congressional intent. Although this zig presumably is not attributable to the power of the tobacco lobby, in the longer history of tobacco control, this decision may be viewed as a reversal in the overall thrust of policy decisions at the end of the century. Another zig toward the support of tobacco companies is the growing fiscal dependence of states on monies from the MSA. States—and not only those in tobacco-growing areas—now have a clear financial stake in the continued survival of the tobacco companies, and logically, for those companies to survive in the tobacco business, they must sell cigarettes.

Although we may reasonably assume most smokers and potential smokers have heard that smoking is bad for one's health, much of the post-1964 era has been a battle of the messages. While companies no longer tout the health benefits of smoking, as they did in the decades immediately prior to 1964, messages continue to imply that smoking a given product is macho, feminine, or otherwise cool. Although difficult to quantify, the battle of the messages has surely served to mitigate the effectiveness of the corresponding growth in the antismoking campaigns.

Judged in terms of the number of laws and regulatory policies implemented, the movement toward tobacco control has been a success. But gauged in terms of outcomes, the record is much more mixed. One impediment to effective policy implementation, at least until the MSA was implemented in late 1998, was the lack of funding to enforce the laws and regulations. The tobacco settlement agreement reached by forty-six states and the major tobacco companies offers more direct support for enforcement. The main and largely pragmatic argument for using litigation in this context is that legislative and regulatory policies have failed.

Today's smokers in their late forties, fifties, and sixties started smoking in an era of public information *without* clear negative signals. They spent several decades listening to cloudy public messages that grew more negative, but not decisively so, until the MSA of 1998. It is too early to tell how the information conveyed by this agreement will affect longtime smokers, nor can we judge whether it will have dramatic effects on those just starting. One reason for undertaking this research is to learn whether it is possible to design an information program that will motivate longtime smokers to stop.

CHAPTER

4

Can Smokers Expect Personal Health Signals? An Evaluation of the Health Impact of Cigarette Smoking

Smoking unquestionably reduces life expectancy. If there is ongoing scientific debate on this effect, it is only about its magnitude. But the impact of smoking on morbidity and disability, as well as the effects on nonsmokers who live or work near smokers and therefore are subject to secondary smoke, are far more uncertain.

As we will discuss in this chapter, smokers can expect to experience health shocks in advance of facing a shortened life span. A small number of studies have been done on the relationship between smoking and acute and chronic health events. New evidence from the Health and Retirement Study indicates that these health shocks occur disproportionately in late middle age with smokers.[1] Especially to the extent that adverse health events can be associated with smoking—events such as the onset of difficulty in breathing or limited cardiovascular fitness more generally—they represent highly personalized warnings to the smoker. These warnings are much more personal than many, if not most, of other the types of messages about the harms of smoking to which smokers are typically exposed.

Not only do adverse health events take the form of the onset of specific diseases such as lung cancer and emphysema, they also may lead to disability and hence limit the ability of people to carry out normal activities at home or work. In this chapter, we examine new evidence among the HRS respondents that smoking is linked to higher rates of disability. In our empirical work, we consider changes in HRS respondents' activities of daily living (ADLs), a common metric for disability, as well as other measures less widely used in research. To develop this evaluation, we examine the relationship between *changes* in respondents' subjective reports of limitations and their smoking patterns. Since the HRS is a longitudinal data set, we are able to study rates of onset of limitations among persons who did not have such limitations at baseline. In our analysis, we limited the sample to persons who were between the ages of fifty-one and sixty-four at baseline. Thus, the analysis focuses on a sample of persons of about the age when many of the deleterious effects of smoking first arise.

All these analyses help develop our argument that personal health conditions contribute to each individual's information set. Knowledge about the health risks of smoking should be treated as a composite of the background, publicly available information and the set of unique, personal experiences. Both types of information—the public and the personal—contribute to each individual's subjective risk perception for continued smoking, measured as a longevity expectation.

Before discussing the role of each source of smoking risk information in later chapters, here we consider whether personal health shocks do occur more frequently with smokers, which would mean that their own health experiences might signal what is coming. If adverse health events do occur more commonly among smokers, then risk messages tied to these experiences may help personalize messages, reducing the likelihood that a smoker will expect his own experience to be "better than the average" and decide to continue to smoke.

Cigarette Smoking and Mortality

Smoking Experience from the HRS

In wave 1 of the HRS (the 1992 baseline interview), nearly 26 percent of the men and 46 percent of the women reported never having smoked. Figure 4.1 shows the percentage of men and women who said they currently smoked and groups former smokers according to the number of years since they quit at the time of wave 1. A large fraction of the HRS respondents smoked at some time during their life: 74 percent of men (54 percent having smoked within the past fifteen years) and just over half (54 percent) of the women.

A number of public information campaigns promoting cessation have emphasized the ability to avoid a reduction in life expectancy by quitting. We can use the HRS's records about current and past smoking, together with the deaths over the time of the panel, to examine whether smokers die

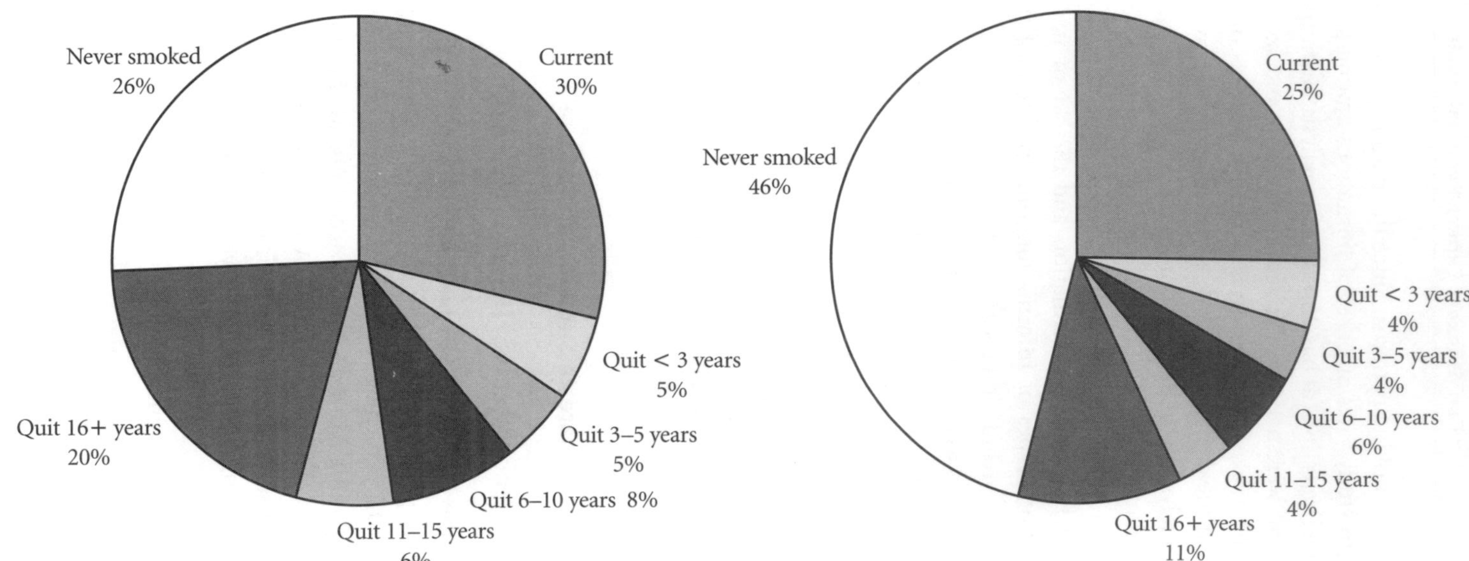

Figure 4.1 Smoking status at wave 1 of the Health and Retirement Study

at a higher rate than nonsmokers and whether the time since a smoker stopped matters with respect to mortality.

Table 4.1 uses the respondent's smoking status at wave 1 (1992) to classify the sample's losses due to death through wave 4 (1998). The deaths are grouped using the quitting intervals in Figure 4.1: those who had quit for less than three years, three to five years, six to ten years, eleven to fifteen years, and sixteen years or more. Using current smokers (by gender) as the reference, we tested the mortality experience of each group. Clearly the mortality rate for smokers is higher than for those who never smoked. By wave 4, six years later, it was nearly four times as great for men, a statistically significant difference. The percent dying appears to decline nearly monotonically with the years since quitting, as reported by the men at wave 1. Only the group who had quit less than three years before the baseline seems to have had a mortality experience comparable to current smokers. Overall, for men the data clearly show that smoking cessation reduces the risk of premature mortality.

Women's experiences in the HRS sample are less dramatic. The mortality rate for former smokers is higher than for current smokers among those who quit within the three years before wave 1, a finding likely explained by the fact that the onset of serious illness is often a catalyst for a

Table 4.1 Deaths between waves 1 and 4 (1992–1998) by smoking status at wave 1

	Deaths (%)	
Smoking status	Men	Women
Current smoker	13.80	7.63
Former smoker		
Quit <3 years	11.35	12.45[b]
Quit 3–5 years	7.81[a]	6.40
Quit 6–10 years	5.81[a]	4.98
Quit 11–15 years	7.53[a]	3.98[b]
Quit 16+ years	4.66[a]	3.24[b]
Never smoked	3.49[a]	2.85[b]
All	7.81	4.82
N	401	257

[a] Statistically significant at 0.01 level or better (two-tail test).

[b] Statistically significant at 0.05 level or better (two-tail test).

midlife attempt to quit smoking. Also, the rates of death for women are lower for former smokers who quit more than three years before wave 1 than they are for men. Statistically significant differences between current and former smokers exist for women only when the interval of quitting reaches eleven to fifteen years or more.

While these results appear as striking evidence in support of the benefits of quitting and also would seem to suggest that the overall perception of reduced longevity with smoking is warranted, our sample sizes are small. Of the 5,134 men, in the study, 401 died by wave 4, and 257 of the 5,327 women died. Given these small numbers, it is important to consider whether the literature is consistent with our evidence for mortality rates and whether it provides smoking-related disease connections that support our estimated death rates.

One of the most publicized recent studies of the effects of smoking on mortality is Doll et al. (1994), which is based on the British Doctors Study (Doll and Hill 1952). In 1951, all physicians in Britain were asked whether they smoked. Most of smokers were men. In 1951, smoking was much less common among women, and, furthermore, the vast majority of physicians were men. In the 1994 study, the authors reported on a forty-year follow-up of male respondents to the 1951 survey, finding forty-eight specific causes or groups of causes of death in men.

Doll and colleagues found that, overall, the death rate for the forty-year period (1951 to 1991) was twice as great for continuing cigarette smokers compared with those who had never smoked. Relative risk is defined as the ratio of two probabilities, the one for the group in question divided by the one for the omitted reference group. The relative risk of death for continuing smokers versus those who never smoked was highest for the age fifty-five to sixty-four cohort, for which the relative risk was 2.1. The relative risk for men age forty-five to fifty-four was only slightly lower for continuing smokers than for those who never smoked. However, in absolute terms the death rates were less than half as large, because death is a much rarer occurrence in the midforties to midfifties than in the midfifties to midsixties. Overall, at age thirty-five male smokers who would continue the habit throughout life had a life expectancy 7.5 years lower than that for men who would never smoke regularly. For those alive at age seventy, the probability of surviving to age eighty-five was 0.41 for nonsmokers versus 0.21 for smokers. The British Doctors Study provides clear epidemiological evidence that continued smoking shortens life span.

Other Empirical Evidence on Mortality from Smoking-Related Diseases

Cancer is the second leading cause of death in the United States. Based on many epidemiological studies, tobacco consumption is known to cause these cancers: lung, mouth, pharynx, esophagus, larynx, stomach, pancreas, kidney, liver, and leukemia, especially acute myeloid leukemia (Boyle 1997; Gaffney and Altshuler 1988; Moolgavkar, Dewanji, and Luebeck 1989; National Cancer Institute 1997; Peto et al. 1994; Siegel 1993; Zhang et al. 1996; U.S. Department of Health and Human Services 1990). Very heavy rates of smoking (but not smoking per se) have been associated with susceptibility to non-Hodgkin's lymphoma (Freedman et al. 1998). Also, excess mortality and morbidity from peripheral artery disease, coronary artery disease, cerebral vascular disease, and chronic obstructive pulmonary disease (COPD) are attributable to smoking. The relative risks of contracting noncancer diseases are lower than for most cancers.

Since the U.S. surgeon general announced that adequate research had been conducted to demonstrate that smoking was systemically related to mortality (U.S. Department of Health, Education, and Welfare 1964), the evidence of a relationship continues to accumulate. Although many deaths are attributed to smoking, the underlying physiological mechanisms are not well understood (Benowitz 1997). For example, nicotine might activate the sympathetic nervous system and in this way could contribute to cardiovascular disease (Benowitz 1997).

Lung cancer is the single most important cause of death from smoking (Thun and Heath 1997) and is rare in individuals who never smoked. Ninety percent of lung cancer deaths in men and 79 percent in women are attributable to cigarette smoking. The existing literature and experience from public health data indicate that lung cancer incidence rises with the amount smoked daily and with duration of the smoking habit (U.S. Department of Health and Human Services 1991, p. 137).

Chronic obstructive pulmonary disease, characterized by permanent airflow obstruction and associated with chronic bronchitis and emphysema, is the fifth leading cause of death in the United States and a major cause of morbidity and disability. Cigarette smoking accounts for 82 percent of deaths from COPD. Death rates from this disease have increased during the past three decades. Growth of COPD-caused mortality parallels the growth in the rate of lung cancer deaths (U.S. Department of Health and Human Services 1991, p. 138).

Mortality from smoking increases with both duration and intensity of smoking. In a recent epidemiological study of 877,000 respondents to the Cancer Prevention Study II (CPS II), Taylor et al. (2002) found that the number of cigarettes smoked per day reduces time to death from any cause. Among current smokers in 1982, the relative risk (compared with lifelong never smokers) of dying in the next fourteen years was more than double for men who smoked up to a pack of cigarettes per day. For men over age fifty smoking more than a pack a day, the relative risk of dying was more than triple that for never smokers. Patterns for female current smokers were similar, but the relative risk for women under age fifty who smoked a pack or less was less than that for men (1.5). But even a relative risk of 1.5 represents a 50 percent increase in the probability of death relative to those who never smoked.

The magnitude of the life expectancy differential depends in part on the specification of mortality models. Having more covariates reduces the effect of smoking per se. There are also interactions between smoking and other health behaviors, such as exercise, that affect the life expectancy differential attributable to smoking (Ferrucci et al. 1999). By engaging in positive health behaviors other than not smoking, it is possible for people to mitigate some of the adverse effects of smoking on survival. Nonetheless, these activities do not completely offset the negative effects of smoking.

Longevity Benefits of Quitting

Analysis of the HRS sample also suggests that quitting early can have substantial benefits. This finding has been confirmed with other, larger samples, including recent empirical work conducted by two of the authors of this book (Taylor et al. 2002). Using data from a very large database, the CPS II, Taylor and colleagues found that there are longevity benefits from quitting. For example, a man who quits at age sixty-five gains just over an additional life year, while women gain more than two additional years. Of course, quitting earlier is better in terms of increased longevity; this study shows that smokers who quit by age thirty-five avoid nearly all the early morbidity that accrues to continuing smokers, a similar finding to that of Doll et al. (1994).

In Doll et al. (1994), men who stopped smoking before age thirty-five (at a mean age of twenty-nine years) had a life expectancy that did not differ significantly from that of nonsmokers. For those who stopped later, life expectancy was between that of never and continuing smokers, but the gain in life expectancy was considerable nevertheless. The authors cautioned that the benefit of stopping later in life was probably underestimated, because men who stopped later plausibly would be more likely to have done so in response to the onset of a smoking-related disease.

Morbidity Attributable to Smoking

Previous Literature

Compared with studies of mortality, the literature on morbidity attributable to smoking is relatively limited. This is especially true for minor illnesses. Nonetheless, these types of effects are precisely what we are arguing might serve as personal health warnings. They are the first signs of ill health a smoker might encounter, potentially many years prior to a more serious health shock. A rather long list of diseases has been associated with smoking. For some, such as pulmonary disease, the causal link is clear. For others, there is a statistically significant association but the underlying causal mechanisms are not well understood.

The effect of smoking on pulmonary function is well established. Several longitudinal studies have shown that age-related decline in pulmonary function is more rapid in smokers than in nonsmokers (see the literature review in Sparrow 1984). After age and weight, cigarette smoking accounts for 80 percent of the explained variation in pulmonary function (Weiss 1984). Cross-sectional studies have indicated that ex-smokers perform better on conventional pulmonary tests than do current smokers. However, longitudinal studies of smoking cessation's effect on pulmonary function have yielded mixed results, with no consensus as to time lag between quitting and the realization of improvements in pulmonary function (Sparrow 1984; U.S. Department of Health and Human Services 1990).

In a study of 154 men and 263 women conducted from 1986 to 1989 in Salisbury, England, Cohen et al. (1993) found that smokers were more susceptible to the common cold than were nonsmokers. Their analysis controlled for demographic characteristics, body weight, virus type, and environmental, immunological, and psychological factors, as well as for alcohol consumption.

Almirall et al. (1999) found an increase in community-acquired pneumonia with smoking status, number of cigarettes smoked per day, and longevity of the habit. Smokers who consumed more than twenty cigarettes per day had three times the risk of acquiring such pneumonia compared with those individuals who never smoked. Adjusting for other factors related to the person's medical history and medical treatment lowered the relative risk for this group of smokers only very slightly.

Evidence from the HRS on Onset of Morbidity and Its Link to Smoking

To examine whether morbidity effects can be linked to smoking, we exploited the longitudinal strength of the HRS by considering whether disease incidence in the first four waves of the survey (1992 to 1998) varied with reported smoking status in wave 1 (1992). As noted above, we limited the sample to persons who were between the ages of fifty-one and sixty-four at wave 1. By wave 4, these persons were at most seventy years old.

We segregated the sample by gender and smoking status. We distinguished between current smokers, former smokers, and those who had never smoked. We further disaggregated the former smokers according to number of years previous to the survey they had quit. We examined relationships between smoking and health outcomes, controlling and not controlling for other determinants of such outcomes to test the robustness of any findings.

Table 4.2 reports our estimates of the rate of *new occurrences* for each of six smoking-related diseases (lung disease, cancer, heart attack, congestive heart failure, angina, and stroke), based on the self-reported records between waves 1 and 4. All cases of preexisting conditions identified at wave 1 were excluded from both the numerator and the denominator in computing these rates (for example, persons with the disease at wave 1 were not counted as having a new case later in the sample). The estimates were developed distinguishing men and women. For purposes of gauging statistical significance, the omitted reference group is current smokers.

The link between smoking and morbidity is striking. Comparing current smokers with the other groups for lung disease, we found significant differences between current, former, and never smokers for both men and women. These differences pertained to those who had recently quit (within the past three years) as well as all other categories of former smokers. In men, the incidence of lung disease among current smokers was more than

Table 4.2 Newly occurring smoking-related diseases, waves 1–4, by smoking status at wave 1 (percent)

	Lung disease		Cancer		Heart attack		Congestive heart failure		Angina		Stroke	
Smoking status	Men	Women	Men	Women	Men	Women	Men	Women	Men	Women	Men	Women
Current smoker	9.0	8.7	7.7	5.6	6.9	4.5	3.5	2.9	3.8	3.4	3.6	3.5
Former smoker												
Quit <3 years	3.2[a]	4.7[b]	5.3	3.0	3.5[b]	1.3[a]	3.5	3.0	3.9	5.6	2.1	3.0
Quit 3–5 years	3.9[a]	3.9[a]	5.9	3.0	2.0[a]	3.9	1.6[b]	3.0	7.0	4.9	2.0[b]	3.4
Quit 6–10 years	6.0[a]	2.7[a]	3.5[a]	5.0	4.9[a]	4.0	3.3	1.7	4.9	4.0	0.7[a]	3.0
Quit 11–15 years	2.1[a]	4.5[a]	4.5[a]	3.0[b]	3.9[a]	2.0[b]	2.7	0.0[a]	4.8	4.0	3.6	2.0
Quit 16+ years	2.5[a]	2.4[a]	5.6[a]	3.8	2.7[a]	0.7[a]	1.6[a]	1.4[b]	3.3	4.1	2.6	1.2[a]
Never smoked	1.7[a]	3.1[a]	4.1[a]	3.4[a]	3.2[a]	1.5[a]	1.7[a]	1.3[a]	3.4	2.9	1.8[a]	1.7[a]
All	4.6	4.6	5.6	4.0	4.3	2.4	2.5	1.8	3.9	3.5	2.5	2.3
N	234	244	286	214	221	129	127	97	202	185	130	122

[a]Statistically significant at 0.01 level or better (two-tail test).
[b]Statistically significant at 0.05 level or better (two-tail test).

five times that observed for those who never smoked (9.0 percent for current smokers versus 1.7 percent for never smokers). The discrepancy for women was large and statistically significant but not as dramatic, mostly because a higher percentage of female never smokers reported onset of lung disease between waves 1 and 4.

For newly occurring cancers in men, there were statistically significant differences between current smokers and former smokers who had quit six or more years previous to wave 1, as well as for never smokers. For women, the only statistically significant differences in newly occurring cancers were found between current smokers and former smokers who had quit eleven to fifteen years before the wave 1 interview and between current and never smokers. There was also a difference in cancer onset between female quitters who had stopped smoking sixteen years or more before wave 1 and female current smokers, but this difference was not statistically significant at conventional levels. Not only is smoking rarer among women than among men but also these women started smoking later. Thus, we did not have a sufficiently large sample of long-term female quitters to detect a statistically significant difference.

We also found statistically significant differences between current and never smokers for congestive heart failure and stroke. Angina rates tended to be higher for wave 1 current smokers and recent quitters, but none of the differences among categories was statistically significant at conventional levels.

Overall, then, for five of the six diseases the rate of new occurrence was higher among current smokers than among those who had never smoked. The one exception was angina pectoris (chest pain). Moreover, in the disease categories most often associated with smoking—lung disease, heart attack, and cancer—for men there are discernable and statistically significant differences in the rates of occurrence between current and former smokers classified by years since they quit. The record is not as decisive for women. However, in their case we are dealing with a smaller number of women who smoked. As Figure 4.1 indicates, only about half of the HRS sample of women ever smoked, compared with 75 percent of the men.

Self-Reported Disability as a Measure of Smoking Impact

At each wave of interviews in the HRS, respondents were asked about their employment status. In wave 1 about 9 percent of the men and 8 percent of the women reported that a disability kept them from working. Changes in disability status over time may indicate the onset of health effects caused disproportionately by smoking. We test this hypothesis in Table 4.3 by comparing the percent of respondents newly disabled at any time between waves 1 and 4.

Table 4.3 reports these results disaggregated by gender and, for former smokers, by years since quitting. Comparing the incidence of new disabilities, male current smokers were more than twice as likely to have become disabled than those who had never smoked. For women the differences are not as pronounced. For both men and women, the difference disability rates for current versus never smokers was statistically significant at better than the 1 percent level. There was no significant difference in new disability rates between former and current smokers for women except for those who had quit for sixteen or more years at wave 1. All groups of women experienced numerically higher rates of disability than men, a result contrasting with the existing group of disabled respondents at wave 1, where disability rates were numerically higher among all men. Retirement rates were unrelated to smoking history.

Table 4.3 Onset of disability and retirement in waves 1–4, by smoking status at wave 1 (percent)

	New disability		New retirement	
Smoking status	Men	Women	Men	Women
Current smoker	11.20	12.11	28.00	24.32
Former smoker				
Quit <3 years	7.78	9.82	33.33	23.31
Quit 3–5 years	6.81[b]	10.32	29.84	25.16
Quit 6–10 years	4.35[a]	11.69	32.61	27.27
Quit 11–15 years	6.12[a]	10.56	31.02	30.43
Quit 16+ years	4.91[a]	5.18[a]	36.52[a]	31.75[a]
Never smoked	5.14[a]	6.65[a]	31.05	26.04
All	6.93	8.54	31.58	26.35
N	258	352	1,176	1,086

[a]Statistically significant at 0.01 level or better (two-tail test).
[b]Statistically significant at 0.05 level or better (two-tail test).

Smoking and Functional Status

Morbidity and deficient functional status are distinct concepts, although the former typically precedes the latter. Morbidity refers to clinical symptoms and diagnoses. Impairments in people's physical or mental ability to perform various tasks at home or at work occur for a variety of reasons, of which disease is just one. For some smoking-related diseases, such as lung cancer, death most often occurs soon after the onset of the disease. To the extent that smoking causes this type of disease, it primarily reduces the length of survival rather than increasing the number of years with a disability. But other smoking-related diseases, such as those affecting the cardiovascular system, may cause years of disability. For example, a person with severe congestive heart failure might experience difficulty in getting around for a number of years before finally dying of a heart attack.

Past Evidence on Smoking and Physical Disability

Evidence from past research that smoking causes disability is inconclusive. Using data from the Alameda County (California) Study, a longitudinal study that allowed researchers to track changes in functional status among persons over age sixty-five for a six-year period, Kaplan, Anderson, and Ganiats (1993) tracked changes in limitations in ADLs and limitations in instrumental activities of daily living (IADLs). The ADL limitations included difficulty in bathing, eating, dressing, using the toilet, walking, transferring from bed to chair, and grooming (Jette and Branch 1981; Katz et al. 1970). The IADL included cooking, shopping, and housework (Lawton and Brody 1969); physical performance measures were pushing or pulling a large object, crouching and kneeling, lifting a ten-pound weight, lifting one's arms over the head, and picking up small objects (Nagi 1976). The physical mobility items were walking a half-mile and climbing up a flight of stairs (Rosow and Breslau 1966). To assess the change in function between 1984 and 1990, Kaplan and colleagues subtracted the 1984 function score from the 1990 score. Smokers in 1984 experienced a marginally significant decrease in physical function over the six-year period ($p = 0.06$).

Analysis of data from the MacArthur studies of successful aging (Seeman et al. 1994; Seeman et al. 1995) used a sample of persons age seventy to seventy-nine at baseline, but limited the sample to persons judged to be relatively high-functioning individuals (in the top third in terms of physical and cognitive function). Decline in physical function over a three-year period was related to education, weight, lack of emotional support, and other factors, but neither cigarette smoking nor alcohol intake had a statistically significant impact on decline in physical function.

Reed et al. (1998) studied men of Japanese ancestry in Hawaii. The most consistent predictors of healthy aging (survival and remaining free of chronic illness and physical or cognitive impairment) were not smoking cigarettes, not being obese, having low blood pressure, and having low serum glucose.

Another type of study has assessed the general impact of health behaviors on disability. Vita et al. (1998) used longitudinal data from 1,751 alumni of the University of Pennsylvania who were students during 1939 and 1940. The average age of study subjects in 1994, the end of the observational period, was seventy-five. The measure of disability was an index of ADL limitations: dressing, rising, eating, walking, grooming, reaching, gripping, and performing errands. Subjects were classified as high, moderate, and low risk based on their body mass index (BMI), amount of exercise, and smoking pattern. The authors found that not only was a person's risk level related to survival, but also that disability was postponed and compressed into fewer years among persons with a better risk-factor profile. The implication of their findings is that persons who engage in unhealthy behaviors, including smoking, have an earlier onset of disability and more years of disability.

Evidence from the HRS

The existing literature has offered somewhat mixed evidence for the effects of smoking on ADL limitations. To address this uncertainty, we conducted empirical work using the HRS reports on ADL limitations to consider how smokers compare with former smokers and those who had never smoked. The important dimension of our implicit argument that the onset of disability and functional limitation serve as personal health information is that, over time, smokers would begin to notice limitations at a higher rate than those who never smoked. We investigated this question by considering the rate of *new* reported difficulties between wave 1 and wave 4 for current smokers (as of wave 1), never smokers, and former smokers classified by years since they quit as of wave 1.

In each of the five categories considered (walking across a room, getting out of bed, bathing or showering, eating, and dressing), current smokers had higher rates of limitation onset between waves 1 and 4 than persons who never smoked (Table 4.4). Relative to the shares of people reporting limitations in ADLs at baseline, there were substantial increases in some types of new limitations in the six years following wave 1. All differences in rates of onset between current and never smokers were statistically significant at conventional levels. This was particularly true for difficulty in dressing. Although not monotonic with respect to the number of years the person had not smoked by wave 1, there were a number of statistically significant differences between current and former smokers.

Considering more physically demanding activities, such as walking one block or more, climbing stairs, or lifting or carrying ten pounds, rates of onset of difficulty between waves 1 and 4 were higher in absolute value for current than for never smokers, with one exception (among women, in climbing one flight of stairs) (Table 4.5). In this one case, onset of difficulty for women in climbing one flight of stairs, the difference was not statistically significant. These findings persisted even after we tested a variety of specifications designed to account for potential endogeneity of disability and covariates.

The ability to delineate differences based on the time since quitting (as reported in wave 1) was more limited. For men, the differences were most apparent in onset of difficulty in walking one block, and for women, in lifting or carrying ten pounds.

Nonetheless, our results stand in fairly sharp contrast to the literature. Between current smokers and those who never smoked, we found clear differences in morbidity effects, self-reported disabilities affecting a respondent's ability to work, and ADLs as measures of functional status. These distinctions were most pronounced for men, but there were comparable numerical distinctions for women, and often the rates were significantly different.

Especially important from our perspective, the new evidence over the six years of the HRS panel was related to current smoking status at wave 1, and we could often distinguish an effect based on years since quitting. The persistent link between the health outcomes, the types of functional limitations, and the chronic diseases linked to smoking all are consistent with our hypothesis that smokers do receive personal health shocks that serve as de facto sources of personal health risk information.

Table 4.4 Onset of difficulty in performing routine activities in waves 1–4, by smoking status at wave 1 (percent)

	Measure: Difficulty in									
	Walking across room		Getting out of bed		Bathing or showering		Eating		Dressing	
Smoking status	Men	Women	Men	Women	Men	Women	Men	Women	Men	Women
Current smoker	5.90	8.79	7.50	10.74	6.10	7.71	4.20	4.10	12.70	11.33
Former smoker										
Quit <3 years	5.00	5.52	4.44	7.98	3.89	8.59	2.78	3.07	13.33	10.43
Quit 3–5 years	2.09[a]	4.52[b]	4.71	9.03	2.62[b]	7.10	1.57[b]	5.81	7.33[b]	12.26
Quit 6–10 years	2.17[a]	9.09	6.83	10.39	4.66	9.96	2.17	3.03	10.25	15.15
Quit 11–15 years	4.08	7.45	6.12	8.07	3.67	2.48[a]	2.04	0.62[a]	9.39	11.18
Quit 16+ years	3.27[a]	4.54[a]	5.54	4.97[a]	3.27[a]	3.67[a]	1.26[a]	2.59	7.56[a]	7.78[b]
Never smoked	3.73[b]	4.68[a]	3.93[a]	6.19[a]	2.52[a]	5.04[a]	1.71[a]	2.60[b]	7.76[a]	8.78[b]
All	4.08	6.07	5.69	7.67	3.97	5.95	2.39	3.06	9.61	9.95
N	152	250	212	316	148	245	89	126	358	410

[a]Statistically significant at 0.01 level or better (two-tail test).

[b]Statistically significant at 0.05 level or better (two-tail test).

Table 4.5 Onset of difficulty in performing physically demanding activities in waves 1–4, by smoking status at wave 1 (percent)

	Measure: Difficulty in									
	Walking several blocks		Walking 1 block		Climbing >1 flight		Climbing 1 flight		Lifting or carrying 10 lbs.	
Smoking status	Men	Women	Men	Women	Men	Women	Men	Women	Men	Women
Current smoker	15.50	18.85	11.70	14.16	13.00	15.92	20.20	16.21	16.20	20.51
Former smoker										
Quit <3 years	12.78	18.40	11.11	7.98[a]	8.89	13.50	15.56	16.56	12.22	20.25
Quit 3–5 years	12.04	23.23	7.33[b]	12.90	8.90	13.55	16.75	15.48	12.04	25.81
Quit 6–10 years	14.29	17.32	7.45[b]	13.42	9.63	14.72	17.70	19.05	10.87[b]	12.99[a]
Quit 11–15 years	11.02	9.94[a]	5.71[a]	8.07[b]	5.31[a]	9.32[b]	16.73	17.39	11.84	13.66[b]
Quit 16+ years	12.34	13.17[a]	6.68[a]	8.42[a]	6.93[a]	12.31	14.36[a]	16.63	11.34[a]	14.25[a]
Never Smoked	9.68[a]	15.23[b]	4.94[a]	7.38[a]	7.36[a]	11.85[a]	15.42[a]	15.49	9.07[a]	15.80[a]
All	12.57	16.23	7.81	9.78	9.00	13.10	16.84	16.11	12.11	17.11
N	468	669	291	403	335	540	627	664	451	705

[a]Statistically significant at 0.01 level or better (two-tail test).
[b]Statistically significant at 0.05 level or better (two-tail test).

Logit Analysis

Our findings thus far have focused on binary comparisons by gender, without attempting to control explicitly for factors aside from smoking that may influence health outcomes. One reason for not controlling for other factors is that those factors might also be affected by smoking. The explanatory variable for the BMI, which we include as a covariate in the analysis presented below, is a case in point. Fear of weight gain is a deterrent to smoking cessation (see Chapter 6). At the same time, however, it is important to gauge the sensitivity of results to the inclusion of covariates.

In the logit analysis that follows, in addition to including explanatory variables for smoking status at wave 1, we included explanatory variables for: age at wave 1 (fifty-five to fifty-nine, and over sixty, with under fifty-five omitted); race (white = 1); marital status at wave 1; education in years as reported at wave 1; BMI of thirty or greater in the previous wave; exercise in the previous wave (classified in categories based on frequency: one to three times monthly, one to two times weekly, three or more times weekly, and less than once monthly, and never as the omitted category); alcohol consumption in the previous wave (one to two drinks daily, more than two drinks daily, less than one drink, and never as the omitted category); and indication of an alcohol problem at wave 1.[2] The observations were stacked so that the dependent variables for waves 2 through 4 were matched with explanatory variables for waves 1 through 3. The dependent variables were defined as a binary variable indicating onset of a specific adverse outcome between waves. Thus, we studied the onset of particular conditions between adjacent waves, which were two-year intervals, given that the condition did not exist at the beginning of the two-year period (that is, at the prior wave).

Table 4.6 provides logit results for newly occurring health problems measured in terms of onset at least one limitation in ADLs (versus none), becoming work-disabled, onset of difficulty in climbing more than one flight of stairs, and onset of difficulty in walking several blocks. The adjusted odds ratios give the relative risk of observing the outcome represented by the dependent variable, given that the other covariates are included in the analysis. An adjusted odds ratio of 1.40 means that the outcome is 40 percent more likely to be observed in the group in question (a smoking category) than the omitted reference group. If both upper and lower bounds on the 95-percent confidence interval are either above

Table 4.6 Logit analysis of impacts of smoking and other factors on newly occurring problems in health and functional status

	Men				Women			
		95% CI[†]				95% CI		
	Adjusted odds ratio	Lower bound	Upper bound	*p*-value	Adjusted odds ratio	Lower bound	Upper bound	*p*-value
ADL limitation								
Former smoker								
Quit <3 years	0.95	0.67	1.35	0.51	1.12	0.79	1.59	0.77
Quit 3–5 years	0.62	0.42	0.93	0.27[b]	0.82	0.58	1.16	0.02
Quit 6–10 years	0.77	0.58	1.03	0.40	1.13	0.85	1.50	0.08
Quit 11–15 years	0.80	0.57	1.11	0.87	0.97	0.68	1.38	0.18
Quit 16+ years	0.70	0.55	0.88	0.00[a]	0.67	0.51	0.87	0.00[a]
Never smoked	0.64	0.52	0.80	0.00[a]	0.70	0.59	0.83	0.00[a]
Work-disabled								
Former smoker								
Quit <3 years	0.79	0.50	1.23	0.80	0.95	0.62	1.45	0.30
Quit 3–5 years	0.51	0.31	0.83	0.05[a]	0.64	0.41	0.99	0.01[b]
Quit 6–10 years	0.30	0.19	0.47	0.65[a]	0.92	0.65	1.31	0.00
Quit 11–15 years	0.55	0.35	0.85	0.79[a]	0.94	0.62	1.44	0.01
Quit 16+ years	0.52	0.39	0.70	0.00[a]	0.41	0.29	0.59	0.00[a]
Never smoked	0.45	0.34	0.60	0.00[a]	0.46	0.38	0.57	0.00[a]
Difficulty climbing >1 flight of stairs								
Former smoker								
Quit <3 years	0.82	0.62	1.07	0.83	1.03	0.80	1.33	0.14
Quit 3–5 years	0.60	0.46	0.77	0.75[a]	1.05	0.80	1.38	0.00

Table 4.6 (continued)

	Men				Women			
		95% CI†				95% CI		
	Adjusted odds ratio	Lower bound	Upper bound	*p*-value	Adjusted odds ratio	Lower bound	Upper bound	*p*-value
Quit 6–10 years	0.74	0.60	0.90	0.04[a]	0.78	0.62	0.99	0.00[b]
Quit 11–15 years	0.64	0.51	0.80	0.01[a]	0.67	0.50	0.89	0.00[a]
Quit 16+ years	0.50	0.42	0.59	0.00[a]	0.76	0.64	0.90	0.00[a]
Never smoked	0.50	0.43	0.58	0.00[a]	0.69	0.61	0.79	0.00[a]
Difficulty walking several blocks								
Former Smoker								
Quit <3 years	0.89	0.66	1.21	0.03	0.72	0.53	0.97	0.45[b]
Quit 3–5 years	0.59	0.43	0.81	0.19[a]	0.83	0.63	1.09	0.00
Quit 6–10 years	0.57	0.44	0.74	0.05[a]	0.77	0.59	0.99	0.00[b]
Quit 11–15 years	0.50	0.37	0.69	0.00[a]	0.45	0.32	0.63	0.00[a]
Quit 16+ years	0.60	0.50	0.73	0.00[a]	0.52	0.42	0.64	0.00[a]
Never smoked	0.51	0.42	0.61	0.00[a]	0.50	0.44	0.58	0.00[a]

Note: In addition to smoking, we included explanatory variables for age at baseline (55–59; 60+; under 55 omitted), race (white), marital status (married), and education in years, all at baseline; body-mass index of 30 or greater at previous wave; exercise at the previous wave (exercise one to three times monthly; once or twice weekly; three or more times weekly; less than once a month; or never, omitted); alcohol consumption at previous wave (one to two drinks daily; more than two drinks daily; none, omitted); past drinking problem at baseline.

† confidence interval.

[a]Statistically significant at 0.1 percent level (two-tail test).

[b]Statistically significant at 0.5 percent level (two-tail test).

or below 1, the adjusted odds ratio is statistically significant at the 5 percent level or better. We report results only for the smoking variables that reached this level of statistical significance.

Never smokers and those who had quit sixteen or more years before wave 1 were much less likely to experience new problems between wave 1 and wave 4. Compared with male current smokers, never smokers were 64 percent as likely to have experienced onset of an ADL limitation, 45 percent as likely to have become work-disabled, 50 percent as likely to have experienced onset of difficulty in climbing more than one flight of stairs, and 51 percent as likely to have experienced onset of difficulty in walking several blocks. For women, the differentials in the probability of onset of adverse health conditions between current and never smokers varied somewhat from those of men, but the overall conclusion is the same. Smokers, in much larger numbers than never smokers, received highly personalized messages in the form of deteriorating health. In general, the adjusted odds ratios for former smokers who had quit sixteen or more years before wave 1 were similar to those for never smokers. The adjusted odds ratios for other groups of former smokers were somewhere between current and never smokers (the adjusted odds ratio on current smokers being 1.0).

Conclusions

Previous research has established a clear link between the amount of smoking and life expectancy. The effects of smoking on morbidity, disability, and functional limitations have been documented much less frequently.

Our analysis of the effect of smoking on disability and health indicates that smoking *is* a major cause of disability, especially among men. This conclusion is strengthened by disability's tendency to decrease with an increase in the number of years since quitting smoking, which suggests that disability can be avoided with behavior modification. In fact, however, disability for former smokers who had quit ten or fewer years before 1992 between 1982 and 1992) tended to be more similar to disability for current smokers, implying that for many years after smoking cessation, disability effects of smoking are not completely reversible. There do appear to be clear positive health effects in terms of morbidity, functional status, and ultimately improved prospects for longer survival, but for ex-smokers' experiences to resemble those of people who had never smoked, they must have stopped at an early age. When we consider those who had quit before 1982, their disability rates more closely resemble those experienced by people who had never smoked. Multivariate analysis confirmed our comparison of current smokers with those who had never smoked, as well as with former smokers.

This body of results confirms that smokers experience personal health shocks in the form of higher-than-typical morbidity, greater functional limitation, and greater evidence of disability. These health shocks provide information that may well be ignored. However, it does not have to be. Indeed, as we discuss in the coming chapters, nonmortality health effects seem to have a large impact on smokers' consideration of cessation, and risk messages that accentuate the impact of smoking on quality of life may well be the most effective in promoting cessation. A strategy that would align public information with the private signals smokers receive could well help to increase the salience of the antismoking message. As a result, it could limit the prospects for the cognitive dissonance associated with a smoker's belief that he or she will experience a better than average set of health outcomes.

CHAPTER

5

Determinants of Risk Perception

Smoking seems an especially hard choice to align with rational behavior. As we acknowledged in Chapter 2, this is one of several reasons why smoking behavior has attracted the interest of so many economists. To understand the economic description of these behaviors, we argued, one must begin with the recognition that informed choices do not have to be aligned with those of an external expert, but they do have to respond to relevant information. In Chapters 3 and 4, we discussed the public information on smoking's health consequences that has been available to smokers over the past half-century, as well as private or personal information about oneself that accumulates from living.

In this chapter and the next we begin the process of investigating how the effects of that information are realized. That is, we consider whether information does influence smokers, and if so, what the insights from this evidence imply for efforts to structure effective ways of delivering information.

Many psychologists and economists have used measures of subjective risk perceptions to evaluate how people interpret information about the sources of risk they face. The use of risk perceptions no doubt has its roots in the expected utility model, and most economists probably would suggest that this strategy has been an effective vehicle for understanding the ways new information ultimately influences behavior. While some observers might interpret the evidence from psychological research as indicating that risk perceptions may not be as consistent with the subjective probabilities as we would like for implementing an expected utility model, the record, with appropriate caveats, supports using an integrated risk perception/choice framework.

One important distinction that affects people's reports of their subjective risk perceptions is whether the activities involved are voluntary or involuntary. Many people feel that if they are in control, the average risk experience as estimated by experts is not relevant to them. We see this kind of judgment in choosing to ride a motorcycle rather than drive a car, or selecting a hazardous recreational sport such as scuba diving or rock climbing. In each case, participants might believe their abilities are better than average and thus their level of risk is lower than average. Additionally, they often can influence the actual risks they face via mitigating activities. For example, one can choose to ride the motorcycle only while wearing a helmet, only at certain times of day, and only on certain roads. In hazardous recreational sports, extensive training and use of two-person teams can reduce risks.

Involuntary risks, on the other hand, are imposed on people. Examples are the health risks from exposure to pollution, having a new landfill established near one's home, or consuming food produced via hazardous practices undisclosed to the consumer. In each case, mitigation might be possible but the risk itself cannot be completely avoided, as with voluntary behavior, at least in the short run. In the longer run, many of these high-risk situations may be averted.

A conceptually distinct question from individual rationality is who is to blame for ill health from smoking. Given the doctrine of consumer sovereignty, one would place much of the blame on the individual smoker. Yet even in the United States, where we typically rely on individual judgment for consumption decisions, many would blame some other party—in particular, tobacco companies—for providing an unsafe product. From this perspective, if people want to smoke, producers should provide them with a "safe" cigarette. The presumption that tobacco companies are to blame underlies the mass and individual tort litigation against them, and the perception of deep corporate pockets still attracts litigants. However, tobacco companies' culpability seems to diminish to the extent it can be shown that individuals have the capacity to make complex judgments.

In this chapter, we address four issues and conclude with a discussion of their implications for public policy. First, we discuss the link between public policy on smoking, public health information, and personal risk perceptions. Second, we evaluate a question from the Health and Retirement Study that allows us to consider whether the types of personal health shocks discussed in Chapter 4 actually influence people's risk perceptions.

All respondents in each wave of the HRS were asked what they believed to be the likelihood that they would live to seventy-five years of age or older. For several reasons this question is ideal for evaluating the effects of personal health information, but the most important reason is that it does not explicitly identify smoking as a potential influence on longevity.

Daniel Hamermesh (1985), who originally proposed the question, found his respondents provided remarkably accurate estimates, on average, of their odds of surviving to age seventy-five or beyond. Comparing their estimates with life tables, he found the average responses were quite close for most groups, by age and gender, although he did suggest there was some tendency to attach too much weight to the experience of relatives. We assess whether the question in the HRS captures what it is supposed to measure, the individual's subjective probability of surviving to a future age. Based on our own empirical evidence, we conclude the question does in fact elicit accurate information about the subjective probability.

Third, we assess how well people can predict their own mortality. Are they overoptimistic or underoptimistic? Does relative optimism differ according to an individual's smoking status? In our analysis, we compared subjective perceptions and actual outcomes. This consistency was evaluated through a comparison of subjective probabilities of death, elicited by the HRS, with actual life table probabilities of death in the same sample of individuals. With HRS data, we also performed a micro-level analysis of longevity expectations of those respondents who died between waves 1 and 2 (1992 to 1994), waves 2 and 3 (1994 to 1996), and waves 3 and 4 (1996 to 1998).

Fourth, we focus on how people update their personal longevity expectations in response to new information and their personal experiences. Here we have paid particular attention to the role of personalized risk messages in the form of newly occurring health events (health shocks) for the individual. The panel feature of the HRS allows us to do this by observing how new health events changed respondents' perceptions and behavior.

Policy Context

The public debate over smoking policies in the United States is fundamentally about what constitutes an informed choice and therefore who is responsible for the harm resulting from smoking. Many observers question whether those continuing or starting to smoke, in the presence of what appears to be an overwhelming set of evidence documenting serious health consequences, are actually making informed decisions.

Becker and Murphy's (1988) rational addiction model suggests that people make a rational choice about whether to start consuming an addictive product based on available information (Chapters 2 and 8). In Chapter 8, we will show that extending their model to include risk of premature death related to the addictive good could, theoretically, alter the influence of addiction and consumption behavior. The actual outcome depends on the relative sizes of the influences of (1) the addictive effect and (2) the individual's perceptions of how smoking contributes to the risk of premature death. We must start with this risk perception process to understand both how risks are subjectively evaluated and how different types of public and private information are used in that process.

An equally important consideration is that, even if the initial choice is rational, smokers may experience regret later, as new information from smoking research becomes public or as people learn about their own susceptibility to more specific health effects. Cassandra Tate's (1999) recollection of her mother's attitude at the time of her death (see Chapter 2), and the quotation from our colleague (see the Preface) after a life of cigarette smoking remind us that people differ in how they deal with a time sequence of decisions. No doubt Ms. Tate regrets her mother's choices, but her mother believed that cigarettes had helped her cope with life's circumstances. Not everyone will feel that way.

People are likely to be heterogeneous with regard to the harmful effects of an addictive good (Orphanides and Zervos 1995). Subjective beliefs about the effect of such a good on one's own health are plausibly updated via a Bayesian learning process. Bayesian learning can take place as a smoker consumes the good or observes other smokers who may have common genes, such as close relatives. According to this perspective, those who receive bad news over time use the information to update their perceptions and may, as a result, regret having become addicted.

What individuals perceive about risks underlying their choices are particularly relevant to the concept of informed consent in tort law. Thus, a major issue in tort litigation against tobacco companies involves the extent to which individuals correctly perceive risks inherent in their smoking decisions and whether the companies misled people to believe that smoking was less harmful to personal health than the companies knew (Hanson and

Logue 1998; see Chapter 3). That is, if the injury victim correctly perceived the risks of harm and decided to undertake the activity anyway, he or she is not likely to be entitled to compensation for damages under tort. In contrast, however, is a case in which a party misstated the risks and consequently the injury victim undertook the risky activity, in which he would not have engaged had he had the full information. The party providing the incorrect information may be liable for damages under tort. In sum, the issue comes down to what the injury victim knew or did not know. Kip Viscusi (1992, p. 61) quotes the American Law Institute's *Restatement of the Law of Torts* (second edition) to emphasize this legal point:

> The article sold must be dangerous to an extent beyond that which would be contemplated by the ordinary consumer who purchases it, with the ordinary knowledge common to the community as to its characteristics. Good whisky is not unreasonably dangerous merely because it will make some people drunk, and is especially dangerous to alcoholics; but bad whisky, containing a dangerous amount of fusel oil, is unreasonably dangerous. Good tobacco is not unreasonably dangerous merely because the effects of smoking may be harmful; but tobacco containing something like marijuana may be unreasonably dangerous.

In short, if consumers know a product is dangerous and decide to consume it anyway, that is their business. But if in some way the seller has misled the consumer into believing that the product is safer than it truly is, that is a tort. It has been argued that tobacco companies withheld pertinent health information from the public and engaged in misleading advertising (Chapter 3).

Claims and counterclaims raise an important empirical question: To what extent have individuals been able to make informed decisions about smoking in the presence of diverse, sometimes conflicting information, especially prior to 1964, when the U.S. surgeon general issued the first report on the dangers of smoking? The answer depends on how individuals use information to form expectations about their risks from smoking. In this chapter we offer answers based on evaluations of the information available to smokers—from public sources, conveyed through the media, as well as from more personal signals, such as changes in their own health and the health of other people they know. If smokers do perceive their risks accurately, then they should be expected to bear the cost of smoking-related diseases. Conversely, if as a result of misleading claims by tobacco companies smokers systematically underestimate the risks from smoking, including the probabilities of acquiring smoking-related diseases, then instead the companies should be found culpable.

Previous Research on Health Information and Risk Perception

Education, Health Information, and Risk Perceptions

Well before scholars probed the relationship between health information, risk perception, and health behavior, studies reported a relationship between health and schooling. Grossman (1975) hypothesized that more schooling makes individuals more efficient producers of health, possibly because better educated persons are better able to assess health care options, process information about their own health, or improve self-control (Thaler and Shefrin 1981); schooling might affect the discount rate people implicitly use in making personal decisions (Chapter 2); or educational attainment might be a proxy for unmeasured ability.

Using a sample of persons age seventeen to twenty-four and a method to look behind the observed simple correlation between smoking and schooling, Farrell and Fuchs (1982) rejected the view that schooling per se was responsible for variations in smoking behavior, thereby leaving open the possibility that one or more variables not included in their analysis but affecting both educational attainment and schooling were responsible for the simple correlation between smoking and schooling. Based on their evidence, they rejected the explanation that social class was an omitted variable. They also argued that the omitted variable was not likely to be mental ability, but they had no direct measure of ability. They speculated there was a difference between highly educated and less educated persons in the discount rates used for making personal choices, but they had no proxies for discount rates.

More recently, Kenkel (1991a) studied whether health knowledge affected cigarette smoking, heavy drinking, and exercise. Respondents to the national U.S. survey used by Kenkel (1991b) were quite knowledgeable about the adverse effects of smoking. More knowledgeable people were less likely to smoke, even when knowledge was treated as a variable jointly determined with the decision to smoke. His results also suggested that healthy behaviors tend to occur together in healthy people (that is, those who do not smoke or drink excessively are more likely to exercise).

Education might affect individuals' willingness to take action in response to personal risk messages. A recent study by Wray, Herzog, and Willis (1998), based on the first two waves of the HRS, provides some evidence on this. Limiting the sample to persons who were between the ages of fifty-one and sixty-one at wave 1, they focused on the effects of education, occurrence of a heart attack, and the interaction of education and having a heart attack on smoking cessation. Unlike previous researchers, they found no effect of education on smoking cessation per se. However, better educated persons were more likely to have reported that they never smoked at wave 1. By contrast, having had a heart attack between the two waves did encourage quitting. Among smokers who experienced a heart attack, higher levels of educational attainment raised the probability of quitting, which provided further support to the notion that education increases individuals' responsiveness to health signals.

One of us (Smith 1997), in research on the impact of information about an involuntary risk from another source, indoor radon (a naturally occurring gas found to be directly linked to lung cancer), found that the effects of education on behavior can be quite subtle and exhibit thresholds. The study investigated the effects of two different public information campaigns and their ability to promote monitoring homes for radon. Two communities each received one of the two campaigns and a third served as the control. Approximately 500 households in each community were interviewed before and after the campaigns.[1] One campaign was active, involving community leaders, periodic news updates and community meetings, and a highly visible program to test homes. In the second campaign, printed information was simply distributed by mail and general public service announcements were made. Analysis of the results, using a subsample of the original data and focusing on respondent's education level, suggested that the general information program (the second campaign described) improved scores on a multiple-choice quiz about radon, given before and after the general program, for those individuals with a high school education or less. Moreover, this learning measure was a positive and significant factor in home testing decisions for this same group. This suggests that education might well be important for how people respond to information messages, but the information messages might be more effective for some groups than others; in this case, the messages were more effective for less educated persons.

As we will discuss in Chapters 6 and 8, we found comparable distinctions in how those without some college education responded to the information about smoking's health effects.

Psychological Research and the Bias toward Optimistic Outcomes

Several psychologists have conducted research on perceptions of smoking risk and individuals' tendency to view risks of various behaviors as lower for themselves than for others engaging in similar behaviors. Because the effect of smoking is underestimated, individuals engage in higher levels of the harmful activity than they would if they were fully aware of the consequences of their actions.

In the most recent study of bias as excess optimism, Arnett (2000) interviewed 200 adolescents age twelve to seventeen and 203 adults age thirty to fifty in the state of Washington, using an intercept survey. The youths were paid $10 each for participating; adult respondents were not paid. Since our study focuses on smoking by adults, we limit our discussion to responses from the adults.

Arnett asked respondents to rate their level of agreement with each of the following statements. "Most people who smoke all their lives eventually die from an illness caused by smoking" (85 percent of nonsmokers and 74 percent of smokers agreed slightly or strongly with this). "I doubt that I would ever die from smoking even if I smoked for 30 or 40 years" (7 percent of nonsmokers and 22 percent of smokers agreed slightly or strongly). "Most people who smoke for a few years become addicted and can't stop" (here the percentages were closer—86 and 81 percent, respectively). "I could smoke for a few years and then quit if I wanted to" (25 percent and 48 percent, respectively). The responses to the third and fourth questions are particularly intriguing. By age thirty and above, the vast majority of smokers must have been addicted, and many must have tried to quit and failed. There is no issue of projection to the future here. The first two questions involve an element of projection, especially the second question.

Using multivariate-model logistic analysis, Arnett also examined the extent to which elements related to the optimistic bias, demographic variables, and socioeconomic status predicted a person's smoking status. The bias-related variables were responses to questions assessing perceived personal risk of death from smoking and perceived personal risk of addiction from smoking.

The variable for optimistic bias based on the addiction question had a positive and statistically significant impact on the probability that the person had smoked during the past thirty days. The measure of bias based on the question about the relationship of smoking to mortality also had a positive impact on the probability of smoking, but was statistically significant only at the 10 percent level. Arnett concluded that optimistic bias is an important cause of smoking in adults. He did not attempt to control for endogeneity of the variables he defined as "optimistic bias variables." Thus, one must be cautious in attaching a causal interpretation to the results.[2] We present new results on optimistic bias in our analysis of smoking cessation and relapsing in the next chapter.

Another study by Ayanian and Cleary (1999) used a national survey of more than 3,000 adults (age twenty-five to seventy-four), 700 of whom were current smokers. Respondents were asked to assess their risk of heart attack or cancer, relative to other persons of the same gender and age. Most of those surveyed had no history of either. For current smokers, the authors used logit analysis to estimate an indicator of perceived risk. The dependent variable was based on the following question: "Do you think your risk of a heart attack (or cancer) is higher, lower, or about the same as other (men/women) your age?" A value of 1 was assigned to respondents who thought that their risk was higher than average. Only 29 percent of the men and 40 percent of the women who were current smokers believed they had a higher-than-average risk of a heart attack or cancer, and only 30 percent and 49 percent of heavy smokers (men and women, respectively) acknowledged these risks.

Elderly current smokers were much less likely than younger people to perceive their risk of a heart attack as higher than average. College-graduate smokers perceived an increased personal risk of cancer. Heavier smokers were more likely than lighter smokers to perceive a higher risk of heart attacks and cancer. Smokers in fair or poor physical health were more likely to state that they had a higher probability of a heart attack. Those who were in fair or poor mental health were more likely to believe that they had a higher than average risk for cancer. In Ayanian and Cleary's study, education had a plausible role on risk perception, as did intensity of smoking. In a letter commenting on Ayanian and Cleary's article, Gerace (1999) suggested that some heavier smokers might have used information about their own shortness of breath to assess their risk without ever thinking about smoking.

The bottom line from past research, especially as it relates to risk perceptions associated with smoking, is that formal education seems to increase the accuracy of risk perceptions (as judged on the basis of consistency with the experts' estimates). However, the underlying mechanisms have not yet been adequately documented.

Viscusi's Research

The well-cited research on smoking and risk perceptions by Viscusi (1990, 1992) considered two questions. First, to what extent are smokers' perceptions of the probability of harm from smoking consistent with what the objective record of smokers' experience implies? Second, does the reported risk perception affect actual smoking behavior—that is, are persons who perceive the probability of harm as relatively high less likely to smoke? One reason for addressing the latter question was to gauge the validity of Viscusi's measure of smoking risk. In a companion study, (Viscusi 1991), he also evaluated the extent to which risk perceptions vary by age.

To assess risk perception, Viscusi used a Bayesian updating model, as do we in analysis described later in this chapter. In this framework, the individual is assumed to have had a prior estimate of the probability, P_{t-1}, that a particular event will occur. The current probability, P_t, is hypothesized to be a weighted function of a respondent's initial assessment, P_{t-1}, along with the risk equivalent, r_t, implied by any new information that motivated the revision. Respondents assign a degree of confidence, θ, to the prior (or baseline) assessment, $P_{t-1.}$ They also assign a degree of the confidence (technically, credibility), γ, to the beliefs implied by the new information, r_t. The posterior or current assessment of his or her odds of experiencing a particular event (such as living to seventy-five or longer), P_t, is then a weighted average of prior beliefs, scaled by the relative "information" associated with that prior assessment $(\theta/(\theta + \gamma))$ and the new information, expressed as a risk equivalent, r_t, weighted by its relative precision $(\gamma/\theta + \gamma)$:

$$P_t = \frac{\theta P_{t-1} + \gamma r_t}{\theta + \gamma} \tag{5.1}$$

At this level of generality, the model does not attempt to differentiate how different types of information contribute to r_t. The news may come from general sources, such as a U.S. surgeon general's report or a newspaper account of the report, or more indirectly through conversations about general information with friends and relatives. The news could also be more personal, such as the experiencing of shortness of breath for the first time after climbing several flights of stairs, or worse, a health shock, or from the personal experiences of friends and relatives. However, it is essential that what is referred to as "new" information in fact be "news" to the individual, for all prior information is incorporated in P_{t-1}.

Viscusi (1990) studied responses from a national survey conducted in 1985 that asked people the following question: "Among 100 cigarette smokers, how many of them do you think will get lung cancer because they smoke?" In telephone surveys conducted in Durham, North Carolina, in 1990 and 1991, Viscusi varied the question to explore the sensitivity of the risk response to changes in question formulation, particularly to changes in the base number of smokers (Viscusi 1992, p. 76). In contrast to our work as well as to other applications of the framework (see Smith et al. 1990), Viscusi had only one observation for each respondent. As a result, the effects of P_{t-1} were assumed to be captured through demographic characteristics included in his risk perception variables, and *not* from observing changes in P.

Recently, Viscusi and collaborators (Antoñanzas et al. 2000) repeated the same type of detailed appraisal of risk perceptions for smokers in comparison with former smokers and those who never smoked, using a random sample of Spanish citizens age eighteen and older. Conducted in 1997 using a single telephone survey, this research followed the basic format of Viscusi's earlier work, asking third-person questions about risks from smoking. However, this study did include risk perceptions for more health effects of smoking, including lung cancer, heart disease, and diabetes, as well as a life-expectancy loss question. The risk perception questions (translated into English from Spanish) were:

- *Relative risk:* For each nonsmoker who dies of lung cancer (heart disease), how many smokers die?
- *Life expectancy loss:* Imagine twin brothers who have lived their entire lives in the same way, in the same city, with the same customs and habits, except one has smoked a pack of cigarettes a day for twenty years and the other has never smoked. Until what age do you think the brother who does not smoke will live? Until what age do you think the brother who smokes will live?

Several of Viscusi's early findings have received considerable attention. First, he compared responses to the question we cited at the onset of this discussion (Among 100 smokers, how many do you think will get lung cancer because they smoke?) with actual probabilities from life tables. Compared with the actual probabilities, smokers and nonsmokers both tended to *overestimate* risks of smoking. That is, they were too *pessimistic*, and thus not prone to the optimistic bias suggested in some of the psychology literature. In addition to assessing responses to the lung cancer question, Viscusi analyzed responses to a more general question, "Among 100 cigarette smokers, how many of them do you think will die from lung cancer, heart disease, throat cancer, and all other illnesses because they smoke?" Individuals also overestimated this probability but by less than in the lung cancer question. Viscusi anticipated less overestimation of the probability that smoking leads to lung cancer, for two reasons. First, lung cancer risks had received relatively more publicity. Second, overestimation is bounded by 1.0. This constraint should compress overestimation of subjective probabilities greater than the one for lung cancer.[3]

The implication of his overall finding is that the various health messages about the dangers of smoking have gotten through to the public, both smokers and nonsmokers alike. Smokers are *more* than fully informed, and they have decided to smoke anyway. Viscusi's results would seem to imply that the tobacco companies have not fooled the public. Viscusi (1992, p. 83) concludes, "Despite the provision of extensive smoking information, individuals have biased perceptions, not accurate risk beliefs. These biases may reflect the character of societal information transfer and the social pressure against smoking. The warnings that were in place at the time of the national survey declared that 'smoking causes lung cancer.'"

To accept Viscusi's findings we must agree with his implicit logic that we can learn about each individual's subjective risk assessment by asking about the risk to 100 smokers. Moreover, in concluding that their appraisals overestimate the risk, we are comparing these reports to the experience in the overall population. It is fine in this context to compare the population average with the estimate given by respondents—considering in effect how well they know the facts. However, when we take the next step and suggest this estimate is what people believe is relevant to themselves, we are on shaky ground.

Viscusi takes this step in his interpretations. We do not, for two reasons. First, there are both observed and unobserved sources of heterogeneity that affect individual responses—the latter being facts each respondent knows but we do not. Thus, individuals may have sound reasons for believing they are different from the average. We simply do not know these reasons without a more complete record on the amount they smoked, their own and family health histories, and their other behaviors.

Second, consistent with the Bayesian updating framework, reported risk perceptions were greater for the younger age cohorts, among whom overall lung cancer risks were appreciably overestimated. This group presumably based judgments on public information from a variety of sources, including public antismoking campaigns. Older persons, by contrast, may have relied to a greater extent on personal experiences and those of their relatives and close acquaintances.[4] As noted earlier, Viscusi measured risk perceptions only at a single point in time. Thus, he was forced to use indirect methods for assessing whether risk updating by individuals follows a Bayesian process.

Viscusi found that respondents who attached a greater risk to smoking were less likely to engage in such behavior. He thus suggested a link between risk perceptions and behavior. (Thus, risk perceptions are not a matter only for scholarly interest.) Using regression analysis with a number of other covariates, Viscusi (1992) also found that, holding other factors constant, current and former smokers had lower assessments of the lung cancer probability from smoking than did never smokers. This tendency was more apparent for current than former smokers (pp. 125–128). Also, people who had heard messages that smoking "shortens life" were less likely to smoke, but other messages had no impact on the propensity to smoke ("dangerous to health," "bad, not dangerous," "not bad for health"). Some of the explanatory variables representing responses to attitude probes from the national survey Viscusi used also decreased the respondents' probability of smoking. The variables referred to respondent agreement with the following statement: smoking "causes lung cancer," "causes any cancer," "affects health," "know people who died," "has general health effects." Interestingly, people who believed that smoking is "habit-forming" were *more* likely to smoke (pp. 97–98).

Research Inspired by Viscusi's Findings

Data from Taiwan confirm the association between risk perceptions and smoking status that Viscusi found for the United States. In a two-equation analysis, one for smoking and the other for risk perceptions, Liu and Hsieh (1995) found that risk perceptions exerted a significantly negative effect on the probability of smoking. They also found that the Taiwanese respondents overestimated the probability of contracting lung cancer from smoking, although the subjective probabilities were lower than in Viscusi's sample. Younger persons had higher risk perceptions than older persons, again presumably because they had less personal experience with consequences of smoking than did persons in older age cohorts.

Hsieh and colleagues (1996) assessed the impact of antismoking campaigns in Taiwan using the above framework. They found that such campaigns had a statistically significant effect on health knowledge, which in turn reduced the probability of smoking. An anomalous finding, seemingly *inconsistent* with Bayesian updating, was that persons with smoking-related illnesses had significantly lower health knowledge (related to smoking risks).[5] However, this may be an artifact of the authors' having only one cross section.

Hsieh and colleagues' findings are also consistent with a result obtained in the United Kingdom by Jones (1994), who also used a single cross section. In this study, smokers who had (self-assessed) fair or poor health at the survey date were less likely to succeed in quitting smoking, holding the degree of addiction and other factors constant. Again, this may be an artifact reflecting the role that health variables play in a single cross section. In these situations, health measures might be proxy variables for other types of individual heterogeneity unaccounted for by the models' other explanatory variables.

The recent research coauthored with Viscusi in Spain, where smoking prevalence is quite high, extended Viscusi's methodology to that country with a single cross section of 2,571 subjects. Survey evidence for the Spanish population indicated that perceptions of change in lung cancer risk and in life expectancy loss attributable to smoking are similar in Spain and the United States (Antoñanzas et al. 2000). In addition to asking about lung cancer, the survey included questions on the risk of heart attack and diabetes attributable to smoking. The question about diabetes is particularly interesting because no scientific link between smoking and the probability of becoming a diabetic has been established. In fact, to the extent that smokers are less likely to be overweight than nonsmokers, and that excess weight is correlated with diabetes, one can argue that the true relationship between smoking and the probability of becoming a diabetic is negative. Respondents systematically overestimated the effects of smoking. Smoking even increased the *perceived* probability of getting diabetes by 0.25.

Critique of Viscusi's Risk Perception Questions

Viscusi's risk perception questions have been criticized from several different perspectives (see Chaloupka and Warner 2000; Hanson and Logue 1998; Schoenbaum 1997; Slovic 1998). Hanson and Logue, who presented the most extensive critique, identified three general issues that also have been raised by the other critics of Viscusi's conclusions. First, the risk perception question was phrased in a way that could be interpreted as a request for "factual" information about smokers rather than a *personal* assessment of risk. In this context, respondents to the survey used by Viscusi (and Liu and Hsieh) were free to overestimate the health risks of smoking. But at the same time, they may not have felt these overinflated risk perceptions applied to themselves. This point is noted by a study conducted on radon risks, described in Box 5.1.

The second issue of concern is the extent to which brand-specific smoking risk information is available to consumers. That is, even if people do know the generic health risks from smoking, they would also need to know the risks of smoking particular brands and types of cigarettes. This issue is reinforced by recent results from Evans and Farrelly (1998) indicating that smokers responded to higher cigarette taxes by purchasing longer cigarettes and cigarettes with higher tar and nicotine content.

Finally, even if individuals overstate the absolute health risks of smoking, they might also overestimate the risks of other hazards to which they are exposed. To the extent that people's decisions are based on the relative risks of actions leading to comparably serious outcomes, then it is the extent of overstatement across these alternatives that is important to their behavior.[6]

It seems unlikely that the degree of overstatement would be exactly counterbalanced by understatement of other risks over all the risky events and activities people must consider. Evidence from other research conducted by cognitive psychologists confirms our expectations that a fortuitous balancing of errors is unlikely. Lichtenstein et al. (1978) found that people overestimated the probabilities of low-probability causes of death and underestimated the probabilities of high-probability causes of deaths. Although recent research has led to refinements of this conclusion, it has not challenged the general notion that people do overestimate the risk of death as a general matter (Benjamin and Dougan 1997; Viscusi and Hakes 1998; Viscusi, Hakes, and Carlin 1997).

Viscusi's findings, coupled with the settlement of the states' tort case

Box 5.1 Different methods of evaluating risk

As part of a panel study to evaluate the effectiveness of different approaches for explaining the health risks of radon, Smith et al. (1987) compared personalized and general questions. Their objective was to evaluate how different informational materials randomly assigned to subsets of the same group of homeowners would affect their perception of risk from radon. The text of each is given as follows:

Personal Risk Question:
Now I'd like you to think about different risks you and your household face. For each type of risk that I read, please tell me how serious you think the risk is on a scale of 1 to 10. Number 1 on the scale is not at all serious, and 10 is very serious . . . How serious are risks you (and your household) face from being exposed to radon?
General Risk Question:
Compared to other health risks people face, how serious a health risk is radon—on a scale from 1 to 10, with 1 being not at all serious and 10 being very serious?

The study involved 2,300 households in the state of New York. The authors compared personal and general risk perceptions after two interviews had been conducted with the same person. The first was a baseline interview, and the second was a follow-up after individuals had received radon readings from their home, and one of five booklets or a one-page fact sheet describing radon.

Comparison of the responses to the personal radon risk question in the baseline and follow-up surveys indicated substantial differences, while the general risk distribution was largely unchanged. Moreover, in the follow-up interview about 50 percent of the homeowners rated the seriousness of general risk from radon at a level of 5 or higher. Only 25 percent of these same people put their personal risk appraisal in these categories (that is, above 5). While they did receive specific information about their home's condition, this finding is consistent with the questions raised about the format of Viscusi's question. Personal risk, rather than general risk, should be the basis for affecting individual behavior (Fishbein and Ajzen 1975; Slovic 1998).*

* Analysis of individuals' responses to information about radon's health risks, developed as part of a study of the effectiveness risk communication in promoting mitigation, also confirmed this conclusion. See Smith et al. (1989).

against U.S. tobacco firms (see Chapter 3), have focused renewed attention on smokers' risk perceptions. To reconsider Viscusi's conclusions, Schoenbaum (1997) compared subjective probabilities of living to age seventy-five or more for people age fifty to sixty-two. Using data from wave 1 of the HRS, he compared subjective longevity expectations with life table values for never, former, current light, and current heavy smokers. This analysis was conducted separately for men and women. Because of limitations in the life tables, the comparison was confined to white respondents. Schoenbaum found that people *underestimated* the risk of death by age seventy-five given their smoking status in 1992 (current smoker, former smoker, or never smoked).

Box 5.2 summarizes the framing of the risk perception questions used by Viscusi (1990, 1992) and by the HRS. The risk perception questions

---

Box. 5.2 Alternative framings of risk/longevity perception questions

A. Viscusi's Risk Perception Questions*

Basic

Among 100 cigarette smokers, how many of them do you think will get lung cancer because they smoke?

Sample Testing†

Among 100 cigarette smokers, how many of them do you think will die from lung cancer because they smoke?

B. HRS Longevity Expectation Questions

Wave 1

Next I would like to ask you about the chances that various events will happen in the future. Using any number from 0 to 10 where 0 equals absolutely no chance and 10 equals absolutely certain . . .

What do you think are the chances that you will live to be 75 or more?

Subsequent Waves

Now I am going to ask about the chances of various events happening to you. Please answer the questions in terms of percent chance. Percent chance must be a number from 0 to 100, where 0 means there is absolutely no chance, and 100 means that it is absolutely certain . . .

What is the percent chance that you will live to be 75 or more?

---

*Liu and Hsieh (1995) repeated the same question in their survey in Taiwan.

†Viscusi (1992) used this question to evaluate the effects of identifying specifically death due to lung cancer in a small telephone survey conducted in Durham, North Carolina.

used by Viscusi and Liu and Hsieh were identical and differed substantially from the HRS longevity questions used by Schoenbaum. The former investigators asked about one disease, lung cancer (representing 55 deaths per 100,000 among smokers in the United States) and people's perceptions of the risk that smokers would contract this disease because of smoking. Overall, there is widespread agreement that the framing of a risk assessment question will affect the answers. Numerous examples supporting this conclusion can be found in the literature (see, for example, Fischhoff and MacGregor 1983).

Assessment of the HRS's Risk Perception Questions

Previous Research on Perceived Risk of Longevity

The HRS's risk perception questions were inspired by Hamermesh's (1985) research. Hamermesh investigated how well subjective estimates of life expectancy match up with life table estimates. In his study, the role of smoking had only a secondary role, but it is nevertheless useful to begin our discussion with a review of his study to provide a context for our discussion of the controversy over the validity of the HRS questions.

Hamermesh set forth four criteria for assessing accuracy of personal risk perceptions. First, how consistent are subjective survival distributions with actual survival distributions? Second, do subjective estimates of the probability of reaching a threshold age rise with the person's age, and, more generally, do differences in the subjective probabilities among individuals coincide with objective differences in life expectancy for particular demographic factors? Third, do people extrapolate past changes in survival probabilities in forming their own subjective expectations? Fourth, to what extent does the importance people attach to various personal factors, such as longevity of parents, or their own behavior, such as whether they smoke, coincide with empirical evidence on the objective importance of these same variables? Hamermesh used surveys of white male academic economists (who presumably were well-versed in the concept of a probability) and a smaller sample of white males selected from the telephone directory of a medium-size midwestern city.

The subjective estimates of life expectancy exceeded their life table counterparts, but only by one to three years. But for some age groups, the economists actually underestimated the probability of reaching the age of sixty. Subjective life expectancies from the sample of economists did not exceed those in the general sample. For both samples, subjective survival functions were flatter than their actuarial counterparts; that is, for younger ages (living to sixty), respondents relatively underestimated the probability of surviving; for older ages (living to eighty), the reverse was true.

To examine whether subjective estimates of life expectancy are demographically and expectationally consistent, Hamermesh estimated various specifications of an equation with the subjective estimate of life expectancy as the dependent variable, as well as variables for a life table estimate and the forecasted change in life expectancy based on the actual change that occurred between 1940 and 1980. Based on this analysis, he concluded that projections of both the economists and men in the general sample reflected then-current life table estimates, adjusted for improvements in life expectancy over the previous decades. The coefficients on the life table variable were 1.01 in regressions based on both samples, implying that, if anything, subjective estimates are very slightly raised over the actual probabilities; the coefficients on the explanatory variable included to measure expectational consistency were 1.29 and 1.28, respectively, indicating that the men anticipated an acceleration of improvements in life expectancy after 1980 as contrasted with the period from 1940 to 1980. Hamermesh concluded from this that "rational expectations formation with a slight bias toward optimism describes the horizon that the consumer has available for use in planning life cycle behavior" (p. 400).

With the advantage of having two additional decades of historical perspective, we now know that life expectancy did increase appreciably in the last two decades of the twentieth century, especially for men. Life expectancy for men rose from 33.6 years at age forty in 1979 to 1981 to 36.2 years in 1997. Even at age sixty-five, life expectancy for men rose by more than a year, from 14.2 to 15.8 years (U.S. Department of Commerce 1999, Table 128).

In an expanded specification, Hamermesh included explanatory variables for longevity of parents and grandparents, two health behaviors (smoking and exercise), and a binary variable for whether the respondent had a life-threatening illness. If anything, respondents placed too much weight on the longevity experience of their parents and grandparents. Tversky and Kahneman (1974) have labeled this tendency an "availability heuristic," a term describing overreliance on readily available and pertinent information in forming personal expectations.

Hurd and McGarry (1995) appear to have been the first to use the HRS longevity expectations question. They evaluated subjective probabilities of survival in the first wave, considering the likelihood of living both to seventy-five and to eighty-five. Most pertinent to our study, the authors found, considering a subsample of persons who were age fifty-five, that the means of the two probabilities were very close to life table probabilities from a recent life table. The estimate of the probability of living to age eighty-five exceeded the corresponding value from a life table based on data from a decade earlier. This suggests that respondents incorporated likely changes in longevity (due to technological change and other factors) in their forecasts of their own future.

Comparing the pattern of subjective probabilities by respondent age with actual life table values, Hurd and McGarry found different patterns for men and for women. For men, the relationship between respondent age and the subjective probabilities was flat until about age sixty-four, when the probabilities began to rise. The subjective probability of men living to age seventy-five tended to be around the life table estimate. For the subjective probability of living to age eighty-five, however, men were more optimistic than this life table warranted.

By contrast, women tended to be too pessimistic about living to age seventy-five and, if anything, slightly optimistic about their chances of reaching age eighty-five. For women, there was a *negative* relationship between respondent age and the probability of reaching seventy-five or eighty-five until the respondents reached about age sixty. Superficially, the negative relationship might seem inconsistent with Bayesian updating, but again, the respondents may have incorporated beliefs about overall improvements in longevity to occur during their lifetimes. Relatively younger persons would be more likely to benefit from technological changes. Thus, observing a flat or even a negative relationship between respondent age and the subjective probabilities is not a sufficient condition for concluding that the subjective probabilities are invalid.

Another indicator of the quality of the data on subjective probabilities concerns the frequency of 0 and 1 and 0.5 responses. A value of 1 may have resulted from the use of a 10 scale rather than a 100 scale in wave 1 (but not subsequent waves). Someone stating the probability as 0 may have had a terminal illness at the interview date or may have been unduly pessimistic. Recall President Lyndon Johnson's stated reason for not pursuing the presidency in 1968: All the men in his family had died early, and his prediction about himself was later justified by his premature death. Subjective probabilities of 0.5 are not logically impossible, but a mass point at this value *is* implausible.

Only 6.9 percent of respondents said that their probability of living to both seventy-five and eighty-five was 0. At the other end of the spectrum, 9.2 percent said that they had a probability of 1 of living to both ages; 4.7 percent said that the probability of living to both ages was 0.5. More troubling is the 2.5 percent of respondents who gave a higher probability of living to age eighty-five than to age seventy-five. Overall the evidence suggests that most people have realistic longevity expectations, but there are exceptions.

Hurd and McGarry also assessed the impact of various factors on the subjective probabilities of living to ages seventy-five and eighty-five. Directions of effect were generally plausible. The subjective probabilities varied in systematic and reasonable ways with diseases, income, wealth, and schooling, self-assessed health, and indicators of family longevity. The authors concluded:

> The subjective probabilities are in general internally consistent. To the extent that they are not, an analyst should model the process that causes the inconsistency. The process surely includes observation error, and in this regard, subjective probabilities are no different from almost all economic variables. Usually, however, the respondent and the analyst share a common understanding of the meaning of a survey question. This is, undoubtedly, not always true for the questions about subjective probabilities, and that difference needs to be "taken into account." (p. S291)

In a subsequent publication, Hurd, McFadden, and Gan (1998) extended the analysis of the subjective probability questions to the much larger set of risk questions asked in wave 1 of the HRS. These questions dealt with such other issues as the economy and the probability of spending time in a nursing home. They found that some respondents consistently reported probabilities of 0, 0.5, and 1 on several of the eight subjective likelihood questions. These types of responses would be unlikely. They labeled such responses "focal responses." Although suggestive, these patterns do not allow one to distinguish responses that would be judged as "focal" from plausible subjective beliefs.

In our own analysis of focal responses using the HRS, we specified whether focal responses were a function of gender, race, age, education, proxy measures for a respondent's time horizon, indications of changes in fine motor skills, and two tests of cognitive ability (Smith et al. 2001). We found fairly strong support for a link between focal observations and the person's having cognitive limitations. Also, older respondents and those with less than a high school education were more likely to give focal responses.

A Critique of HRS's Survival Probability Questions

In an unpublished paper, Viscusi and Hakes (1998) argued that the HRS longevity questions should not be treated as estimates for individual subjective probabilities. Their work potentially undercuts Schoenbaum's conclusion, based on the HRS, that smokers are optimistic about their survival chances. Also, because we rely on the HRS longevity expectations questions in our research, it is important to consider the substance of the arguments underlying their conclusions.

Like Hurd and McGarry (1995) and Schoenbaum (1997), using wave 1 of the HRS, Viscusi and Hakes found that, for white men, subjective probabilities rose with respondent age; for white women, they found no relationship between age and expecting to live to seventy-five and actually a negative relationship between age and expecting to live to eighty-five. We surmise that Viscusi and Hakes probably limited their analysis to white respondents to make their research comparable to Schoenbaum's.

Viscusi and Hakes stated that the flat relationship for white women might be consistent with a learning model in which, referring to Eq. (5.1), the new information, in this case living another year, has no effect on the subjective probability. But the negative relationship between respondent age and the perceived probability of living to eighty-five cannot be reconciled even on this basis. Thus, Viscusi and Hakes concluded that the HRS subjective probability reflects other concepts, such as a general measure of health status.

A second test of the validity of the HRS questions was to compare the effect of age separately for white males and white females. For both genders, there was a positive relationship between the life table probabilities and age. For men, the effect of age was less on subjective probabilities than on the objective ones. For women, there was no effect on the latter, yielding an ever-widening gap between actual and perceived probabilities as one approached age seventy-five. Viscusi and Hakes noted that, for white women, responses to the survival question were not a monotonic transformation of the actual probability. Viscusi and Hakes found a pattern in the accuracy with which the probabilities were assessed; relatively small actual probabilities tended to be overestimated, and relatively large ones underestimated.

Third, Viscusi and Hakes considered whether respondents correctly perceived the differential probabilities of living to seventy-five and eighty-five. The results may be interpreted as seeing a cup either half-empty or half-full. Viscusi and Hakes took the pessimistic view, stressing the shortcomings of HRS-respondent risk perceptions. Hurd and McGarry (1995), based on similar analysis, tended to the optimistic view, emphasizing aspects of the finding implying that people in late middle age do reasonably well in appraising future chances of (their own) death.

Fourth, Viscusi and Hakes conducted a regression analysis with subjective probabilities as the dependent variable. Like Hurd and McGarry, they found the signs on coefficients of explanatory variables were plausible, but Viscusi and Hakes emphasized that this says nothing about magnitudes of effects of each individual variable.

None of Viscusi and Hakes's criticisms are airtight. Perhaps foremost, we do not have a basis for estimating the "correct" survival probability for individuals at the time they give their subjective longevity expectation. Recall our example of President Johnson's longevity expectations. Any judgment about the multivariate models and magnitudes of the parameter estimates is just that—an analyst's judgment. We can compare the averages of subjective experience, and we summarized this evidence as being more favorable than the Viscusi and Hakes argument might imply. Turning now to the specific explorations offered by Viscusi and Hakes, several responses are warranted.

On the first and second Viscusi and Hakes tests, anticipated changes in technology, among other factors, may obscure the future relationship between age and survival probabilities. Although a younger person has a lower probability of living to age seventy-five, such a person has a better chance of benefiting from yet-to-be-developed life-saving innovations and health systems improvements. Such changes are likely to have a greater effect on the probability of living exceptionally long than on the probability of reaching the age of seventy-five.

Considering Viscusi and Hakes's third test, differentials in the probabilities can be viewed positively as well as negatively. It should not be surprising that people do not have a well-formed view of the probability of living to age eighty-five. Few people live to this age, and respondents were unlikely to know many people of this age or older. This does not necessarily imply that individuals are unreceptive to new information about living this long or about behaviors that enhance the chances of living to eighty-five. With Bayesian updating, subjective probabilities of living to eighty-five should become more precise as the person grows older.

With respect to their fourth test, there is little objective evidence on magnitudes of effect of various determinants of longevity. Published life tables control for very few covariates (age, gender, race, and, only very occasionally, specific diseases) and health behaviors (such as smoking). Thus, the effects of many covariates on survival are unknown.

Also, when people answer a question about what they think the effect of a certain change in behavior, such as smoking cessation, will be, we generally do not know what other factors they hold constant or, conversely, allow to vary. In assessing their own chances of surviving to a certain age in the future, individuals might assume some changes in behavior (a point made in the Viscusi and Hakes paper). For example, in forming their expectations, some persons might reason that they will change their future behavior, such as by quitting smoking. Our focus groups (see Chapter 7) indicated that people have interpreted the published warnings in a way that is consistent with this conclusion.

Our Empirical Analysis of Risk Perceptions

We performed our own analysis of risk perceptions based on the longevity-expectations measure from the HRS. In our analysis we addressed three related questions. First, how good are people at predicting their future health, particularly their own demise? With some important caveats, the answer is, people predict their own deaths quite well. Second, to what extent does the Bayesian updating process differ among current, former, and never smokers? If smokers are more resistant to certain types of information, the design of health messages about smoking and other health risks should incorporate that resistance. Third, are smokers too optimistic about their longevity? With respect to this third issue, we extended Schoenbaum's (1997) analysis with the HRS. We found on balance that smokers are too optimistic about their chances of living to age seventy-five or longer.

Longevity Expectations and Death: Can People Predict Their Own Demise?

In our own analysis of subjective probabilities of death (Smith, Taylor, and Sloan 2001), we considered whether responses to the subjective probability question asked by the HRS can be relied on to include all the information people use to form their subjective survival probabilities. We extended earlier analyses of the role of longevity expectations as a predictor of mortality in several ways, and included two additional waves of interviews. In addition, our analysis accounted for missing or unusable responses to the risk perception measure when testing the predictive value of longevity expectations. To do this, we used the Van de Ven and van Praag (1981) proposal extending Heckman's (1979) selection model to the case of probit with sample selection. We estimated separate models for deaths between waves 3 and 4, taking account of deaths between waves 2 and 3 as well as deaths between waves 1 and 2. By focusing on *new* health events and *changes* in activity restrictions, the estimated models distinguished separate effects over time for changes in health status and household income. Finally, we exploited the unique advantages of the panel to evaluate longevity expectations over time. This was accomplished by considering specific subsamples. For example, to assess the temporal evolution of longevity expectation, we looked at those who died between waves 3 and 4 and examined the time profile of their earlier responses to the question about their expectation of living to age seventy-five.

In one specification, whether the person died between waves 3 and 4 was the dependent variable. Explanatory variables were the subjective probability of living to age seventy-five at wave 3, new health conditions that arose between waves 2 and 3, changes in the count of the respondent's reported limitations in ADLs between waves 2 and 3, smoking status at wave 3, and family income at wave 3. The model also included two selection effects, one for survival to wave 3 and the other for survival to wave 2. The selection models included the same explanatory variables as in the mortality equation except that values were lagged one wave.

Coefficients on all explanatory variables in both the mortality and associated selection equations had signs that agreed with our a priori expectations. The longevity expectation variable had a negative impact on mortality and a positive impact on survival, as expected. Both smoking status and income in the preceding wave were statistically significant determinants of mortality, after taking account of new health shocks and changes in activity restrictions. We assumed that the new health shocks and changes in activity restrictions would not have been anticipated at the previous wave, but income and smoking status at the previous wave were known and might have been incorporated in longevity expectations.

As noted above, previous researchers who used waves 1 and 2 of the HRS reported lower longevity expectations at wave 2 than at wave 1. One would have expected that those surviving to a later wave would have reassessed the odds of living to age seventy-five as higher, not lower. We reexamined this issue from a different perspective, examining the mean responses to the longevity question among (1) those who died between waves 3 and 4 and (2) those who survived to wave 4.

Two results are notable. For decedents, mean longevity expectations *declined* monotonically in each of the waves until death. For survivors, the corresponding subjective probabilities were constant over the first three waves. Also, the mean subjective probabilities in all three waves were appreciably higher for the survivors than for the wave 3–4 decedents. We repeated the exercise for wave 2–3 decedents, and the results supported our results for wave 3–4 decedents and wave 4 survivors.

We then specifically tested whether the longevity-expectation measure reflected all information known to the individual but not necessarily objectively observable by others (including researchers) at the time the probability was elicited by the HRS. We tested this hypothesis by including the mortality status of respondents during the two years *after* they reported their longevity expectations.

We found that longevity expectations appear to be reasonably good predictors of future mortality. People can and do predict their own demise. Such expectations are also consistently updated with new information, but they do not reflect all the information that respondents who subsequently die have about their survival prospects. More specifically, individuals' reported longevity expectations tend to be below the values that the updating model would imply for them, after accounting for new health shocks and activity restrictions. The extent of underestimation of the probability of death is relative. Nevertheless, our findings leave little scope for doubt about whether these subjective probabilities should be taken seriously—clearly, they should.

Are There Systematic Differences between Smokers and Nonsmokers in Risk Updating?

As discussed in Chapter 2, the factors underlying the decision to begin smoking are not well understood. Further, although we can control for several observable characteristics of smokers and nonsmokers, there are undoubtedly unmeasured differences that the data do not capture. In Smith et al. (2001), we asked the following question: How do smokers differ from nonsmokers in the way they incorporate information when forming risk perceptions? This study was based on the first two waves of the HRS. We split the sample into three groups: current smokers, former smokers, and never smokers. Following Viscusi, we assumed a Bayesian updating process as described in Eq. (5.1). In our case, however, we observe the prior (wave 1) longevity expectations, unlike Viscusi. Viscusi's work, both in 1990 and 1992 and with Hakes, assumed that respondents' socioeconomic characteristics incorporate the prior beliefs. Our model used the wave 1 longevity expectation and thus could distinguish the effects of individual characteristics on how new information was used. Without a direct measure of the person's prior longevity expectation, Viscusi and his coauthors could not make this important distinction.

The dependent variable was the respondent's self-reported subjective assessment of living to seventy-five or more years of age. Explanatory variables included demographic variables (age, education, gender, whether parents were alive at the interview date), smoking and nonsmoking-related health shocks, and the previous wave's subjective longevity assessment. The health shock variables, both smoking-related and general, measured unexpected events that we hypothesized would cause respondents to reevaluate their personal longevity expectations. By "shock," we referred to a newly occurring health event; if a person reported having had a heart attack in the past and had a second heart attack between waves 1 and 2, this was not considered to be a shock. The smoking-related health shocks were those health events found to have an elevated relative risk for death among smokers (see Chapter 4). We considered cardiovascular and cerebrovascular diseases, cancers related to smoking, and severe chronic lung disease, such as emphysema, to be smoking related.

Our specification was partly determined by the questions asked in the HRS. In later waves, the HRS unfortunately no longer asked for specific details about which body system was affected by cancer. For this reason, we confined our analysis to the first two waves. Nonsmoking-related shocks reflected the onset of new conditions or other major health events not considered smoking related, such as hospitalization for a hip fracture or the onset of diabetes. Since the HRS provided no information on disease severity, regarding diseases for which there was likely to have been some ambiguity, we considered the event a shock only if the person reported having been hospitalized for at least three days between waves 1 and 2. For newly occurring cases of severe chronic lung disease (bronchitis, emphysema), the respondent had to state that this illness limited his or her ability to do paid or household work. For cancers, we did not use a hospital stay as a screen because the diagnosis of severe disease is clearer and treatment of some cancers is increasingly performed on an outpatient basis.

We first tested the hypothesis that the distribution of longevity expectations for HRS respondents was the same across current, former, and never smokers. The null hypothesis of equality of distribution of responses was rejected, using a chi-square test. Our secondary hypothesis was that persons in the three groups react differently to health shocks. This hypothesis was tested using chi-square analysis for cross-tabulations of the longevity expectations of each of the three groups, classified by the different health shocks. This approach imposes fewer maintained assumptions than a formal risk-updating model. We found that current smokers adjust their subjective probability of death only to smoking-related shocks, while the other groups respond to both smoking-related and nonsmoking-related health shocks.

We then used the empirical counterpart to the risk-updating model (Eq. 5.1) to investigate the updating of risk perception using multivariate analysis. We estimated the models for three separate samples. We also repeated the same three groupings for a paired husband-wife/partners sample. In the latter analysis, there were two observations per household, and the health shock variables were symmetrical. That is, if the primary respondent experienced a health shock, this was recorded as a spouse's health shock for the observation associated with the individual listed as partner or spouse.

Some interviewees gave what we judged to be focal responses (values of 0, 0.5, 1.0, identical probabilities of living to age seventy-five and age eighty-five), and others were unable to answer the longevity questions at all. To account for these types of answers, we treated the focal response as a source of selection effect and adjusted our longevity expectations accordingly. The dependent variable in the selection equations identified the focal and nonresponses compared with other plausible responses. The explanatory variables were gender, race, education, proxy measures for the respondent's time horizon, indications of changes in fine motor skills, and cognitive ability, which were based on two questions from the HRS (see Box 5.2).

The key finding from the selection analysis was that respondents with low scores on the cognitive tests were more likely to have difficulty dealing with the subjective probabilities—that is, they gave focal responses or did not respond. Also, older respondents and those with less than a high school education were more likely to give focal responses or not respond.

The selection models were estimated for the three separate samples (current, former, and never smokers). A likelihood ratio test suggested that the selection models were significantly different for the three groups. In particular, our selection models revealed clear differences between former and never smokers versus current smokers in the role of cognitive ability scores as a determinant of longevity responses. The relationship between cognitive ability and the ability to answer the longevity expectation question was less pronounced for current smokers than for the other two groups. This may imply that, for nonsmokers, the inability to think clearly is an important reason for poor answers. By contrast, many smokers may simply not want to deal with questions about future health.

There are several important differences in these groups' risk-updating processes. First, health shocks of the type that occur much more frequently among smokers were the only pieces of "new information" in the analysis that influenced current smokers' longevity expectations. The other two groups' longevity expectations were influenced by both smoking-related and general health shocks. We also conducted statistical tests to determine for each group whether the smoking and nonsmoking health shocks had the same effect on longevity expectations. The null hypothesis of equality across the type of shock was rejected for current smokers but not for the other two groups of respondents.

Several factors contribute to understanding these differences in risk updating between smokers and the other groups in response to general health shocks. In our focus groups (Chapter 7), we asked participants the HRS risk-perception question for the probability of living to age seventy-five. Each respondent was asked to write his or her answer on a piece of paper. We then discussed their answers. We found that current smokers seemed to be more likely to use the experience of parents or grandparents to discount the relevance of health warnings for their personal decision to smoke. If their grandparents had smoked and lived to a ripe old age, current smokers often acted as though the averages do not apply to them. In contrast, former smokers who were in the same age range as current smokers often said that their relatives had experienced adverse health events attributable to their smoking. In other words, current smokers needed direct personal event to convince them of the danger of smoking and probably were more oblivious to health events not linked to their prior experience.

Smokers may have a different propensity for acquiring new information and may be more anchored in prior beliefs about the probabilities of adverse outcomes stemming from their behavior. We tested the hypothesis that each of the three groups placed different weights on new information, based on their own personal health experiences. We applied each subsample's estimated updating model to the observed experience of all three subsamples to estimate r_t for each group (from Eq. 5.1), as would be implied by their own and others' use of information. To permit testing, bootstrap estimates of the standard errors were computed with 500 replications. These estimates were constructed by sampling with replacement from the paired (spouse/partner) sample of respondents to wave 2.

This approach allowed us to separate the effects of each group's updating weights for information from their actual health-related experiences (what we interpreted as the new information). For example, we could evaluate how current smokers would update if they experienced the health shocks actually experienced between waves 1 and 2 by those who never smoked.

We found that current smokers evaluate all three interwave health records differently from former smokers. In particular, former smokers placed a higher weight on the new health information experienced by each of the three groups (current, former, and never smokers) than did current smokers. Differences between current and never smokers followed the same direction as between current and former smokers, but the differences failed to be significantly different at conventional levels.

These results emphasize the importance of probing into differences in the risk perceptions reported by smokers and other groups. To understand the full implications of these empirical tests for older smokers' choices, we need to look behind the numbers to understand why the risk-updating processes differ between the three groups. Overall, these statistical models provide an approximate road map for the types of information smokers and nonsmokers use in forming longevity expectations. The clear differences in the effects of smoking-related health shocks for current smokers suggest that personalized messages, relevant to their circumstances, are necessary to get their attention and induce changes in their beliefs.

Are Smokers Too Optimistic about Their Own Survival?

In Sloan, Smith, and Taylor (2001), we reanalyzed data from HRS wave 1, using the same sample and life tables as Schoenbaum (1997). We compared subjective probabilities, measured at wave 1, with life table estimates of the probability of living to age seventy-five at an aggregate level. These values were interpreted as objective estimates of the survival probability. Because the life tables were limited to white people, our sample was restricted to this group. Moreover, the life tables stratified current smokers into two groups according to whether they smoked more or less than twenty-five cigarettes per day. We constructed groups corresponding to former smokers and those who never smoked. The panel structure of the data allowed us to observe respondents over time and to compare their subjective responses with the life tables. With the addition of data from HRS wave 2, we were also able to assess how changes in smoking behavior affect personal longevity expectations.

Overall, there was a close correspondence between average longevity expectations and life table values. However, there were important differences in the patterns of subjective assessments of survival rate versus objective probabilities by gender and smoking status. White men who never smoked were remarkably accurate in forecasting their own probability of living to age seventy-five, as defined by life tables. For all but one of the age categories, the perceived probability was within 0.01 or less of the actual probability. Only for the sixty-five to sixty-nine age group were those who never smoked unduly pessimistic about their chances of living to seventy-five: 0.67 for the perceived probability versus 0.75 for the actual probability. (Although primary respondents to the HRS had to have been born between 1931 and 1941, spouses and partners could be of any age.) Overall for white men, the estimated differential between longevity expectation and average value taken from the life tables (subjective probability less the objective life table probability of living to age seventy-five) was small, 0.018, and significantly different from zero, suggesting slight pessimism.

Nonetheless, this should be considered a very close correspondence that is generally consistent with past research for the overall sample (see Hamermesh 1985).

White male former smokers were somewhat less accurate in predicting their life expectancy. Those in their fifties appeared to be overly optimistic and those in older age groups were somewhat pessimistic. Respondents in the sixty-five to sixty-nine age group assessed their probability of living to seventy-five accurately. Of course, persons in this age group were closer to age seventy-five. A similar but somewhat more erratic pattern characterized the responses of current smokers who consumed fewer than twenty-five cigarettes per day in wave 1. Current smokers who consumed more than this amount daily were much too optimistic about their life expectancy. The differentials were particularly great for heavy smokers who were in their fifties, confirming Schoenbaum's conclusion that smokers are optimistic about their chances of reaching seventy-five years of age.

Using the life table as our standard, white women who never smoked were too pessimistic about their chances of living to age seventy-five. Female former smokers were more accurate, while those who were light smokers under age sixty-five tended to be pessimistic. As with the white men, women who smoked twenty-five or more cigarettes daily were much too optimistic in their longevity expectations.

Life tables represent population averages. As mentioned earlier, individuals may differ from population averages because of systematic biases in cognition (see Kahneman and Tversky 1981, 1982). They may also differ because of characteristics that are obvious to them but are "smoothed" in average life tables. To investigate whether smokers differ from former and never smokers in terms of their wave 1 assessments of living to seventy-five, we estimated an equation for the difference between an individual's subjective assessment and the life table average assigned to them based on their age and gender. We specified this difference as the dependent variable. Smoking status was among the covariates. Other explanatory variables included gender, cognition (number of words correctly recalled), and educational attainment.

Holding several other factors constant, current smokers overestimated their probability of living to seventy-five by 0.13. Former smokers, other factors held constant, overestimated this probability by about half as much on average. Men tended to be overly optimistic, overestimating the probability by 0.068. Persons in higher-income households, those with a college degree, and those who scored relatively well on the HRS test of cognitive status also tended to overestimate their probability of living to seventy-five. The latter results may be due to objective increases in life expectancy associated with higher income, cognition, and education. The life tables did not disaggregate on the basis of these variables. The same cannot be said for the discrepancy by gender and smoking status, since the life tables accounted for those factors.

Given that smokers tended to be overly optimistic about their probability of surviving to age seventy-five at the baseline interview, we also examined how subjective probabilities responded to changes in smoking status between the waves. We found subjective probabilities rose and fell in the right directions. That is, persons who quit smoking increased their longevity expectations after they quit, and the converse was true for those who resumed smoking. However, persons who quit seemed to be too optimistic about the health gains from quitting, especially in the short run.

Conclusions

Risk perceptions are important because they may guide health-related choices. At the most fundamental level, the study of longevity expectations and survival probabilities is about individuals' willingness and ability to anticipate the future. These expectations can be expressed as answers to factual questions—such as, what is the probability that a smoker will die from lung cancer?—or they can be put in terms of the personal likelihood of an event for an individual decision maker, as in the risk perception questions included in the HRS.

The life table is not a perfect prediction. What we know about survival probability is based on averages for different groups (for example, white men who smoke). We have less ability to predict how long an individual will survive based on his or her decision to smoke, and prior research had not revealed much about how individuals forecast their own longevity.

To help address this issue, we used the panel structure of the HRS to investigate how personal messages in the form of health shocks affect longevity expectations. Our analysis confirmed that people *do* take account of information related to their own health. We also found evidence, based on the time distribution of responses to longevity-expectation questions for those who later died, that people are able to anticipate their own demise, at least within a few years prior to the event.

Overall, the process of forming longevity expectations seems to be rational, reflecting each individual's personal appraisal of his or her circumstances, and realistic, with little sugarcoating. While predictions are not perfect, people do seem to know a small amount more than they reveal through the expectations questions about their own health and its relationship to their mortality.

Our analysis also revealed some shortcomings in risk perceptions. Current smokers in general, and especially those who consumed many cigarettes per day, were overly optimistic about their chances of survival. Just by considering the relative optimism of smokers compared with others in a cross section, one cannot distinguish between two nonmutually exclusive reasons for the relative optimism of smokers. Are smokers an innately optimistic group of folks? Such innate optimism may not be picked up by the covariates in our model. Or, is there no basic innate difference between smokers and others in optimism? Perhaps current smokers simply have a blind spot when it comes to smoking and systematically underestimate the deleterious effect smoking has on one's health.

With data from a panel of near elderly respondents, we were able to link changes in smoking status to changes in the subjective probability of living to age seventy-five. We found directions of change in the probabilities to be as expected. This much is the good news. Persons who quit smoking revised the probability upward, but they were probably too optimistic about the short-run effects of quitting on longevity.[7] Although our evidence on changes in subjective longevity expectations conditional on quitting suggests that quitters overestimate the effects of smoking cessation on longevity, one could argue that those who quit were those who took their doctors' advice seriously, or, more precisely, too seriously.

When we considered the updating process in response to new personalized information from essentially exogenous events, in the form of changes in various dimensions of health, current smokers did not update their longevity expectations in response to changes in their health as much as did others in this age cohort. This suggests more fundamental underlying differences in risk perceptions among persons who happen to smoke. Such differences may be attributable to differences in cognitive processes that vary systematically by smoking status. We were not able to identify from our analysis *why* the differences in risk updating for current, former, and the never smokers occurred.

Women who never smoked appeared to be too pessimistic about their life expectancy. This biased view of longevity may have nothing to do with their smoking status per se, but may reflect unmeasured personal factors. The conclusion about smokers being overly optimistic about their future longevity held even after we accounted for other plausible determinants of the probability of living to age seventy-five. These findings may be of special interest, because our measure of risk perception was a personalized risk rather than one applicable to an entire population.

Our results differ from Viscusi's for plausible reasons. Our measure of risk was personalized. His measure was not. Also, he studied Bayesian updating of risk perceptions with single cross sections. Panel data, such as that made available to researchers by the HRS, are needed for a more comprehensive study risk updating.

We also differ in the policy inferences we draw from our findings. Viscusi concluded that, if anything, people overestimate the impact of smoking on such health harms as lung cancer, implying that tobacco companies are not culpable in causing smokers to disregard the health risks of smoking. Our conclusion is that heavy smokers do *not* overestimate their personal risks. Moreover, simple blanket generalizations, such as Viscusi's conclusion for all smokers and nonsmokers, are simply unwarranted. Factors influencing longevity expectations are diverse—relating to the observable characteristics of respondents, their cognitive abilities, education, and past experiences—and are correlated with smoking.

In the chapters that follow, we examine the link between risk perceptions and choices.

CHAPTER

6

Do Health Shocks Influence Smoking Behavior? Cessation and Relapse Patterns in Older Adults

Serious health shocks related to smoking do influence the longevity expectations of smokers, but do they do anything about it? The literature tying public and private information to risk perceptions and behavior is sparse. In this chapter and the next, we explore relationships between information obtained from personalized health messages, risk perception, and smoking behavior. To our knowledge, such an integrated treatment was nonexistent before, especially for this age group.

Understanding determinants of smoking cessation in older adults is important for a number of reasons. People over age fifty represent one-fifth of all smokers (Orleans et al. 1994a). They can experience health benefits from cessation regardless of how long they smoked (U.S. Department of Health and Human Services 1991; and see Chapter 4). Moreover, the smoking habits of persons over age fifty have potential financial implications for publicly financed health insurance, most specifically Medicare (Daviglus et al. 1998; Chapter 9). Finally, some states are using funds from the 1998 tobacco settlement to promote cessation, and while this is an admirable goal, current and previous approaches to promote cessation have had only moderate success.

At least 30 percent of smokers in the United States make at least one attempt to quit smoking every year (Fiore et al. 1990). However, about 80 percent of attempts fail within the first month (Hughes et al. 1992). The average smoker cycles three to four times through stages of quitting and relapsing before cessation is maintained for a sustained period. Even in these cases, however, cessation is often not 100 percent successful (U.S. Department of Health and Human Services 1990, p. 24). The difficulty of trying to quit can make smokers feel desperate, as the title of a recent popular book, *Dying to Quit,* implies (Brigham 1998).

Other smokers apparently would rather die than quit. Two multicenter clinical trials of patients undergoing angioplasty for their heart disease revealed that this intervention was insufficient to promote quitting (Tiara et al. 2000). Out of frustration, the author of an editorial accompanying the research report asked, "What is wrong with these people?" (Califf 2000).

At middle age, smoking initiation among those who never smoked before is virtually nil. Almost all cases of initiation are relapses by persons who had quit smoking in the recent past. Most of the variation in aggregate demand for cigarettes is attributable to switches between smoking and not smoking, rather than to changes in the amount of smoking among current smokers.

This chapter is in two parts. First, we review the literature on determinants of smoking cessation and relapse, emphasizing, to the extent possible, evidence for these behaviors among persons over age fifty. Second, we present our own analysis of smoking cessation and relapse based on data from the Health and Retirement Study.

Determinants of Cessation and Relapse

Demographic Factors

Demographic factors—age, gender, race, education, and marital status—reflect a cluster of more fundamental underlying influences—psychological, biological, cognitive, and environmental. While it would be desirable to link the demographic characteristics to these underlying, unobserved personal characteristics, the requisite understanding of how different groups form beliefs and develop smoking habits is currently lacking. For now, we must be satisfied with a description of the role of each demographic factor in smoking cessation and relapse.

At least two factors tend to make the perceived cost of smoking rise with age (Douglas 1998). First, the time remaining until the typical age of onset of smoking-related diseases decreases as one becomes older (see Chapter 8). Any effect of discounting the cost of future adverse health events is reduced. Second, as a person accumulates information about his or her own health, the size and certainty of adverse consequences of one's own smoking practices becomes more apparent.

Age cohorts may differ in their beliefs about the harmful effects of smoking. There might also be differences in the attractiveness of smoking, such as appeal to peers or the lack thereof (stigma), that are correlated with age. Some findings about beliefs about smoking are surprising. Orleans et al. (1992) found that older persons were much less likely than younger persons to believe that smoking harms health. In this study, fewer older current smokers believed there is a strong connection between smoking and illness. Compared with older smokers, many more younger smokers thought they were more likely than nonsmokers to get diseases such as heart disease, lung cancer, bronchitis, or emphysema. The age difference was also evident within the fifty to seventy-four age group, with beliefs that smoking harms health being less prevalent among persons age sixty-five to seventy-four than among persons fifty to sixty-four. In a later study, Orleans and coauthors (1994b) confirmed these observations using data from another source. The differences in risk perception by age cohort may largely reflect different information obtained about smoking during the person's formative years.

These findings might seem to be at variance with our focus group findings, which are that most smokers seem to feel they can continue for a few more years, quit, and be restored to health comparable to that of a nonsmoker (see Chapter 7). However, an explanation may be found in the perception on the part of current smokers that the effects of smoking are fully reversible. These studies may simply be capturing the net effect of smokers' plans. As smokers get older, they get closer to their "planned" time to stop and reacquire excellent health. Under these circumstances, if they answer questions based on a predetermination of this plan, their answers could appear to indicate a belief that smoking is less hazardous to health over time.

Cumulative quit rates, defined as ex-smokers as a percentage of ever smokers, rise with age for both men and women. For example, in one study conducted in six large cities throughout the United States, quit rates rose from 30 percent for men and 28 percent for women at age twenty to twenty-four to 76 percent and 63 percent for men and women, respectively, over age seventy-five (Kabat and Wynder 1987). For men, quitting accelerated dramatically after age forty-five. For women, patterns were much more erratic, with no definitive pattern by age.

Rates of quitting are influenced in part by cohort effects reflecting when smoking was initiated; one source of a cohort effect, differential information about the harms of smoking, was suggested above. With a single cross section, it is impossible to isolate age from cohort effects, and some of the surprising findings on risk perception and preference we reported above may really be cohort effects rather than age effects.

Among respondents age fifty-one to sixty-four at wave 1 who answered all four waves of the HRS, quit rates rose with each successive wave (Table 6.1). Of the 2,835 persons who smoked at wave 1, only 1,669 persons smoked continuously through wave 4 (58.9 percent). This does not include the 308 persons who smoked at wave 1 and died by wave 4 (11.7 percent). By contrast, of the 3,771 never smokers at wave 1, only 116 persons had died by wave 4 (3.1 percent). Dropping decedents from the base substantially increases the number of wave 1 smokers who smoked continuously between waves 1 and 4, from 58.9 percent to 66.0 percent, or nearly two-thirds of wave 1 smokers.

This is a case of a cup half empty versus a cup half full. Although 1,669 persons who were smokers at wave 1 continued to smoke throughout waves 1 to 4, or from 1992 to 1998, another 252 who smoked during 1992 (8.9 percent of wave 1 smokers) reported not smoking in each of the subsequent waves. This leaves 606 wave 1 smokers who did not smoke continuously and did not die (21.4 percent of wave 1 current smokers). These people vacillated, perhaps on their way to permanent quitting, but our six-year follow-up period did not allow us to observe this. This is the cup half full.

This evidence is consistent with the model in Suranovic, Goldfarb, and Leonard (1999) that suggests that the shape of an individual's adjustment-cost function influences patterns of quitting behavior. When adjustment costs associated with reducing levels of smoking increase at a decreasing rate for consumption levels near zero but at an increasing rate for consumption levels near the habitual level, their model describes a smoker's cigarette consumption as consisting of three stages: "In the initial stage the smoker would consume at a fixed positive level. Eventually the smoker will enter a second stage in which a gradual reduction in average consumption ensues. Finally the smoker would quit smoking cold turkey for some positive level" (p. 17). The authors noted that this overall pattern is consistent with smokers who attempt to quit numerous times before being successful. Once consumption levels reach the low level, the cost of quitting may not be large. Looking at the cup as half empty, a higher proportion of wave 1 current smokers died between waves 1 and 4 than quit (presumably) permanently for the years between waves 1 and 4.

Table 6.1 Smoking transition matrix, waves 1–4

Wave 1	Wave 2		Wave 3		Wave 4	
					Smoking	1,669
			Smoking	2,001	Dead	81
					Not Smoking	251
			Dead	92		
					Smoking	49
	Smoking	2,328	Not Smoking	235	Dead	16
					Not Smoking	170
Current Smoker, 2835	Dead	82				
					Smoking	76
	Not Smoking	425	Smoking	110	Dead	3
					Not Smoking	31
			Dead	21		
					Smoking	29
			Not Smoking	294	Dead	13
					Not Smoking	252
					Smoking	62
			Smoking	89	Dead	8
					Not Smoking	19
			Dead	7		
					Smoking	6
	Smoking	133	Not Smoking	37	Dead	3
					Not Smoking	28

Table 6.1 (continued)

Wave 1	Wave 2		Wave 3		Wave 4	
Former Smoker, 3855	Dead	72				
					Smoking	32
	Not Smoking	3,650	Smoking	55	Dead	1
					Not Smoking	22
			Dead	67		
					Smoking	30
			Not Smoking	3,528	Dead	76
					Not Smoking	3,422
					Smoking	8
			Smoking	14	Dead	1
					Not Smoking	5
			Dead	1		
					Smoking	1
	Smoking	21	Not Smoking	6	Dead	1
					Not Smoking	4
Never Smoker, 3771	Dead	35				
					Smoking	1
	Not Smoking	3,715	Smoking	1	Dead	0
					Not Smoking	0
			Dead	41		
					Smoking	7
			Not Smoking	3,673	Dead	37
					Not Smoking	3,629

Among the 3,855 former smokers at wave 1, 3,422 persons, or about 89 percent, remained nonsmokers throughout the six-year observational period. When the 234 former smokers who died after wave 1 are dropped from the base, the nonsmoking retention rate increases appreciably, to 94.5 percent. This leaves 199 vacillators (5.2 percent of wave 1 former smokers). The pool of wave 1 former smokers contained many persons who had quit smoking many years before the baseline interview.

Why was the share of persons who continued to smoke as high as it was? We offer two possible explanations. For one, older smokers might reason that since they have already made it to an advanced age, smoking cannot be bad for them. Alternatively, as our focus groups of current smokers indicated, they may believe the health effects are completely reversible.

A second demographic factor is gender. With data from the Lung Health Study, the largest trial to evaluate the long-term efficacy of smoking cessation programs in initiating and sustaining smoking cessation in both men and women, Bjornson et al. (1995) found that women have greater difficulty than men in quitting smoking. However, other demographic factors and smoking history were more important than gender per se in explaining variations in success of sustained smoking cessation. Men are more likely to quit than women. Gender differences in smoking cessation increase after controlling for possible confounders such as age, education, and amount smoked (Osler et al. 1999), although the reasons for the differences by gender are not at all well understood. A high rate of smoking initiation occurred with later birth cohorts for men than for women (Escobedo and Peddicord 1996); further, among current smokers, consumption is lower for women than for men.

On the dimension of race, African Americans have higher smoking prevalence rates and lower smoking cessation rates than white Americans (Novotny et al. 1988; Royce et al. 1993; Wagenknecht et al. 1993). One possible explanation for racial differences in smoking and quit rates is that prolonged social distress and marginalization might lead to a greater likelihood of engaging in detrimental health practices, such as smoking, or of resisting the adoption of disease prevention behaviors, including smoking cessation (King et al. 1998). Another possible explanation relates to competing risks. To the extent, for example, that African Americans face a greater risk of death from causes other than smoking, they might have less disincentive to engage and continue engaging in harmful behaviors such as smoking. Still another possibility is that some of the consequences of quitting are worse for smokers at higher ages. For example, Becona and Vazquez (1998) found higher rates of weight gain among quitters over age thirty-five than for adults below this age.

Evidence on the effect of marital status or partner or spousal support on cessation is conflicting. Many of the studies have used highly selected and small samples. With a very small sample (twenty-one smokers and their partners), Ginsberg, Hall, and Rosinski (1991) found that failure to quit was predicted by smokers' negative behavior, including pro-smoking statements, interrupting the partner, and criticism or rejection of help, and by their partners' suggestion that they quit the quitting process. In a one-year longitudinal study of nearly 200 adults who tried to quit on their own, subjects were administered a measure of expected partner support before starting the quitting process and a measure of received partner support one month after their quit date (Cohen and Lichtenstein 1990). Partner support was measured by ten positive and ten negative partner behaviors. Examples of positive behaviors were: "compliment you on not smoking," "help you think of substitutes for smoking," and "help you to calm down when you are feeling stressed or irritable." Examples of negative behaviors were: "asking you to quit smoking," "comment that smoking is a dirty habit," and "comment on your lack of willpower." The study found that the ratio of positive to negative behaviors was an important determinant of continuous abstinence.

Price

Although price is a key variable in economic models of consumer choice, there is surprisingly little empirical evidence on the effects of cigarette prices on cessation behavior. To our knowledge, no empirical evidence focuses on price's effect on the quitting behavior of older persons.

Douglas (1998) used data from a single cross section, the 1987 National Health Interview Survey, to form an artificial panel. With the panel, he studied the hazard of starting and stopping the habit of smoking. He used cigarette price data from the Tobacco Institute for states and years. He found that the future price, but not the current or previous period's price, affected the rate of quitting; a 1 percent increase in the future price would increase the rate of cessation by about 1 percent. His results imply a substantial response of cessation to price, but the article is unclear regarding price's link to the panel. There is some ambiguity about the years for which past, current, and future cigarette prices were defined. To link the price data to the survey, he had to assume that respondents remained in the state of their youth. In analysis of longitudinal data for much younger persons, Taurus (1999) and Chaloupka and Wechsler (1997) concluded that higher prices increase the probability of first-time cessation for young adult men and women. The authors did not exclude from their category of quitters persons who subsequently restarted.

The bottom line is that cigarette prices seem to influence smoking cessation. However, the absence of research on this issue, especially regarding older smokers, indicates an opportunity to consider the roles that the prices of smoking and quitting day in these smokers' behavior.

Risk Perception

To our knowledge, no study has explicitly studied the impact of risk perception on smoking cessation and relapse. As we noted earlier (Chapter 5), Viscusi (1992) used a single cross-sectional interview to study smokers' risk perceptions. He then evaluated the impact of those risk perceptions on the probability of smoking. Viscusi repeated this type of single cross-section study in Spain, with many of the same types of questions and with broadly similar conclusions.

He found that higher values for the perceived risk of developing lung cancer from smoking reduced the likelihood that the person smoked. This result was robust to changes in equation specification. His analysis considered various alternative specifications to assess the probability that individual survey respondents smoked. He included health information and attitude variables.

Many of the negative and positive attitudes had plausible and statistically significant impacts on the probability of smoking, but there were also some implausible relationships. From the perspective of our analysis, the most important aspect of Viscusi's evaluation of these attitude variables was the stability in the sign and statistical significance of the effect of risk perceptions on the likelihood of being a smoker. Since his results suggested that smokers overestimated rather than underestimated the risk of getting lung cancer, he computed the change in smoking prevalence if persons knew the true risk of getting lung cancer. Not surprisingly, more people would smoke if they knew the true risk.

His findings clearly challenge the conventional wisdom and suggest that information programs that bring smokers' perceptions in line with the actual risks will cause *more* smoking, not less. However, several issues should be raised regarding his arguments. First, Viscusi did not actually study cessation, but rather studied the probability of smoking by comparing different individuals in a single cross section. Because both sets of responses are given contemporaneously, there is the potential that both are jointly determined, with causation flowing from the state of being a smoker to the risk perception rather than the reverse, as was assumed in his probability-of-smoking models. Second, smokers die from diseases other than lung cancer. Their decision to quit smoking is plausibly motivated by the increased risk of contracting a number of diseases, becoming disabled, and dying prematurely. While contracting lung cancer is virtually a death sentence, getting lung cancer is not as great a threat to a person's functional status as is chronic obstructive pulmonary disease, the disease we used in our own information treatments (Chapters 7 and 8), or the congestive heart failure that may follow one or more heart attacks. Lung cancer often leads to a rapid death and therefore often does not have a sustained impact on a person's quality of life. Third, Viscusi's risk variable is subject to several criticisms (see Chapter 5). Use of a panel rather than a single cross section allowed us to consider the evolution of risk perceptions, as measured in our case by longevity expectations, and thus we could disentangle the potential for endogeneity by considering longevity expectations as reported in the waves that preceded the wave when a respondent decided to stop smoking.

Adverse Health Events

Serious health events (such as a heart attack or cancer) are the most salient form of personal information an individual can receive about his or her health. We have argued, based on the longevity expectations, that this information is more salient to smokers than a general message to the effect that smoking is bad for you. In Chapter 5 we presented empirical evidence indicating that smokers do connect smoking related health shocks to their longevity expectations. The next step is to consider how they respond. Information suggesting that the quality of their life could change (associated with these types of health shocks) was a powerful motivator.

Surviving a serious health event such as a heart attack may increase an individual's likelihood of smoking cessation for at least two reasons. First, the health shock may serve as a wake-up call, both in terms of the implications of behavioral decisions in general and in terms of a greater recognition of one's own inherited susceptibility. Second, some persons may seek to forestall further health damage. But another possibility is that health shocks might *encourage* smoking or relapsing. In this case, an individual who was a former smoker might relapse and begin smoking again following a serious health event because he believes he is too far gone to benefit from cessation.

The death of a parent also reveals information relevant to an individual's expected longevity, but the effect on cessation, although similar, is expected to be weaker than an adverse health event occurring to the smoker himself. The death of a parent of the same gender may be more salient, given (at least perceived) gender-specific differences in the effect of smoking on health. The transmission of genes to children is not gender specific, but genetics and gender may interact to affect smoking behavior in ways that currently are not understood.

Unfortunately, the HRS provided information only about deaths of parents and parents-in-law and did not provide any information on their smoking history or the causes of death for these individuals; we could not consider these types of informational signals in detail.

Comparatively little empirical evidence links adverse health events to subsequent smoking cessation. Several early studies, summarized by Garvey (1984), investigated this issue. Pertinent quotations from this review are found in Box 6.1. Most of these studies did not have a control group.

The most thorough analysis of effects of adverse health events on smoking cessation to date is by Wray et al. (1998). This study was based on the first two waves from the HRS. Unlike previous researchers, they found no effect of education on smoking cessation, although education did raise the probability of being a never smoker at baseline. By contrast, having had a heart attack between the two waves did encourage quitting. Among smokers who experienced a heart attack, higher levels of educational attainment also raised the probability of quitting.

Other Health Behaviors

Smoking is a very risky activity, but other risky activities may serve as either complements to or substitutes for smoking. Being overweight due to lack of exercise or overeating is an example of a substitute. An example of a complement is heavy drinking. With the increase in restrictions on advertising for tobacco products, cigarette companies tend to focus their advertising efforts on special groups, such as patrons of bars (Sloan et al. 2000). Pearson et al. (1987) showed a strong positive correlation between smoking and heavy drinking. A negative relationship between body weight and smoking has been reported in several studies (Klesges et al. 1998).

Ussher et al. (2000) reviewed articles published between 1980 and 1999 on the effect of exercise-based interventions on smoking cessation. The review focused on randomized controlled trials, including both healthy indi-

---

Box 6.1 Some persons continue smoking despite health shocks

Arthur Garvey (1984) summarized several studies of the reaction of smokers to health shocks:

> For a one-year period Mausner (1970) followed smokers being treated by chest physicians in Philadelphia for respiratory problems (but not lung cancer) and found that only 58 percent were ex-smokers.
>
> Croog and Richards (1977) followed heart-attack patients over a period of eight years and found that approximately 50 percent of them stopped smoking.
>
> Burt and colleagues (1974) found, when they followed their sample of smokers who survived acute myocardial infarction over a period of one to three years, that 62 percent of them quit smoking.
>
> Daughton and associates (1980) studied cessation among patients with chronic obstructive pulmonary disease and found that 67 percent had stopped smoking over a period of five months to nine years after discharge [from a hospital, presumably for treatment of this disease].
>
> Weinblatt et al. (1971) is of particular interest because it is the only known study of quitting rates after an illness that provided a control group of healthy individuals, thereby allowing smoking-cessation rates in the two groups to be compared. These investigators found that approximately 50 percent of smokers with heart disease stopped smoking after a period of five years of follow-up, while only 20 percent of the control group of healthy smokers quit in the same period. (p. 191)

viduals and those with specific medical conditions. Overall, no effect of such interventions was detected.

In an analysis of the relationship between smoking and other risky behaviors, Hersch and Viscusi (1998) found that smokers were less likely to take preventive health actions, such as using a seatbelt, flossing, and checking their blood pressure. They not only selected riskier jobs but also were more likely to be injured on the jobs. Also, they were more likely to be involved in an accident in their home, and were more likely to have an accident overall. Because Hersch and Viscusi's analysis relied on individual cross sections, it was not possible to discern whether changes in the other risky activities influence smoking cessation.

Determinants of Smoking Cessation and Relapse in the HRS

Overview

In Chapter 5 we assessed determinants of longevity expectations as a measure of risk perceptions, under the presumption that if one could motivate people to form more realistic risk perceptions, some current smokers would be encouraged to quit. To begin our analysis of this issue, we first consider determinants of cessation measured by changes in smoking status between waves of the HRS panel.[1]

The HRS has both strengths and weaknesses for assessing cessation and relapse. On the positive side, the HRS is a nationally representative sample. Its panel feature allows for analysis of behavioral change over time. However, behavior is recorded at two-year intervals. Thus, we must track longer-run changes. We assess abstinence over a two-year period, as recommended by some experts, but we do not know whether abstinence during the time interval was continuous. Also, the HRS does not contain information on mechanisms used for quitting, such as self-help or pharmacological interventions. Finally, the HRS does not contain some measures, such as self-perceived efficacy (Shiffman et al. 2000).

In our analysis of cessation and relapse, we assessed the probability that persons who smoked at the preceding wave had quit by the next wave. For former smokers at the preceding wave, we also evaluated the probability of relapse. The sample was limited to those respondents between the ages of fifty-one and sixty-four at wave 1.

Within the four waves of the HRS considered in our analysis, there were three transitions, each for a two-year time interval: waves 1–2, waves 2–3, and waves 3–4. Thus there were up to three observations per person. Standard errors were adjusted for clustering. For the cessation analysis, an observation was included if the person smoked at the beginning of the two-year period. For the relapse analysis, an observation was included if the person did not smoke at the beginning of the two-year period. Those respondents who reported themselves as never smokers at wave 1 were eliminated from both analyses. If an individual smoked at wave 1, did not smoke at wave 2, smoked at wave 3, but did not smoke at wave 4, he would have been included in the cessation analysis for waves 1–2 and for 3–4 and in the relapse analysis for waves 2–3. The samples used in the regression analysis were smaller than in Table 6.1 because observations were dropped in the case of missing values on explanatory variables.

Of the 2,961 observations in the cessation analysis, we recorded 461 instances of cessation, implying a 15.6 percent quit rate. In the relapsing analysis, there were 4,973 observations, but only 67 instances of relapsing, or a 1.3 percent relapse rate.

Although relapsing is common, the vast majority of relapsing occurs very soon after quitting. Thus, a current smoker at one wave could have quit and relapsed several times between adjacent HRS waves. The structure of the HRS interviews makes the study incapable of capturing this behavior; instead we focused on long-term changes in smoking behavior. The dependent variable was set to one if the person smoked at the end of the two-year interval and zero if the person did not smoke then. Thus cessation was represented by a dependent-variable value of zero and relapse by a value of one.

To develop our analysis of cessation and relapse behavior, we considered smokers' attitudes. Following past psychological research on smoker optimism (Chapters 2 and 5), we hypothesized that the most important attitude variable would be a measure of optimism or pessimism about longevity. Smokers who are optimistic about their health might believe that, because of their genes or other physical characteristics, continuing to smoke will not seriously harm them.

The first step in constructing our optimism measure was to predict the objective probability of living to age seventy-five for each respondent. Men and women were stratified into separate samples. We estimated logit models for the probability of surviving within a two-year time interval, combining data from waves 1–2, 2–3, and 3–4. The results were then converted to life tables.

Explanatory variables for the probability of surviving, in addition to smoking status at the beginning of the two-year interval, were self-reported health, high blood pressure, cancer, diabetes, lung problems, heart attack, angioplasty, stroke, arthritis, body mass index, history of problem drinking, alcohol consumption at the beginning of the two-year interval, risk tolerance, marital status, race, age, educational attainment, and binary variables for health insurance the person had at the beginning of the two-year time interval. Thus, our life tables were developed from a much more comprehensive model than the age-gender-race distinctions generally used to construct conventional life tables.

In our specification for the empirical analysis of cessation and relapse, for our explanatory variable optimism/pessimism we defined a continuous variable, the difference between the subjective and objective probabilities at the preceding wave. In an alternative specification, we defined two binary variables: "optimistic" for persons in the top fifth of the distribution and "pessimistic" for persons in the bottom fifth of the distribution (least optimistic). Frequency distributions were computed separately for current smokers (cessation) and former smokers (relapse).

Holding other factors constant, a rise in the price of cigarettes should increase the probability of quitting and reduce the probability of relapsing. We used the price measure based on Bureau of Labor Statistics data (described in detail in Chapter 8). We included two price variables: price in the year between the waves (for example, in 1993 if the observation measured a change in behavior from wave 1 to wave 2), and the change in price between the year between the wave and the year after the wave (the change in price between 1993 and 1995, for example, if the observation measured change in behavior from wave 1 to wave 2).

The remaining explanatory variables fell into the following categories: smoking history, personal health information between the waves, divorce between the waves, time-invariant personal characteristics, and binary variables identifying each of the waves. Smoking history was measured in different ways for the cessation and the relapse analysis. In the analysis of smoking cessation, we included variables for the amount smoked per day measured in packs at baseline. Smoking less than a pack per day was the omitted reference group. We anticipated that heavy smokers would be less likely to quit. For relapsing, we included binary variables for the length of time the person had quit smoking as of the baseline interview. The categories were: quit for three to five years, six to ten years, eleven to fifteen years, and sixteen or more years. The omitted reference category was quit for less than three years. We expected that more recent quitters would be more likely to relapse.

With follow-up data on the same persons who were interviewed at baseline (wave 1), the HRS allowed newly occurring serious health events experienced by respondents to be identified and collected via self-reporting. For the analysis of quitting, we defined three binary variables for health shocks that occurred between the waves: (1) smoking-related health shocks other than cancer (lung problems, heart attacks, congestive heart failure, angina pectoris), (2) cancer, and (3) other health problems leading to a hospital stay of at least three days between the waves ("hospitalization"). In each case, for the event to be coded as one, we required that the disease was not experienced in the past.

In addition, we defined variables for (1) onset of limitations in one or more activities of daily living, (2) onset of fair to poor health, (3) onset of difficulty in climbing several flights of stairs, and (4) onset of difficulty in walking several blocks. Limitations in ADLs are deficits in carrying out many personal activities, such as dressing, bathing, and eating. We accounted for a maximum of six such limitations.

For the smoking-related shocks other than cancer, we also imposed a three-day hospitalization screen. Thus, for example, if the person reported having angina but did not spend this much time in the hospital between the waves, we did not consider it a smoking-related health shock. For cancer, although the HRS asked for the body system involved with the cancer in wave 1, unfortunately this question was dropped in subsequent waves.

Given the relatively small number of relapsers, we could not include such a detailed measure of health shocks in the relapsing analysis. Thus, we collapsed the three health variables from the cessation analysis into a single binary variable, "major health problem," and again required that the condition included as a major health problem be newly occurring.

Death of a parent is also likely to convey vulnerability about one's future personal health (see Hamermesh 1985; Chapter 5). In the age group under study, death of parent is a relatively frequent event. Learning about one's own parent's life span provides information that is potentially important in helping individuals characterize their own health risks. In our focus groups, we found that persons in this age range gave considerable credence to the death of their same-gender parent, and that such a death often triggered smoking cessation attempts (see Chapter 7). We included two variables for death of a parent between the waves: (1) death of the same-sex parent and (2) death of the opposite-sex parent. This specification assumes that the death of the same-sex parent may have a greater impact on risk perceptions and other conditions leading to a change in smoking behavior than the death of the other parent.

Our focus groups suggested that divorce or separation was a major stressor that resulted in smoking relapses even after extended periods of cessation (see Chapter 7). To measure the contribution of divorce or separation in smoking decisions, we included a binary variable equal to one when a person was divorced or separated between adjacent waves. The other time-variant personal characteristic was age. Age was classified into three groups: fifty-one to fifty-five, fifty-six to sixty, and sixty-one or older (omitted).

We also controlled for education, race, marital status, gender, risk tolerance, and the time horizon a person used to make important financial decisions, as reported at the wave 1 interview. Education was indicated by two binary variables. The first identified individuals with less than a high school education, and the second identified respondents who had completed college or more, with intermediate educational status as the omitted reference group. We defined binary variables for black and white races, with other nonwhite races as the omitted reference group. Marital status was defined as a binary equal to one for those persons who were married in wave 1.

We controlled for the time horizon the respondent stated at the baseline interview that he or she used for making important family financial decisions. The HRS included the following question: "In deciding how much of their (family) income to spend or save, people are likely to think about different financial planning periods. In planning your (family's) saving and spending, which of the time periods listed in the booklet is most important to you [and your husband/wife/partner]?" Separate binary variables were defined, the first equal to one a time horizon of less than one year and the second equal to one for a time horizon of ten years or more, with time horizons between these two as the omitted reference category.

We included a set of binary variables to describe the person's risk tolerance. The HRS included a set of general questions to measure risk tolerance. These questions were based on a question related to an employment risk and did not directly relate to smoking (Barsky et al. 1997). The mutually exclusive risk-tolerance categories were: highly risk tolerant, somewhat risk tolerant, and somewhat risk averse, with very risk averse as the omitted reference group. Using this measure from the HRS, Barsky and coauthors found that persons who were risk tolerant were more likely to smoke. We limited our analysis of quitting and relapsing to persons who were current smokers or former smokers. The relationship between risk tolerance and smoking should still hold; however, given that we had the condition of some history of smoking, the relationship is not likely to be as strong as in Barsky and colleagues' research. We anticipated that more present-oriented and more risk-tolerant people should be less likely to quit and more likely to relapse.

We used logistic regression to model cessation and relapsing between the waves. We obtained robust standard errors that accounted for clustering of persons in the same household using the Huber/White estimator of variance in Stata (Stata Corp. 2001). T-tests of difference in means were used to test bivariate relationships.

Descriptive Results: Characteristics of Current, Former, and Never Smokers at Baseline

As a first step, we examine the sample frame from which potential quitters and relapsers were drawn. We distinguish between current smokers, former smokers, and never smokers at wave 1 (Table 6.2).

Among former smokers at wave 1, 12 percent had quit less than three years earlier. The majority (57 percent) had quit eleven or more years earlier. Among current smokers, 27 percent smoked m two or more packs a day, 36 percent smoked one to two packs a day, with a minority, the remaining 27 percent, smoking less than a pack a day (the omitted reference group).

There were many statistically significant differences in characteristics of smokers, former smokers, and never smokers at wave 1 (Table 6.2). Current and former smokers were more likely than never smokers to have experienced a smoking-related health shock other than cancer. Current smokers were more likely to be divorced than either former or never smokers. Current smokers tended to be less educated. Overall, current smokers tended to be more present-oriented than those in either of the other two

Table 6.2 Sample characteristics by smoking status at wave 1

	Smoking status at wave 1				
Characteristic at wave 1	Current	Former	*p*-value[1]	Never	*p*-value
Quit 3–5 years		0.12			
Quit 6–10 years		0.19			
Quit 11–15 years		0.14			
Quit 15+ years		0.43			
Smoke 1–2 packs	0.36				
Smoke 2+ packs	0.27				
Live to 75 difference	0.04	−0.02	0.000	−0.10	0.000
Cancer	0.05	0.05	0.366	0.05	0.323
Smoking health shock other than cancer	0.03	0.04	0.041	0.02	0.002
Hospitalization at least 3 days	0.03	0.04	0.131	0.04	0.242
Major health problem	0.11	0.13	0.181	0.10	0.159
Same-sex parent dead	0.70	0.73	0.055	0.66	0.001
Opposite-sex parent dead	0.71	0.66	0.001	0.73	0.116
Divorced	0.18	0.11	0.000	0.11	0.000
Male	0.49	0.60	0.000	0.34	0.000
Less than high school education	0.35	0.25	0.000	0.24	0.000
College education or more	0.11	0.21	0.000	0.21	0.000
Black	0.18	0.13	0.000	0.16	0.093
White	0.79	0.84	0.000	0.80	0.295
Age 51–55	0.50	0.41	0.000	0.45	0.001
Age 56–60	0.39	0.42	0.016	0.42	0.015
Married	0.71	0.82	0.000	0.79	0.000
Time horizon 10+ years	0.08	0.10	0.027	0.08	0.651
Time horizon < 1 year	0.23	0.16	0.000	0.17	0.000
Highly risk tolerant	0.40	0.35	0.037	0.33	0.004
Somewhat risk tolerant	0.28	0.30	0.335	0.32	0.137
Somewhat risk averse	0.32	0.34	0.228	0.35	0.131

Note: p-values test for differences in mean values between former and current smokers and between never and current smokers.

Table 6.3 Continuing smoking and relapsing sample characteristics: Comparison of means across subsamples

	Continue smoking			Relapse		
Variables	Yes	No	*p*-value	Yes	No	*p*-value
Variables changing between adjacent waves						
Cancer	0.02	0.04	0.001			
Smoking-related health shock other than cancer	0.03	0.10	0.000			
Nonsmoking health shock	0.08	0.14	0.000			
Same-sex parent died	0.04	0.05	0.393	0.05	0.04	0.173
Opposite-sex parent died	0.06	0.06	0.660	0.10	0.06	0.036
Divorce	0.03	0.02	0.083	0.04	0.02	0.032
Health shock				0.15	0.13	0.260
Variables defined for beginning of two-year time interval						
Married	0.65	0.69	0.033	0.68	0.78	0.000
Age 51–55	0.15	0.13	0.105	0.13	0.10	0.198
Age 56–60	0.46	0.40	0.001	0.43	0.39	0.077
Smoke 1–2 packs daily	0.36	0.27	0.000			
Smoke 2+ packs	0.22	0.14	0.000			
Quit 3–5 years ago				0.22	0.09	0.000
Quit 6–10 years ago				0.15	0.19	0.222
Quit 11–15 years ago				0.07	0.15	0.000
Quit 16+ years ago				0.13	0.52	0.000
Time-invariant variables						
Male	0.49	0.52	0.095	0.56	0.59	0.287
Less than high school education	0.36	0.31	0.003	0.26	0.26	0.906
College education or more	0.10	0.14	0.004	0.17	0.21	0.046
Black	0.17	0.20	0.028	0.18	0.14	0.037
White	0.80	0.76	0.018	0.79	0.84	0.026
Time horizon 10+ years	0.08	0.07	0.612	0.06	0.09	0.031
Time horizon < 1 year	0.24	0.21	0.083	0.19	0.17	0.194
Highly risk tolerant	0.14	0.16	0.197	0.17	0.13	0.051

groups. Judging from the results for the variable live-to-seventy-five difference, relative to the other two groups, current smokers were more optimistic about their chances of living to age seventy-five (the subjective probability minus the objective probability equals 0.04) than either former or never smokers. The never smokers tended to be the most pessimistic (with a live-to-seventy-five difference of -0.10). We found no statistically significant differences in the proportions for the risk tolerance categories.

The strongest predictor of someone's not continuing to smoke was health shocks, smoking-related as well as others (Table 6.3). Divorce and the death of the opposite-sex parent were the strongest unadjusted predictors of relapsing among former smokers.

Results of Multivariate Analysis

Cessation

New adverse health conditions led persons to stop smoking (Table 6.4). A new smoking-related shock, such as a heart attack or stroke, had a dramatic impact on smoking cessation. As we noted earlier (Chapter 4), an odds ratio is the probability of an outcome for the group in question relative to the corresponding probability for the omitted reference group. This type of ratio allows one to gauge the effects of health shocks on decisions to stop smoking. For example, current smokers who experienced a smoking-related health shock other than cancer were less likely to continue smoking. The estimate of probability that people would continue to smoke was only 14 percent of that for those who currently smoked and did *not* experience a comparable shock. Nonsmoking-related health shocks also reduced the probability of choosing to continue to smoke, but not as much as the smoking-related shocks did. The relative odds of continuing in this case were 43 percent. Functional limitations, measured by reported ADL limitations and subjective assessments of health status, were also associated with a reduced chance of continuing to smoke.

Persons who were more optimistic about their chances of living to age seventy-five relative to the objective probability were less likely to continue to smoke, but this relationship was not statistically significant at conventional levels. The adjusted odds ratio, 0.81, implies that raising the difference between subjective probabilities by one reduces the probability that the person will continue to smoke by about one-fifth. This result is not consistent with the view that optimism is a deterrent to quitting. Higher tobacco prices led persons to quit; this result was almost statistically significant at conventional levels ($p = 0.11$).

Smoking intensity at the beginning of the two-year time interval had important effects on the probability of continuing to smoke. For persons

Table 6.4 Predictors of continuing to smoke and relapsing

	Continue to Smoke 95%				Relapse 95%			
		Confidence interval				Confidence interval		
	Odds ratio	Lower bound	Upper bound	*p*-value	Odds ratio	Lower bound	Upper bound	*p*-value
Variables changing between adjacent waves								
Onset of cancer	0.64	0.32	1.31	0.224				
Smoking-related health shock other than cancer	0.14	0.09	0.21	0.000				
Nonsmoking health shock	0.43	0.31	0.59	0.000				
Onset of ADLs	0.63	0.42	0.95	0.028				
Onset of work disability	0.70	0.38	1.29	0.252				
Onset of fair/poor health	0.67	0.45	1.00	0.047				
Onset of climbing stairs difficulty	0.89	0.64	1.23	0.463				
Onset of walking several blocks difficulty	1.02	0.67	1.54	0.945				
Same-sex parent died	0.76	0.49	1.20	0.243	0.61	0.14	2.66	0.513
Opposite-sex parent died	0.77	0.51	1.17	0.221	2.26	1.07	4.76	0.032
Divorce	1.44	0.69	3.02	0.336	2.75	0.76	10.02	0.124
Health shock					0.58	0.25	1.39	0.222
Variables defined for beginning of two-year time interval and price								
Live to 75 difference	0.81	0.59	1.11	0.190	1.39	0.65	2.96	0.395
Tobacco price	0.87	0.74	1.03	0.105	0.84	0.61	1.15	0.273
Married	0.80	0.60	1.06	0.123	1.11	0.48	2.59	0.810
Age 51–55	1.20	0.87	1.65	0.274	1.38	0.67	2.85	0.387
Age 56–60	1.48	1.18	1.86	0.001	1.08	0.61	1.89	0.798
Smoke 1–2 packs daily	1.90	1.48	2.43	0.000				

Table 6.4 (continued)

	Continue to Smoke 95%				Relapse 95%			
		Confidence interval				Confidence interval		
	Odds ratio	Lower bound	Upper bound	*p*-value	Odds ratio	Lower bound	Upper bound	*p*-value
Smoke 2+ packs daily	2.15	1.57	2.93	0.000				
Quit 3–5 years					0.49	0.22	1.08	0.076
Quit 6–10 years					0.20	0.09	0.46	0.000
Quit 11–15 years					0.09	0.03	0.24	0.000
Quit 16+ years					0.05	0.02	0.13	0.000
Time-invariant variables								
Male	0.89	0.71	1.11	0.298	1.62	0.92	2.85	0.093
Less than high school education	1.23	0.97	1.56	0.093	0.65	0.33	1.27	0.209
College education or more	0.70	0.50	0.97	0.031	1.04	0.55	1.97	0.897
Black	0.90	0.47	1.73	0.755	0.99	0.21	4.72	0.989
White	1.05	0.57	1.94	0.881	0.62	0.14	2.72	0.523
Time horizon 10+ years	1.29	0.87	1.94	0.210	0.81	0.31	2.07	0.653
Time horizon < 1 year	1.14	0.87	1.50	0.348	1.68	0.89	3.17	0.109
Highly risk tolerant	1.11	0.82	1.52	0.496	1.78	0.90	3.52	0.096
Somewhat risk tolerant	1.36	0.94	1.96	0.106	1.66	0.81	3.44	0.169
Some risk averse	0.98	0.71	1.33	0.875	1.34	0.62	2.86	0.457

Note: p-values are for tests of the null hypothesis of no effect on cessation relapsing. ADLs-activities of daily living.

who smoked one to two packs daily at the beginning of the time interval, the odds ratio was 1.90, suggesting that such persons were almost twice as likely to continue to smoke than were persons who smoked less than a pack per day. The odds ratio for persons who smoked more than two packs a day was even higher, 2.15.

Only one of the time-invariant variables had a statistically significant effect on the probability of continuing to smoke. The odds ratio corresponding to persons who had a college degree or more education was 0.70 ($p =$ 0.031), suggesting that persons with more education were more likely to quit. Since time and risk tolerance were also included in the analysis, interpreting education's role is not easy. Perhaps college-educated smokers are better at assimilating newly acquired health information.

Relapse

Although persons who experienced a new health shock were less likely to restart smoking, with an associated odds ratio far less than one (0.58), the estimated effect was not statistically significant. Persons who experienced the loss of a parent of the opposite gender were much more likely to relapse. This was also true of persons who divorced, although the effect did not attain statistical significance at conventional levels ($p = 0.12$).

Other factors contributed to relapse as well. More optimistic persons were more likely to relapse, but this effect was not significant ($p = 0.40$). As in the cessation analysis, where higher cigarette prices encouraged cessation, higher prices seem to discourage relapsing, but the estimated effect was not significant ($p = 0.27$). Persons who quit many years before the beginning of the two-year time interval were much less likely to relapse. For persons who had quit eleven to fifteen years previously, the odds ratio was 0.09. For those who had quit sixteen or more years earlier, the odds ratio was even lower, 0.05.

Smoking Intensity and Cessation

We found a significant relationship between smoking intensity at the beginning of the two-year interval and the propensity to quit. To examine this relationship further, we stratified the sample according to amounts smoked by current smokers at baseline. Then we examined the frequency distributions by smoking intensity category in each of the subsequent waves, noting in particular the percentage of persons in each baseline smoking category who quit by the end of the wave. Based on data on the number of cigarettes smoked per day, we also computed the mean number of cigarettes smoked in each of the waves subsequent to wave 1.

For each of the baseline smoking intensity categories, the percentage of persons who quit smoking rose monotonically with each subsequent wave (Table 6.5). For example, of persons who smoked more than two packs daily at baseline, 8.1 percent had quit by wave 2, 13.0 percent had quit by wave 3, and 22.8 had quit percent by wave 4. However, for persons who smoked less than a pack a day at baseline, the percent quitting was two to three times greater. By the fourth wave, 40.9 percent of those smokers had quit. The mean values display a similar pattern.

While the reasonably high percentage of quitters seems to be good news,

Table 6.5 Relationship between baseline smoking intensity and subsequent smoking intensity

		Wave 2		Wave 3		Wave 4	
Wave 1 packs per day	Subsequent packs per day	*N*	%	*N*	%	*N*	%
2+	2+	168	58.95	125	43.86	106	37.19
	1–2	82	28.77	87	30.53	89	31.23
	<1	10	3.51	20	7.02	22	7.72
	0	23	8.07	37	12.98	65	22.81
Mean no. cigs. per day			37.14		34.23		32.75
1–2	2+	90	9.14	52	5.28	53	5.38
	1–2	577	58.58	502	50.96	456	46.29
	<1	176	17.87	204	20.71	230	23.35
	0	134	13.60	172	17.46	243	24.67
Mean no. cigs. per day			21.33		19.64		19.21
<1	2+	13	1.72	9	1.19	6	0.80
	1–2	105	13.93	93	12.33	86	11.41
	<1	447	59.28	389	51.59	346	45.89
	0	183	24.27	231	30.64	308	40.85
Mean no. cigs. per day			11.62		11.10		10.78

Note: Using the wave 1 <1 category as the reference group, all mean numbers of cigarettes smoked are significantly different at the .001 level. In addition, persons in the omitted reference group were more likely to have quit than persons in the other groups, at the .001 level.

almost two-fifths of persons who smoked more than two packs a day continued to smoke as much through wave 4. About 5 to 10 percent of persons who smoked one to two packs daily actually increased their smoking intensity. An even higher percentage of smokers who consumed less than a pack a day at wave 1 increased their smoking intensity.

Discussion

The most important determinants of smoking cessation and relapse are a person's smoking history and, for cessation, major health shocks. Tobacco prices and optimism about longevity, at least in the age group studied, are not among the major determinants of continuing to smoke or relapse.

Our findings on how smoking history influences cessation choices have important implications for public health policy. Over the six-year period in which we observed the near-elderly persons in the HRS subsample, current smokers who started the six-year period smoking less than a pack a day had more than a 0.4 probability of quitting.

That health shocks lead to quitting is both good and bad news. The good news is that those individuals do quit. The bad news is that it seems to take a major health shock to get them to quit. General information about the adverse health effects of smoking does not seem to motivate older smokers. In Chapter 5 we reported that longevity expectations changed in the interview immediately following a serious health shock. Introducing an expectation change variable in our analysis of cessation and relapse would have introduced considerable multicollinearity without additional insights. We did perform a sensitivity analysis to determine whether our results on optimism depend on how we specified the variable. Replacing the optimism variable with the subjective longevity perception without accounting for the corresponding objective probabilities had no appreciable effect on the results.

Previous psychological research indicates that persons who are more optimistic about their longevity are be less likely to continue smoking or to relapse (see Chapters 2 and 5). We did find that smokers tend to be relatively optimistic. This result is consistent with previous psychological research. However, in multivariate analysis of the probability of cessation and relapse, we could not isolate statistically significant relationships. Thus, based on this chapter's analysis, we cannot say conclusively that messages designed to encourage a more realistic assessment of the adverse effects of smoking would encourage people to stop smoking and not restart. We consider this issue more deeply in the next two chapters, using a controlled situation in which we evaluate how older smokers react to different types of information.

The HRS is rich in descriptors of individuals' preferences, including measures of personal time horizons and risk preferences. In descriptive analysis, we found some plausible differences in such preferences according to smoking status and changes in smoking status. Yet these effects largely disappeared in the multivariate analysis. Of course, these variables were time-invariant, and we explored the reasons for a change in smoking status. Thus, it is not surprising that time-varying variables had more explanatory power. An exception to this generalization about time-invariant variables is that more highly educated persons were more likely to quit. They were also less likely to smoke in the first place.

On average, current smokers were more likely to be highly tolerant of risk. This attitude contrasts with both former and never smokers. However, there were no differences in terms of the percentages of persons who were risk averse. Current smokers also tended to have a shorter time horizon, as measured by the percentage of persons who had a time horizon of less than one year. While we found statistically significant differences, the magnitudes of these differences in risk preferences and time horizons were not that large. Judging from these indicators, measured on mature individuals, not much mileage can be gotten from examining risk tolerance and myopia as determinants of smoking, particularly because many of these effects disappear in multivariate analysis.

Conclusions

We have described the dynamic nature of smoking decisions found in a nationally representative population, using a model that is consistent with the concept that new information as key to smoking decisions. Millions of persons in the United States smoke past the age of fifty. For these individuals, one of the most important health-enhancing public policies that could be undertaken would be to promote smoking cessation and deter relapsing.

Our results indicate that an informational message that mimics the message individuals receive from the onset of a serious health event might encourage smokers to quit. The current broad-based messages (such as the surgeon general's warnings on cigarette packs) are unlikely to be important or personal enough to alter individuals' smoking behavior.

One limitation of our analysis is that serious health events were collected via self-reports, although we took steps to define the serious nature of these events; it seems unlikely that persons would forget to report serious conditions. Our study cannot conclusively prove that the onset of a serious health event was the catalyst for smoking cessation without retrospective interview data that are not available. However, the longitudinal nature of our design reduces the likelihood that an omitted variable explains our findings.

In our own research for this chapter, we were unable to demonstrate with an appropriate level of statistical confidence that higher cigarette prices lead smokers to quit. We will assess further the impact of prices in Chapter 8. In Chapter 3 we argued that past informational campaigns and bans have been of limited effectiveness; we do not imply they are not worth implementing, only that they are not panaceas. Another approach to promoting to community-based smoking cessation would be to target health professionals, encouraging them to counsel individual patients who smoke. While such efforts may be useful, the devil lies in the details of implementation. It is one thing to write and promulgate guidelines. It is another to get them to work in practice.

Finally, the fact that serious health events are major catalysts for cessation indicates that the message that it is never too late to quit is in one sense false. While it is clear that benefits from cessation can accrue to virtually any smoker who stops (see U.S. Department of Health and Human Services 1990), and that life extension can accrue even to elderly quitters who are not already ill (Taylor et al. 2002), it is also clear that for many it will take a serious health event to convince them of the risks of smoking and thus to initiate cessation attempts.

CHAPTER

7

Personalized Health Messages and the Perceived Risks of Smoking

Serious health shocks change people's beliefs about how long they will live. These shocks should be recognized as a source of information that can lead people to change their behavior. In Chapter 5, we described how shocks change the longevity expectations of different groups, and in Chapter 6 we presented evidence that these health shocks contribute to cessation decisions. In some respects, these changes may come too late in the life cycle. An important reason for warning people about the hazards of smoking is to avoid or forestall these serious new health conditions that we described as shocks.

Long-term smokers seem immune to the persistent risk-based messages that today are so present in the public media. Perhaps survival is the wrong emphasis. After all, smokers may well reason that everyone has to die some time and in some way.

In this chapter we consider whether it is possible to design information messages that mimic the information conveyed to middle-aged smokers by such health shocks. We investigate the factors that may make a personal health shock an especially salient message for smokers. To be sure, when it happens to *you,* the events are no longer abstract but are quite tangible. Moreover, the experience seems to highlight an issue of special concern to older adults—reductions in their functional independence. Increased dependency can follow the onset of smoking-related diseases, such as dependence on oxygen in the case of emphysema or on help from relatives following a stroke. The clear association between these losses and the onset of diseases associated with long-term smoking got the attention of the older smokers we surveyed. An implication of our findings is that risk messages for smokers might need to be reoriented from a focus on the ultimate outcome, death, to one on the quality of one's life at the end of life. Smoking is associated with the onset or increased frequency of physical limitations and disabilities. Messages conveying this type of information might be more salient than those emphasizing life extension alone. Although messages to this effect have been printed on cigarette packages for years, they are general, not personalized.

Three sets of results support this conclusion. First, smokers and former smokers in the focus groups we organized were quite concerned about the quality of life at the end of life. Second, results from a survey of smokers that we conducted in Raleigh, North Carolina, in the summer of 1999 were consistent with this view. Finally, we also found that the short-term revisions in longevity expectations of the type elicited by the Health and Retirement Study were sustained in a six-month follow-up to our summer 1999 survey. This is important because these changes in risk perceptions may be permanent and may be associated with reduced smoking.

Focus Groups

A focus group provides an opportunity for researchers to learn how people describe their beliefs and explain their behavior. Generally, such groups are small (eight to twelve individuals) and are organized to discuss a predesigned menu of topics over a short period (for example, ninety minutes). The group is guided by a moderator who encourages an open discussion. Questions are specific, but the responses are much more open-ended than is typical in a structured interview, the approach usually used in surveys conducted by social scientists. While focus groups do not substitute for survey research, they nonetheless can provide valuable insights into how people make decisions and interpret information. These insights can be of direct use and provide guidance for survey design.

We organized three focus groups in Raleigh in late 1998, two with current smokers and one with former smokers. The sessions had four objectives: (1) to learn about smokers' knowledge of the risks of smoking; (2) to elicit smokers' reasons for continuing to smoke and, in the case of former smokers, for quitting; (3) to learn how current and former smokers interpret the longevity-expectation questions used in the HRS; and (4) to gauge smokers' reactions to different types of information about the health risks of smoking.

Participants were recruited from a marketing research firm's database. To be included in a focus groups, a person had to be age fifty to sixty-four and a high school graduate, and to have not participated in a market research project in the previous two years. Former smokers had to have stopped smoking within the past six years to be eligible.

Two types of insights emerged from these sessions. The first were based on anecdotes about smoking, examples of which are in Box 7.1. These statements were volunteered in slightly different forms by both groups of smokers, as well as by some former smokers. We also presented participants with a set of statements culled from the literature that might characterize a smoker's experience and asked them how the specific statements described their own feelings about smoking (Table 7.1). Responses were elicited in three categories: whether each statement "often," "sometimes," or "never" captured their feelings.

After each respondent provided a personal longevity expectation in the format used in the HRS, we probed the reasons for their responses, using a written exercise followed by a discussion of the role of factors such as lifestyle, parents' genetic endowment, relatives' experience with smoking, and health. Consistent with earlier findings (Chapter 5), smokers in particular tended to place considerable emphasis on their parents' longevity in assessing their own future longevity. Indeed, it appeared that smokers searched their family experiences for relatives who had a long life despite a history of smoking. For example, one participant replied, "Good genes. Both my grandmothers were in their nineties. My grandfather was in his seventies and my mom is eighty-one. I think I'll go on for a while yet." Another responded, "I chose 8 [out of 10, where 10 is certain to live to seventy-five]. I

Box 7.1 Statements about Smoking

Addictive feature:
"I'm addicted. I would dearly love to quit and I can't."
"'Daily rituals' describes my smoking. I smoke first thing in the morning and after every meal."
"My wind is shot; my lungs are bad. I'm an idiot, but I can't quit."

Smoking's comforting aspect:
"The thought of not having the friend of the cigarette overwhelms."
"When I am in a stressful situation I want to smoke because I can get comfortable and [take time to] calm down. But it [the addictive craving] doesn't happen all the time, just some of the time."

Table 7.1 Attributes associated with smoking

Attributes[a]	Group	Often	Sometimes	Never	*p*-value[b]
I reached for a cigarette when I need a lift.	F[c]	7	3	0	
	C[c]	2	7	1	0.068
I felt more comfortable with a cigarette in my hand.	F	5	5	0	
	C	2	6	2	0.185
Smoking cigarettes was pleasant and enjoyable.	F	6	4	0	
	C	4	6	0	0.371
I wanted a cigarette most when I was comfortable and relaxed.	F	3	5	1	
	C	6	2	2	0.276
Smoking relaxed me in a stressful situation.	F	5	4	1	
	C	7	3	0	0.478
When I was depressed I reached for a cigarette to feel better.	F	6	4	0	
	C	4	5	1	0.47
I was very aware of not smoking when I didn't have a cigarette in my hand.	F	2	8	0	
	C	0	7	3	0.079
When I hadn't smoked for a while, I got a craving for a cigarette.	F	7	2	1	
	C	7	3	0	0.549

[a] Condition is described here in past tense for former smokers. For current, it was described in present tense.

[b] p-value for chi-square test of equivalent distribution.

[c] F refers to count of responses from former smokers; C is count of responses from current smokers.

thought if I would stop smoking and exercise, then I can do it. There is longevity in my family."

The second quotation illustrates a second feature of current smokers' responses. They tended to ignore their current smoking habit and focused on their *intended* behavior when assessing their longevity expectations. They cited good health histories for relatives and argued that "everything in moderation" was more important than their one "vice." By contrast, former smokers seemed to identify pessimistic family histories and the related smoking patterns. One noted, "I lost four first cousins from heart attacks or strokes in the last ten years."

Some responses related to their current quality of life and how it could be maintained as they aged. This concern was also expressed in terms of avoiding dependency on others. One smoker noted, "Quality of life is most important. I have an aversion to being a burden to anyone. I don't want to be a burden . . . My quality of life will deteriorate . . . I'll take the shorter [route]." Former smokers expressed the same concern—in one person's words, "a deadly fear of dependence." Given the importance of these consequences to participants in the first two focus groups, we expanded this dimension of our questions in the third focus group, which consisted entirely of current smokers. We found that the ability to leave the house, participate independently in activities, and care for oneself were aspects of quality of life that were important to the participants.

The second general insight to emerge was that smokers seemed to assume that their own experience would be different—that is, better than average. Thus, risk information presented in the third person was interpreted as being relevant to the experience that *other* smokers might have (see Chapter 5). Smokers in the focus groups usually combined their family experience with other aspects of their own health to explain their responses to the messages. For example, one respondent, reacting to the risk information, explained that longevity depends on "lifestyle and genetics . . . My dad's family lived to their mid-eighties and -nineties. Dad died at eighty-five . . . I don't think smoking will kill me . . . Dad smoked and it didn't kill him. If it was going to kill anyone, he was a good candidate."

The focus groups also confirmed an insight from our analysis of the HRS smokers. Heavy smokers did not adequately evaluate their behavior's likely consequences on survival. They were more optimistic than the actual experience of heavy smokers warrants. Smokers try to find a source for optimism in their family history and use then that personal context to explain and adjust the messages they hear. Thus, while they appear keenly aware of the health warnings, they seem to find a way to discount the relevance of the messages to their own personal situation.

New Information Messages

Based on the insights from the focus groups and our own research findings (see especially Chapter 5), we formulated two distinct types of information messages to be administered in the survey of smokers we conducted in the summer of 1999. The first message concerned personalization of the adverse health effects of smoking. The experience of a health shock reminds smokers it is not only "the other guy" who can experience these consequences. Equally important, the shocks often demonstrate that such health events do not provide an "easy passage" to death—a normal life one day, with the full independence and discretion one is accustomed to having, and then gone the next. Rather, the transition may be very different. Conveying each of these ideas in a succinct form to smokers who had not personally experienced a smoking-related health shock was a major challenge.

To describe the loss in quality of life following such a health shock, we listed the symptoms and limitations in daily activities that are commonly associated with such a health event. For simplicity, we limited the message to one smoking-related disease, chronic obstructive pulmonary disease, a general category of serious lung diseases including chronic bronchitis and emphysema. By including material on loss of quality of life, we did not intend to avoid consideration of the increased risk of death but instead to highlight that the road to death may be a difficult and unpleasant one. The information as presented to respondents is shown in Box 7.2. This was our first information treatment.

Box 7.2 First information treatment: symptoms and activity restrictions

Please consider the following points in the next series of questions: The use of cigarettes often results in chronic lung diseases. While not all smokers get such diseases, virtually no nonsmokers get them. These specific lung diseases are called chronic obstructive pulmonary disease (COPD) and include chronic and acute bronchitis and emphysema. Following is a description of what your life would be with a chronic lung disease.

Common symptoms and activity limitations:

- Mucus-producing cough, lasting indefinitely without underlying disease
- Cough so severe it wakes you from sleep several times each night
- Gasping for air when speaking
- Wheezing and difficulty breathing during ordinary activities, such as walking up one flight of stairs
- Repeated respiratory infections
- Unable to push a baby stroller for several blocks or walk 9 holes of golf
- Weakness and weight loss
- Pain in upper chest which worsens during a coughing spell
- Fever
- Increasing severity, eventually resulting in the need for supplemental oxygen and being wheelchair bound
- Decreased ability to engage in sexual activity for men

Our second information treatment focused on the probabilities of death from specific smoking-related diseases. The computer screen respondents saw is reproduced as Box 7.3. Early in the survey, respondents were asked various questions about their background. Based on their responses, a simple algorithm incorporated in the survey program filled in the appropriate changes in the underlined portions of column one. Examples of the inserts are "substantially higher," "somewhat higher," and so on. Thus, assessments of personal risk were cast in qualitative terms relative to the general population, and the underlined phrases were particularized for the individual respondent. The woman who saw the screen in Box 7.3, for example, had a substantially higher risk of stroke, but this was not true of other respondents. Separate versions of the question were developed for men and women. Data on mortality rates by gender, race, and levels of cigarette consumption came from the 1990 surgeon general's report (U.S. Department of Health and Human Services 1990).

One measure of the impact of each of our information treatments was its effect on an individual's assessment of his or her probability of living to age seventy-five or older. An effective message should have the effect of reducing this probability. On average, smokers are too optimistic about living to age seventy-five. So a reduction in longevity expectations not only is more realistic but also, one hopes, would lead to some smokers to quit. We initially asked the longevity expectation question during the screening interview that preceded the 1999 survey. We also asked the same question after participants received the information treatment, as part of the interview, and finally, we asked it in the six-month follow-up interview. Asking about longevity expectations in the 1999 survey, immediately after the information treatment was administered, allowed us to measure the change in longevity expectations immediately following the message.

Design and Implementation of Our Survey of Current Smokers

Our experiment presented these two information treatments to older smokers and evaluated their responses. We recruited a sample of smokers and interviewed them three times, in the screener interview, in the main survey, and in a follow-up interview conducted six months later. Early in the summer of 1999, participants completed an interview as part of the recruiting process. The purposes of this screening interview were to identify persons eligible for the main survey, to be conducted later that summer; to

Box 7.3 Second information treatment: personalized relative risk

You said that you were most likely to die from ______________________________ [insert choice from previous question]. Below is a table that describes the average death rates in your sex and age range and, given your race, gender, and smoking habits, your relative chances of dying from stroke, lung cancer, heart disease, and chronic obstructive pulmonary disease (COPD) compared to these averages. The average death rate in your age range is given in the third column. Please take a few minutes to read through this table, then click "Next Screen" to continue with the survey.*

Your chances relative to the average	*Disease*	*Deaths per 100,000*
Your chances are substantially higher than *26* out of *100,000*	Stroke	26 out of 100,000 women will die of stroke
Your chances are somewhat higher than *55* out of *100,000*	Lung cancer	55 out of 100,000 women will die of lung cancer
Your chances are substantially higher than *120* out of *100,000*	Heart disease	120 out of 100,000 women will die of heart disease
Your chances are approximately *average*	Chronic obstructive pulmonary disease	24 out of 100,000 women will die of COPD

* The probabilities were personalized based on the respondent's gender, age, race, and smoking habits. Using aggregate data, we constructed a simple regression model for each cause of death and computed lower bounds for the effects of cigarette consumption. If the predictions for each respondent's mortality rate were higher than the average, we adjusted the words describing the risk as higher than average ("somewhat" or "substantially," and so on), depending on the extent to which the risk exceeded the average. Confidence intervals of 68 percent and 95 percent were used to modify the descriptor used to characterize each person's risk of contracting each disease in relation to the overall average. This process was repeated for each cause of death and tailored to each respondent's individual actions, race, and gender. As in the case of the activity limitation treatment, the information treatment associated with personalized risk was followed by the HRS longevity expectations questions.

collect demographic information; to ask about the person's longevity expectations for the first time; and, for those who were judged to be eligible, to request their participation in the main survey.

The experimental information messages were administered during the main survey. One half of the participants were randomly assigned receive to the first information treatment. The other half received the second. The interviews were computer assisted and were conducted at a central location in Raleigh.

Sample

We surveyed current smokers age fifty to sixty-four. We used several strategies for recruiting the sample: (1) placing recruiting flyers on automobiles in parking lots, (2) running newspaper ads, (3) direct telephoning of numbers listed in the Raleigh telephone directory, and (4) drawing names from a marketing firm's database. Of the 2,128 contacts we made in the screening process, 287 individuals met eligibility criteria and agreed to participate, and 244 individuals actually completed the main survey.

Comparing the HRS sample of smokers to our sample of 244 smokers, we found three differences pertinent to our analysis of the effects of information treatments: (1) the amount smoked was higher for our sample; (2) respondents to our survey were more optimistic about the probability of living to age seventy-five; and (3) our sample of smokers, on average, was more educated than were HRS smokers. We adjusted for the HRS sample to develop control groups for our analysis of the effects of the two information treatments.

Survey Design

The computer-assisted survey had five sections: (1) smoking patterns, including amount smoked, the year the respondent started smoking, and two attitude questions about smoking; (2) a stated-preference or conjoint survey to evaluate each respondent's trade-off between life extension and quality of life;[1] (3) the information treatments; (4) the respondent's health history; and (5) characteristics of the respondent's family, including parents' current health status (and cause of death if appropriate) and age (or age at death).

The section presenting each of the information treatments had several components. We began by asking about common causes of death. Respondents were asked to pick one cause as the most likely source of their own death. Following this question, one of the two information treatments was randomly assigned to each respondent and, after reading the screens presenting the assigned information treatment, each respondent was asked questions about his or her own expectations of living to age seventy-five and to age eighty-five.

Control Group

Assessing the effects of the information treatments requires evaluating how people receiving them changed their beliefs and behavior in comparison with those who did not receive them.[2] We did not reserve some participants for a control group—smokers who did not receive a message. In accordance with guidelines for the protection of human subjects, we had to explain to potential participants that the purpose of our survey was to gauge the impact of information about the effects of smoking. Also, the very process of involving participants in a survey specifically about smoking would have reinforced the discussion of the study's purpose, and the responses to questions about longevity expectations likely would have been influenced by the other questions about the person's smoking.

Rather than use a subsample of respondents to our survey as controls, we used a matched sample of respondents to the HRS as controls. The HRS is a lengthy survey about many matters. Questions about smoking constitute much less than 1 percent of the HRS.[3]

Using responses from the HRS was feasible for three reasons. First, we used the exact format of the HRS longevity expectations questions (subjective probability of living to age seventy-five or more) and smoking questions. Second, HRS respondents were not administered the information treatments, although they admittedly could have heard antismoking messages from others, as could have respondents to our summer 1999 survey of smokers. Third, we matched the characteristics of the sample of HRS controls to our main survey samples. Changes in longevity expectations and amount of cigarettes consumed could be used to gauge the effect of each information treatment.

Observing such changes required that we establish a baseline for the participants as well as the control group. Our research design required that we have information about each respondent's longevity expectations before receiving the information as well as after each information treatment.

To meet this objective, as noted above, we conducted three separate interviews and we asked about longevity expectations three times: in the telephone interview used to recruit individuals for the sample, as a part of the body of the main computer-assisted survey, and six months after the main survey, in a telephone follow-up survey. We included in this telephone follow-up a small group of individuals who had been recruited for the computer-assisted survey but did not actually come to the interview. In fact, this small group was contacted twice (in addition to the recruiting interview), shortly after the computer-assisted interviews, and then as part of the six-month follow-up. While this group was too small to provide a basis for gauging the effectiveness of the information treatments, we did use it for one of the control groups.

As already noted, we concluded it would not be possible to recruit a completely neutral control group. Instead, we randomly sampled respondents from the HRS to match our sample. This strategy also allowed all respondents to our survey to be assigned to one of the two information treatments.[4] Compared with HRS smokers, the smoker respondents to our main survey were more educated, believed their prospects for living to seventy-five or older were better, and smoked more. Each of these attributes could influence our evaluation of the effects of the information treatments. For example, as reported earlier (Chapter 5), we found that a simple Bayesian updating model offered an effective basis for describing how longevity expectations were revised with new information. Thus, the baseline or initial beliefs about longevity have been shown to have an effect on revised longevity expectation. The same observation could be made about the influence of an individual's cognitive ability on how these types of questions were answered.

Fortunately, these distinctions could be taken into account with the sampling process used to compose the control sample from the HRS sample of smokers. We imposed several eligibility restrictions and evaluated three different sampling criteria to compose our controls. Participants' ages and health events were selected so that the control individuals from the HRS sample on average looked like our experimental group. The first of the conditions, age, was controlled by requiring the same age interval as in our experimental sample. The second, past health, was handled similarly. Over the period we selected to observe the HRS participants' behavior (from wave one to wave two), HRS control individuals could not have experienced serious health shocks.

Even with these two criteria imposed, we still faced the possibility that, at baseline, the treatment and control groups differed on the basis of optimism about longevity, educational attainment, or smoking intensity. To address these concerns, we selected smoker controls from the HRS in the different ways. One approach was to match the distribution of their longevity expectations in HRS wave one to the distribution reported in our experimental group in their initial interview. On average, then, each group displayed the same level of optimism. A second control sample matched the joint distribution of education levels and the typical amount smoked between the control and the experimental samples. A third control sample was simply a random sample of HRS smokers satisfying the eligibility criteria. We included this group to determine whether there was merit to our concerns about baseline differences between treatment and control groups. Further detail on selection of control groups is reported in Smith et al. (2002). Because our findings were not affected by the control used, we limit our discussion here to one case—controls matched on the basis of longevity expectations of the experimental sample.

As a further gauge of the effectiveness of our control strategy, we included the updating of longevity expectations from our sample of recruited participants who did not take the main survey ($N = 34$). These smokers were not administered either of the information treatments. While they might be considered a logical control group, the size of this group was too small. Moreover, one could not be sure that some factor preventing the person from coming to the interview, such as forgetfulness, would not be a source of bias in evaluating the effects of the information treatment. Comparison of the results for the information treatments with both types of control samples offers an important cross-check on findings.

Expected Effects of Information

Our two information treatments provided smoking-related health and risk information in different ways. We hypothesized that both types of messages would lower individuals' longevity expectations. The framing of the relative risk message (the second information treatment) provided the clearest link between the information and the revision in subjective probabilities. It explained how each individual's circumstances and behavior led to a personalized risk assessment relative to the average.

For the first information treatment, which described various dimensions of reduced quality of life following the onset of COPD, the connection was less clear-cut. We described the events that precede death under a specific condition. We provided a more complete description of the event at risk, not new information about its probability (the risk itself). The expected utility model distinguishes the probabilities of events at risk from the preference weighting of the events themselves. Thus, using this framework, we might not necessarily expect smokers to alter their longevity expectations. However, as we argued earlier, this inference seems too simplistic. People define events for themselves and may well interpret "longevity" as length of life with their *currently experienced* daily activities.

Under this view, the COPD information could lead individuals to reduce their longevity expectations. That is, we expect the quality of life information to induce respondents to report a diminished chance of experiencing life to seventy-five *under current living conditions.* We do not have specific documentation for this interpretation, but it is consistent with the focus group participants' explanations of their longevity expectations. Furthermore, at a general level it is consistent with a substantial literature in cognitive psychology suggesting that people reporting their subjective risk perceptions often combine a pure risk assessment with subjective weighting of the events of risk (see Slovic, Fischoff, and Lichtenstein 1977).

Results

First Information Treatment: COPD

The simplest test of the effects of an information treatment on longevity expectations is a chi-square test comparing the distribution of responses to the longevity expectation question for our experimental group in comparison with the HRS control group as of wave two.[5] For the first information treatment, the results are direct and highly significant differences ($\chi^2(18) = 36.2$, $p = 0.007$), implying that the information treatment did affect longevity expectations. These results are consistent across the two other HRS control samples. The results are direct and highly significant ($\chi^2(18) = 31.6$, $p = 0.000$) for the case where the control sample matches the baseline distribution of longevity expectations. The results are comparable using the two other criteria to develop the control sample. We also tested our results by recoding longevity expectations to a ten-point scale to take account of the difference between the zero-to-ten scale used in our survey (and in wave 1 of the HRS) and the scales used in other HRS waves. The results were maintained regardless of this recoding.

The findings are important because they do not require that we accept the updating model of the interaction between the information treatment and smoking. Of course, they do not allow us to unambiguously assign a direction to the adjustment in longevity expectations. Thus, it is important to consider parametric models as well.

We estimated two different models with the subjective probability of living to age seventy-five as the dependent variable (Table 7.2). For the first, we combined the respondents to our experimental sample for the first information treatment with a sample composed of two control groups—the no-shows to our main smoker survey and the matched statistical control from the HRS baseline distribution of longevity responses. The second model compares the experimental sample's longevity updates with those of the small group of no-shows. Results for the two models are shown in columns 1 and 2, respectively.[6]

The Bayesian updating model was used to explain how people revised their beliefs. Starting from their initial longevity expectations, expectations are updated on the basis of the information treatment, personal characteristics, and smoking behavior.

The effect of the information treatment was represented by three explanatory variables (rows 2–4 in Table 7.2). The first was a binary variable included to identify respondents who received the information treatment. For the control group, the sample of HRS participants and the no-shows, this variable took the value zero. The second and third explanatory variables were, respectively, the interaction between the binary variable for receipt of the information and the person's score on the cognitive test and the interaction between the binary variable for treatment and the number of packs smoked. Other explanatory variables were a binary variable distinguishing persons in excellent health from others, a binary variable identifying respondents with at least one living parent, and a binary variable identifying persons who did not show for the main survey.

The rationale for including the binary variable for the no-shows requires further discussion. If the experimental controls (taken from the HRS) are not a perfect match for the treatment group in ways we cannot measure with explanatory variables ("omitted heterogeneity"), the results on the effect of the information treatment may be biased. Our specification permitted us to check for this. We used the small sample of no-shows to our main survey to satisfy this objective. In contrast to the HRS, which is a national sample, the no-shows were all smokers who lived in the Raleigh area. Thus, it seemed likely that the no-shows would share some unmea-

Table 7.2 Longevity updating with HRS baseline matching: Evaluation of information treatment

	COPD		Relative risk	
	Model 1	Model 2	Model 3	Model 4
Dependent variables	Live to 75[t]	Live to 75[t]	Live to 75[t]	Live to 75[t]
Explanatory variables				
1. Longevity expectations at baseline	0.606 (11.62)	0.797 (12.45)	0.415 (7.19)	0.581 (8.98)
2. Information treatment (= 1)	0.173 (2.88)	0.211 (0.97)	0.051 (0.80)	0.096 (0.46)
3. Interaction of information treatment and cognitive score	−0.07 (−1.81)	−0.07 (−1.83)	0.077 (2.12)	0.061 (1.70)
4. Interaction of information treatment and number of packs smoked	−0.14 (−2.53)	−0.075 (−0.48)	0.016 (0.30)	0.045 (0.29)
5. Number of packs smoked	0.035 (1.02)	−0.013 (−0.09)	−0.027 (−0.80)	−0.039 (−0.26)
6. Self-reported health rating (excellent = 1; otherwise = 0)	0.043 (1.07)		0.105 (2.27)	
7. At least one parent living (=1)	0.014 (0.51)		−0.008 (−0.27)	
8. Respondent did not take computer-assisted interview (no show)	−0.099 (−1.40)		−0.063 (−0.85)	
Intercept	0.175 (3.07)	−0.014 (0.07)	0.350 (6.09)	0.176 (0.86)
R^2	0.336	0.516	0.203	0.425
Number of observations	331	139	312	115
Hyp. 1: Addictive effect of COPD reflects unobserved heterogeneity[a]				
Pr > F	0.441		0.903	

Table 7.2 (continued)

	COPD		Relative risk	
	Model 1	Model 2	Model 3	Model 4
Hyp. 2: Information effect depends on amount smoked[b]				
Pr>F	0.017	0.046	0.754	0.877
Hyp. 3: Information effect includes amount smoked and cognitive score[c]				
Pr > F	0.009	0.029	0.097	0.242

Note: Numbers in parentheses are *t*-ratios for null hypothesis of no association. COPD = chronic obstructive pulmonary diseases.

[a] This hypothesis tests for a baseline effect—that is, the information term taken alone reflects differences in the experimental group and the control. We test whether the sum of this parameter (row 2) and the parameter for no-shows (row 8) (that is, no treatment but same group) is zero.

[b] This hypothesis tests whether the sum of the parameters for the effect of the number of packs (row 5) and the interaction effect of information and number of packs (row 4) is zero.

[c] This hypothesis tests whether the first restriction (sum of parameters in row 4 and row 5 = 0) and the parameter for the interaction effect of information and cognitive score (row 3) is zero.

sured characteristics in common with the smokers in our treatment group. To evaluate the success of our statistical controls, we also included a binary variable identifying these no-shows.

If the effects of the information treatment and the no-show variable are offsetting, then there is reason to expect that the parameter estimate on the binary variable identifying respondents who received the information treatment is misleading. We might erroneously attribute effects to the information treatment that were really due just to unmeasured differences between the treatment and the control groups. We labeled this hypothesis the "baseline effect" (since if the treatment and control samples were not fully comparable in ways we could not explicitly measure, this would affect initial differences in longevity expectations). We suspect that such omitted heterogeneity might have been the source of the positive sign on the parameter estimate for the binary variable for the information treatment in the longevity-updating model (the positive sign on the coefficients for the first information treatment), when a negative sign would have been expected.

To the extent that the binary variable used to identify an information treatment actually reflected unobserved differences in the baseline characteristics of the survey sample compared with the HRS (rather than the information treatment), we would expect the coefficient on the no-show binary variable to be negative and opposite in its effect on longevity expectations. The no-show binary would offset the implausible effect attributed to information. This is exactly what happened when we included it. The sum of the two coefficients was not significantly different from zero (Hypothesis 1; see bottom of Table 7.2).

Among personal characteristics, the information treatments should be more effective for respondents with higher cognitive abilities. As reported in Chapter 5, HRS respondents with higher cognitive scores gave more carefully reasoned answers to the live-to-seventy-five question. Thus, we anticipated that the sign on the coefficient of the treatment-cognition interaction variable would be negative. We would also expect the message to be more salient for heavy smokers who, on average, are at higher risk for adverse health outcomes. Again, for this reason, the expected sign on the parameter estimate for the treatment-smoking interaction term should be negative. Both scores reveal the anticipated effect on the longevity-expectations measure in Table 7.2.

There are some potential offsetting influences. In the case of number of packs smoked, this variable, when not interacted with the treatment, has a positive and statistically insignificant effect on longevity expectations. As a result, one might conclude that the interaction variable between the information treatment and number of packs smoked simply reflects the effects of smoking (as perceived by the respondents). It is important to ascertain whether the joint effect of smoking intensity is negative and statistically significant, and in fact, the joint effect was found to be negative and significant (Hypothesis 2 in Table 7.2).

Finally, we considered whether the composite effect of all explanatory variables including the information treatment binary variable was negative and statistically significant (Hypothesis 3).[7] The results are clear-cut, with a *p*-value of 0.009 (column 1), indicating that the COPD information treatment was effective in reducing smokers' longevity perceptions.

The second column in Table 7.2 eliminates the control observations randomly drawn from the HRS and compares the experimental group with the no-shows as a control for the first information treatment. Despite the small sample, we confirmed our finding—the information treatment significantly reduced longevity expectations. This included a negative and significant impact that depended on the amount smoked (Hypothesis 2), as well as on the cognitive score (Hypothesis 3), and the separate effect associated with the parameters for the qualitative variable identifying the people receiving this treatment. The composite test for the information treatment in this case involves the three parameter restrictions for these separate effects, and it was rejected at a *p*-value of 0.05.

Two aspects of these estimates are important. First, the information treatment effect was insignificant on its own (and this held regardless of the inclusion of the interaction terms). This confirms the specification we used in our earlier samples with the HRS control sample. Second, the influences of information through the amount smoked and, as a composite, between amount smoked and the cognitive score, was confirmed. Thus, even with this limited sample, we conclude that the COPD information treatment should lead to significant reductions in smokers' longevity expectations. None of the covariates for influences other than information had statistically significant effects on the updating of longevity expectations. Very likely these factors are already being captured in the baseline longevity value that is also included in the updating model.

Second Information Treatment: Personalized Relative Risk

The results for the second information treatment, the personalized and relative risk information, require less discussion. Columns 3 and 4 in Table 7.2 repeat the same basic structure for the experimental sample receiving the relative risk information treatment. First respondents are analyzed in comparison to a set of control individuals drawn from the HRS to match the distribution of initial longevity expectations as well as the no-shows (column 3). Then we compare the group receiving the relative risk information to the no-shows alone (column 4).

Our attempt to personalize the risk message was largely unsuccessful. There was no significant effect of the information treatment on longevity expectations. We repeated the multivariate modeling of longevity expectations done for the first information treatment, using the same logic to construct the control samples (Table 7.2). We used three statistical controls from the HRS sample of smokers as well as the no-shows control. Column 3 reports our findings using the statistical controls matching the baseline longevity expectations of the sample receiving the relative risk information. Column 4 considers a sample composed only of participants receiving the relative risk information and the no-shows. When the model was limited to the interaction terms with the cognitive score variable, the information effects were positive, not negative as hypothesized. When considered as a composite test, the null hypothesis that the information treatment had no effect could not be rejected at the 5 percent level with any of the control samples.

There are several potential explanations. The message in this treatment was more complex, with multiple health outcomes and comparisons displayed. As a consequence, respondents might have received quite mixed messages, with some risks presented as average and others higher. We did not attempt to take account of these differences in the severity of health outcomes in each person's warning when we evaluated the change in longevity expectations.

Personalization of the message implied that different respondents received different messages, depending on what their age, gender, and smoking behavior implied for their risk of dying from each of the smoking-related diseases. With small samples, we expect (at least in retrospect) that it may be difficult to detect any influence of this type of respondent-specific treatment. A full evaluation of this information strategy would require a much larger sample than our resources permitted.

Longevity Expectations after Six Months

The ultimate objective of providing information about the harmful effects of smoking is not to make individuals unhappy or simply to affect their longevity expectations; rather, it is to induce a change in their smoking behavior. The assumption underlying our focus on the effects of information on risk perception is that by altering longevity expectations we can ultimately induce behavioral change. Results from the above analysis suggest that a message worded like our COPD message can change longevity expectations, but to be effective, these changes cannot be ephemeral. An important assumption in this logic is that smokers' immediate responses to new information are sustained over a longer time horizon.[8]

To assess whether the information provided during the main interview had a more permanent impact on longevity expectations, we recontacted the Raleigh sample in January and February 2000, approximately six months after they had completed the computer-assisted, in-person interviews. Telephone interviews were conducted with both those who took the survey and the no-shows. Since there was no instantaneous effect for the second information treatment (the personalized relative risk of onset of different smoking-related diseases), we did not investigate it further.

In the follow-up, we focused on those who received the COPD information and the no-shows. The no-shows completed the screening interview, but because they missed the main interview, they did not receive the information treatment. Of the original 132 respondents who received the information treatment, 78 completed a follow-up interview. Of the 34 no-shows, 14 completed a follow-up interview.

Given this small sample, drawing any unambiguous inferences about the persistence of our informational message is difficult. Nonetheless, four comparisons support a conclusion that the effect persisted for at least six months. Using the sample of respondents who completed all three interviews (screening, main computer-assisted, and six-month follow-up), we made two comparisons. First, we analyzed the immediate change in their longevity expectations, comparing the responses obtained right after receiving the message in the main interview with the expectations obtained earlier in the screening interview. If the informational message was effective, we should observe a different pattern in updates between respondents who did the main interview and received the COPD message and the no-show group. A chi-square test of equivalent distributions for the longevity expectations at baseline and after the information treatment did reveal a difference, as expected. On purely statistical grounds, it was a close call. The test of equality of the two distributions of longevity expectations yielded a chi-square statistic of 26.9 (degrees of freedom = 19). This difference is almost statistically significant at conventional levels ($p = 0.11$). With such a small sample providing responses to all three interviews, we interpret this tendency as quite a strong result.

Second, we assessed the difference in longevity expectations reported at the six-month follow-up in comparison to immediately after the information was presented in the main interview. From results presented above, we know that the COPD information caused smokers to modify their longevity expectations immediately after they were presented with this information.

Results from the follow-up interviews offer quite strong confirming evidence that the change persisted after six months. A comparison of these expectations after six months with those reported in the interview immediately after receiving the information suggest no further change in longevity expectations (χ^2 = 12.1, degrees of freedom = 19, p = 0.84). Thus, the change in longevity expectations induced by the information appears to have been persistent.

In a third comparison, we assessed the longevity expectations at the six-month follow-up as a function of the longevity expectations at the *screening* interview, ignoring the immediate update obtained as part of the main survey. Our sample had only 77 respondents with sufficient information to estimate the mode. All tests failed to reject the null hypothesis of no effect of the information treatment. Given the small size of the sample, we treat this result as a neutral finding—neither supporting earlier conclusions nor offering evidence inconsistent with them.

Finally, we considered whether these respondents reported changes in smoking behavior, measured by the number of packs of cigarettes smoked. Using an interval-based format for the amount smoked, we compared the "before" and "after" responses of respondents who received the COPD information treatment versus the no-shows. A chi-square test indicated the two distributions were different (χ^2 = 12.8, degrees of freedom = 7, p = 0.078), and the direction indicated a decline in the amount smoked.

The results are subject to two important limitations. First, the sample was small, and second, individuals in the group receiving the COPD message did not stop smoking, although they did reduce the amount they smoked. Thus, the direction of the effect is consistent with the fundamental premise linking new information to changes in risk perceptions about longevity to changes in smoking behavior.

Conclusions

Judging from the focus groups we organized for this study, current and former smokers have well-developed views about how long they will survive and why their longevity expectations are what they are. Their views on this issue appear to be heavily dependent on the survival of their parents. Their parents' health and activity limitations prior to death were especially important considerations. In general, the current smokers appeared to be more optimistic about their health than the former smokers, a result consistent with our findings based on the HRS (Chapter 5).

Among focus group participants, the prospect of becoming disabled and dependent on others, together with the possibility of having to live in a nursing home, was both disliked and feared. This implied to us that information messages stressing the adverse impact of smoking on health and the quality of life in the years the person survives are likely to make an impression on smokers. Smoking causes disability as well as premature mortality (Chapter 4). Thus, these types of messages are consistent with what happens to older smokers.

Focus group meetings such as the ones we conducted can be informative, but they do not permit hypothesis testing. For this purpose, we conducted computer-assisted interviews with smokers age fifty to sixty-four and combined their responses with data from the HRS. The HRS data provided control samples to evaluate the impact of two information treatments on smokers' risk perceptions as measured by their reported longevity expectations. The first information message explained the symptoms and activity limitations associated with serious lung disease (COPD) linked to smoking. The second used an individual's demographic characteristics and smoking habits to provide a personalized relative risk message. Only the first message was effective in causing people to modify their longevity expectations. We found some evidence that the message also affected the amount they smoked.

We further hypothesized that the information treatments should be more effective for respondents with relatively good cognition. Our results confirmed that longevity expectations of persons with higher cognitive scores were more responsive to the COPD information message. Longevity expectations of persons who smoked more cigarettes per day were also more responsive to the message about COPD as an outcome from smoking than were those of persons who smoked less.

These findings are reassuring and potentially important for several reasons. The results on cognition substantiate the view that it was the information treatment and not some other omitted influence that reduced longevity expectations. More cognitively aware persons should be better able to digest the information content of messages. Also, the results on cognition are consistent with those of Wray, Herzog, and Willis (1998), who found that more educated persons were more likely than others to quit smoking following a heart attack (Chapter 5). The result for smoking intensity is important because persons who smoke heavily have more reason to listen to such information messages, as they are at greater risk for smoking-related diseases and their adverse effects (Chapter 4).

We tested whether providing information about adverse effects of smoking has persistent effects. We found some evidence that the COPD information treatment was remembered six months after it was administered. Overall, while we feel the results on the effect of the COPD information treatment are encouraging, they should be confirmed with a larger sample. As a result, although our results are suggestive, we are very reluctant to regard changes in behavior as a consequence of a "one-shot" information message as permanent. A more conservative course would involve reminders and reinforcing messages.

CHAPTER

8

Risk, Longevity Expectations, and Demand for Cigarettes

Throughout this book we argue that smoking policies must be based on a complete understanding of how people make the choice to smoke. There is no longer debate about whether smoking is a serious threat to one's health. *It is.* We have presented new evidence that the morbidity patterns and limitations of activities of daily living for older smokers are worse than for those who never smoked (Chapter 4). There is also no longer debate about whether smoking's addictive properties influence cessation decisions of older smokers (Chapter 6).

If the hazards are well known and the consequences life threatening, why do adults continue to smoke? Addiction is only part of the answer. To fully address the question, we must decompose the elements that influence people's choices for these types of goods. We have suggested that information, the formation of risk perceptions, and ultimate choices are intertwined. The panel structure of the Health and Retirement Study allowed us to take these elements apart to see how they might be influenced individually. Now we will put the elements back together to see if it is possible for an information policy to make a difference.

In Chapter 5, we discussed how longevity expectations we updated in response to new information about personal health, including information from smoking-related health shocks. In Chapter 6, we studied how longevity expectations, in particular overestimation or underestimation of personal survival, affect smokers' decisions to quit smoking, finding that overestimation or underestimation per se is at most a secondary influence on smoking cessation. Far more important are the effects of health shocks. Many smokers, it seems, must be struck by a major illness to be induced to quit. Our analysis in Chapter 7 suggests that providing information to smokers about how smoking-related diseases limit the personal activities of individuals afflicted with those diseases could change personal longevity expectations.

In this chapter, we integrate these results with new estimates of the demand for cigarettes. Smokers are concerned about being incapacitated. They do not want to find themselves unable to manage their activities at the end of their life. To the extent they believe diseases associated with these types of health states are more likely with continued smoking, they are more likely to change their risk perceptions. If we can associate these revised risk beliefs with smoking, then we will have a potential gauge of the impact of a new program to reduce smoking.

Our demand analysis in this chapter offers a way to measure the potential impact of information messages—in particular the message we found to affect subjective longevity expectations in Chapter 7, on typical cigarette consumption of mature smokers. By linking the health message to risk perceptions as indicated through a reduction in longevity expectations and in cigarette consumption, we estimate that providing new quality of life information to smokers would reduce daily cigarette consumption by 11 to 15 percent. To achieve the same reduction in demand for persons in this age cohort would require a 40 to 50 percent increase in the price of cigarettes.

This chapter begins with an overview of the conceptual models economists have used to argue why rational, informed consumers continue to use a potentially harmful, addictive commodity. This explanation has taken several forms. One highlights a discrepancy between how "real people" and how economic models consider future consumption. A second focuses on perceptions of the risks from smoking. Using a fairly simple framework, we discuss analytical parallels between the modeling of violations of temporally consistent behavior and treatments of uncertainty in a rational addiction model. In contrast to Chapter 2, where we discuss alternative perspectives on what might explain observed departures from rational behavior, in this chapter our conceptual framework is unambiguously economic. In fact, with the goal of generating empirically testable hypotheses, we put aside some of the economists' concerns discussed in Chapter 2. As stressed there, in the final analysis, the "proof of the pudding" is the results—our empirical findings. If flawed, underlying assumptions lead to flawed hypotheses, and this should show up in our empirical tests of these hypotheses.

Because there exists a very comprehensive recent review of the cigarette demand literature (Chaloupka and Warner 2000), we provide only a brief overview of previous research here, focusing primarily on reasons for differences in price elasticity estimates, including the types of data used to develop those estimated price elasticities. We then describe the price measure we merged with HRS data. To our knowledge, this price measure had not been used in the empirical analysis of smoking demand heretofore. Monthly values for a local price index for tobacco products were made available to us by the Bureau of Labor Statistics. This allowed us to implement a direct, and less restrictive, test of forward-looking behavior than had been used previously.[1] In addition, the price index improves on measures that have traditionally relied exclusively on variation in state excise taxes to assure sufficient price variation to measure the relationship between cigarette consumption and price. Although excise taxes are an important source of intertemporal and cross-sectional variation in prices among states, there are other reasons for price variation, including differences in the structure of the retail market for cigarettes.

Next, we present our demand estimates and use them to evaluate how our information treatment, describing the effects of chronic obstructive pulmonary disease on personal activities, affects longevity expectations and, in turn, reduces the cigarette consumption of this group of mature smokers.[2] Finally, we summarize our findings and comment on their relevance for public policy.

Modeling the Demand for Cigarettes

In economic models of individual demand in the context of an addictive good such as cigarettes, five aspects are relevant: effects of addiction; foresight; discounting of future events; the individual's time horizon; and risk. While past models may not explicitly identify each of these factors, they are all tested in some implicit way that influences how individual preferences and constraints are characterized. We will discuss each in turn in describing how they contribute to the specification of a cigarette demand function.

Addiction

Becker (1992) defined addiction as a strong habit. In this setting, habitual consumption can be described as involving choices of goods where there is a positive relation between past and current consumption of the same commodity. This "temporal complementarity" had been largely overlooked until his work with Murphy (Becker and Murphy 1988) developed the so-called rational addiction framework. The reason stems from the separability assumptions made in most conventional descriptions of behavior. Becker and Murphy's model does not completely relax this assumption. It focuses attention on past choices as contributing to a stock of consumption. This stock influences the satisfaction derived from current consumption. To evaluate the importance of their approach, we can consider the general case where we do not impose restrictions on how past choices influence the utility derived from current or future consumption.

As a general statement of individual preferences, we define a utility function U, with x_1 through x_k representing consumption of k different goods, as arguments (Eq. 8.1). This represents the conventional static model with the timing of consumption not explicitly defined.

Generality is both a strength and a weakness of this description of consumer choice. A strength is that we can accommodate a wide range of situations. On the negative side, when we proceed to implement the model, we need to ask whether the x's are daily, weekly, or monthly levels of consumption. Do they represent rates of consumption? These questions are inevitably answered when one adapts Equation (8.1) along with a description of the constraints to behavior to describe actual choices.

$$U = U(x_1, x_2, x_3, \ldots, x_k) \tag{8.1}$$

To see effects of temporal separability assumptions explicitly, a second subscript, t for the time period, is introduced in the labeling commodities.[3] Eq. (8.2) shows how a general specification of preferences with the "dated" goods (left side) relates to one exhibiting additive separability over time (the right). The latter precludes the complementarity of consumption across time periods. This feature is important because, by allowing for temporal complementarity, the rational addiction model describes strong habits and addictive behavior.

$$U(x_{11}, x_{21}, \ldots, x_{k1}; x_{12}, x_{22}, \ldots; x_{1t}, x_{2t}, \ldots, x_{kt}) =$$
$$U_1(x_{11}, x_{21}, \ldots, x_{k1}) + U_2(x_{12}, x_{22}, \ldots, x_{k2}) + \ldots + U_t(x_{1t}, x_{2t}, \ldots, x_{kt}) \tag{8.2}$$

Eq. (8.2) also allows for the possibility that preferences are different over time by subscripting the separable U_t functions.[4]

To define temporal complementarity, it must be possible to display a relationship between the consumption of x_j at different times. Adjacent complementarity is a special case of temporal complementarity and means just what the name implies : x_{jt} and x_{jt+1} are complements.[5] The precise specification of the left side of eq. (8.2) allows for any possible relationship between each x_{jt}, and the one on the right assumes there is no relationship in consumption decisions over time (except, of course, through a lifetime budget constraint, which is not considered here).

In many respects, the specification on the left side is too general to be informative. Becker and Murphy (1988) imposed restrictions on the utility function to develop an analytically tractable model. As they suggested, addictive behavior is about the general relationship. The specific form of the utility function, given in Eq. (8.3), simply makes empirical analysis tractable. To see how their formulation works, consider a case with two goods ($k = 2$): one an addictive good (x_1) and the other (x_2) a reference, or numeraire, good.

Addiction is introduced with the definition of a stock term for x_1 (Eq. 8.4). This equation describes how past consumption of x_1 has a cumulative effect on the pleasure a person derives from current consumption of the same good. As we said, this is only one way a connection can be made. In this case, a weighted average of past consumption describes how it has an influence. The role is established by specifying the role for the stock term, S_t, in the preference function, as in Eq. (8.4). Under some specifications, we can have current x_1 contributing to preferences directly and through S_t. Others assume S_t reflects only past consumption. Either way, the past decisions have a role in influencing the current trade-off between x_1 and x_2, depending on how S_t affects the utility function. S_t is the mechanism used to describe how consumption of x_1 is linked though time. Its role in preferences determines how the trade-off between x_1 and x_2 is influenced by past consumption of x_1.

Becker and Murphy incorporated addiction through a stock term for x_1 similar to the form in Eq. (8.3), with Eq. (8.4) defining how that stock evolves through time.[6]

$$U_t = u(x_{1t}, x_{2t}, S_t) \tag{8.3}$$

$$S_t = S_{t-1} + x_{1t} - \delta S_{t-1} \tag{8.4}$$

Simplifying Eq. (8.4), S_t can be described as a power series in x_{1t}.[7] Eq. (8.5) describes the general format.

$$S_t = x_{1t} + \alpha x_{1t-1} + \alpha^2 x_{1t-2} + \ldots + \alpha^k x_{1t-k} \tag{8.5}$$

The important implication to be drawn here is from the marginal rate of substitution (MRS) between adjoining years' consumption of x_1, one measure of complementarity.[8] Eq. (8.6) describes how the marginal utilities contributed to the trade-offs between current and past consumption.

$$MRS_{x_{1t},x_{1t-1}} = \frac{\alpha \cdot u_3}{u_1 + u_3} \tag{8.6}$$

$$\text{where } u_j = \frac{\partial u}{\partial j}$$

$$j = \text{position of the argument in the expression, } u(x_{1-t}, x_{2-t}, S_t)$$

As we consider consumption more periods apart, the MRS declines geometrically: as α^T grows large, with T equalling periods separating consumption of the good. The components of S_t imply that $0 < \alpha < 1$. Thus, the effect of past consumption on x declines rapidly.

To implement the model, Becker and Murphy assumed individuals maximize the present value of utility realized over an infinite time horizon,[9] subject to a budget constraint defining their assets. This optimization problem was defined in continuous time. For the case of a quadratic utility function in consumption of x_1 and the addictive stock (assumed separable from the numeraire good), the demand function is given by Eq. (8.7),

$$x_{1t} = \beta_0 + \beta_1 P_{1t} + \beta_2 P_{1t-1} + \beta_2 \theta P_{1t+1} + \beta_3 x_{1t-1} + \beta_3 \theta x_{1t+1} + \ldots \tag{8.7}$$

where: β_2 reflects the depreciation on the addictive stock and θ is a discount factor.

Assuming the depreciation rate on the addictive stock is one ($\delta = 1$), we can drop P_{1t-1} and P_{1t+1} from the demand function.[10] With this restriction the parameter, β_2, affecting their contribution to demand is zero ($\beta_2 = 1-\delta$). This is the form of the rational addiction model frequently tested (see Becker, Grossman, and Murphy 1994 and Chaloupka 1991). Such empirical analysis relies on two additional assumptions we consider next. Until recently, these have received less attention in the literature.

Discounting and Foresight

Discounting and foresight must be treated together. Discounting refers to a simple way that economic models assume people weigh future consumption in relation to current consumption. People prefer to avoid waiting to enjoy something. The rate of time preference is another way of characterizing the trade-off between current consumption and future consumption. Discounting specializes the treatment of waiting by assuming that people use a process comparable to the compounding of interest to adjust future gains. Compared with enjoying something today, they recognize that there is an equivalent future gain reflecting the fact that they could have saved those resources, earned a return, and used it to enjoy more of the good or service in the future. This required return on waiting is the discount rate. Foresight enters the picture because discounting implies a time horizon and with it an ability to anticipate (or estimate) the future values of external variables, such as commodity prices, that influence a person's choices.

Rational addiction relies on forward-looking behavior on the part of a time-consistent consumer whose preferences are adequately described by a conventionally discounted utility function.[11] In discrete terms, with a T period time horizon, this objective function is given by Eq. (8.8) for period t.

$$v_t = \sum_{i=0}^{T} \theta^i U_{t+i} \tag{8.8}$$

$$\text{where } \theta = \frac{1}{(1+r)}$$

r = individual rate of time preference (discount rate)

To implement the model in a simple rational addiction, U_{t+i} would be replaced by Eq. (8.3), and the intertemporal budget constraint would be defined involving current and future prices. This process requires the assumption that consumers be able to forecast future prices.

Gruber and Köszegi (2001) recently sought to determine whether smokers take future prices into account when deciding on how much to smoke at present. They studied the effect of announced increases in state cigarette excise taxes on current cigarette consumption. Their evidence was based on models estimated using aggregate, pooled, time-series cross-sectional data.

They found several interesting responses to tax changes. Announced but not yet effective tax increases led to both increased sales and decreased consumption of cigarettes. To the extent that smokers are forward looking, they would seek to buy cigarettes for future consumption if they knew the price would rise. Hence, if smokers are forward looking, sales should increase. Thus, this first aspect of their findings is clearly consistent with forward-looking behavior. The second finding constitutes indirect evidence of adjacent complementarity. Knowing that prices will increase in the future, they reduce their cigarette consumption now.

Gruber and Köszegi were especially critical of the discounting assumption typically used in economic analysis. As an alternative, they replaced the conventional discounting in Eq. (8.8) with an adjusted form, termed quasi-hyperbolic discounting, as in Eq. (8.9).

$$v_t = U_t + a \cdot \sum_{i=0}^{T} \theta^i U_{t+i} \tag{8.9}$$

The a term was assumed to be between zero and one, reflecting the asymmetry resulting from comparing trade-offs between the current period t and any future period in comparison with trade-offs for similarly spaced future periods. For example, consider t and $t+1$: the effect of discounting on the marginal rate of substitution for these two different consumption choices separated by one year is $a\theta$. Comparing periods $t+1$ and $t+2$, the effect of discounting on consumption in the future, also separated by the one period difference, is θ. This difference in the effects of discounting, comparing present consumption with a future period, versus any two future periods separated by the same amount of time, is the asymmetry. Thus, when we compare the current period to a gain that is k periods ahead, it is given more weight than the model would assign to the trade-off between two future gains separated by k periods.

The formulation hypothesized in Eq. (8.9) could also be used to reflect a risk effect. Suppose, for example, an individual compares current utility with a subjective appraisal of the likelihood he or she would survive to experience the gains represented by the summation of future utility. If T is defined to be the difference between seventy-five and one's current age, then this probability is equivalent to the longevity expectation elicited in the HRS questions and discussed earlier (Chapter 5).

Gruber and Köszegi's discussion of naive agents' consumption of addictive goods provides another interpretation for the specification for our demand model. Their model implies (for values of $a > \frac{1}{2}$) that, holding other factors constant, naive agents will experience greater increases in the demand for cigarettes with a given increase in the past stock than time-consistent agents. In our terms, this would imply that those with higher subjective expectations of longevity over the time horizon (to age seventy-five) are more likely to exhibit adjacent complementarity and strong effects of the addictive stock (which represents the cumulative effect of past smoking) than those who think that their time horizon is shorter.

Before assessing effects of the time horizon, we should emphasize an aspect of the foresight assumption. The ability to test for differences in cigarette consumption across agents in the Gruber-Köszegi framework relies on depreciation rates less than unity ($\delta < 1$ and $\beta_2 \neq 0$). This feature highlights the importance of taking account of future price effects in cigarette demand models. When δ is not unity, future prices will not drop out of the demand function, as Becker, Grossman, and Murphy (1994) and Chaloupka (1991) assumed. Nearly all of the tests of rational addiction have maintained time consistency, full depreciation (and thus no effects of future prices in the function), and a high level of sophistication on the part of smokers in forming future price expectations. The Gruber-Köszegi model and empirical results suggest each assumption needs to be reconsidered.

Time Horizon

While Ippolito's early (1981) research on risk-taking behavior over the life cycle explicitly discussed how a person's life span (or time horizon for decision making) affected behavior, life span has not played a central role in formal versions of the rational addiction framework.[12] Suranovic, Goldfarb, and Leonard (1999) suggested this issue should be reconsidered, especially in terms of the adjustment costs arising from a decision to stop smoking.[13] They described smoking behavior in an intertemporal optimization setting, considering three separate components: current benefits, future losses, and adjustment costs. Future losses involve the present value of the expected utility difference (from a baseline of no smoking) associated with each level of current smoking. Their conceptual analysis acknowledged the addictive effect of smoking and incorporated the effect of age and smoking level on expected longevity. This last component links a person's smoking choices to the time horizon over which the person experiences utility from these choices. A shorter life means less utility, other factors being equal.

They distinguished three types of adjustment costs and assumed a simple form of adjustment costs to describe how current smoking affects an individual's time horizon. More specifically, such costs varied according to the individual's current age and addictive stock (past amounts smoked), and were a constant multiple of the person's current smoking level. They characterized weak addiction as adjustment costs that rise at an increasing rate with the amount currently smoked, and strong addiction as costs that rise at a decreasing rate. With weak addiction, a smoker quits gradually over time, a pattern we observed for many smokers in Chapter 6. With age, the time-horizon effect consistently increases the loss function, and eventually optimal consumption becomes zero—that is, the person quits smoking. By contrast, with strong addiction, "cold turkey" quitting is more likely to occur as a person grows older. The third case, a changing adjustment cost function for different levels of consumption, implies numerous attempts to quit smoking before cessation is successful.

All of these results stem from a model in which current smoking leads to life reduction (a shrinking time horizon) by a constant amount per unit of smoking. Assuming the effect of smoking on life expectancy (and implicitly the time horizon) is not constant, Suranovic and coauthors isolated two effects—an age effect and a smoking stock effect. The former occurs because an increase in age for a given stock reduces the smoker's time horizon or life expectancy and can contribute to raising expected losses from current smoking. The stock effect works in the opposite direction.

The authors' conclusions, which were based entirely on conceptual analysis and a simulation model, are completely consistent with our empirical research on longevity expectations and smoking-related health shocks (Chapter 5) and the results from our focus group and smoker survey (Chapter 7). More specifically, Suranovic, Goldfarb, and Leonard (1999) observed that "results from using a more realistic and complex numerical assumption about how smoking affects probability of dying suggests the importance of incorporating better information into the model about how smokers *actually perceive the health effects of smoking*" (pp. 18–19, emphasis added).

This suggestion is consistent with our own findings. In our empirical analysis, effects of health shocks and new information about smoking were captured by the longevity expectations variable.[14] Our focus group and information experiment suggested that the health effects should not be confined to information about mortality risks. We found that information messages about the adverse effects of smoking on disability and hence on quality of life in late life were highly salient to the smokers we interviewed. Thus, informing smokers about the potential influence of smoking on the quality—not just the quantity—of life is important for promoting more realistic longevity expectations. Not only does such information have a psychological impact, but given this information, smokers are more likely to reduce the amount they currently smoke.

What appears to be happening, in terms of the Gruber-Köszegi model and Suranovic, Goldfarb, and Leonard, is that smokers act as if they assign a subjective belief to a present value of utility gains from smoking. Focusing on quality of life dimensions appears to result in a more effective message. Cast in this form, the message increases perceived losses due to continued smoking. Changes in discounting, longevity expectations, risk perception (expressed as a composite probability of realizing a present value of utility over a defined time horizon), and the time horizon itself all act through the composite term's contribution to the future losses perceived to arise from smoking.

Risk

Smoking is a very risky activity and can, through health shocks, affect longevity expectations (and implicitly the risk of premature death) of smokers compared with nonsmokers. Our discussion in this chapter up to now has been confined to the effects of smoking stock measures on current demand, and the relationship between time horizon, adjustment costs, and patterns of smoking cessation.

Gruber and Köszegi's (2001) empirical evidence suggests that one should observe effects of adjacent complementarity on the current price responsiveness of cigarette demand. That is, expectations of a future price increase should influence the effect of the current price on current consumption. The Becker-Murphy rational addiction framework is readily modified to demonstrate that the magnitude of these price effects is related to whether or not an individual's longevity expectations are affected by smoking. Here, we outline a simple modification of an already simplified version of the rational addiction model that Becker (1992) used to illustrate some of its key insights.

Assume that stock effects work through a type of threshold consumption. That is, for current cigarette consumption to contribute to utility, its utility must exceed some fraction, α, of the depreciation in the existing addictive stock ($x_{1t} > \alpha\delta S_t$ for a positive contribution to individual utility). The formulation replaces the general form of Eq. (8.3) with Eq. (8.10), dropping x_{2t} to simplify the exposition.

$$U_t = u(x_{1t} - \alpha\delta S_t) \tag{8.10}$$

Using a continuous form of the stock accumulation relationship given earlier in discrete form in Eq. (8.4), and focusing on the steady-state demand response ($dS_t/dt = 0$), yields Eq. (8.11).

$$\frac{dS_t}{dt} = 0 = x_{1t} - \delta S_t \tag{8.11}$$

or

$$x_{1t} = \delta S_t$$

Thus, $U_t = U(\bar{x}_1 - \alpha\bar{x}_1)$ with $\bar{x}_1$, the steady-state consumption level, determined by solving the dynamic optimization problem. Becker used this approach to describe how strength of addiction influences the steady-state impact of price on steady-state quantity demanded, $\bar{x}_1$. The term α captures the influence of addiction; α increases as the habit increases. For a given discount rate, addiction affects the influence of a permanent change in the price of cigarettes (P_1) on steady-state demand. Holding marginal utility of wealth over the individual's planning horizon, λ, constant, Becker (1992) described the effect of a change in price on steady state demand as:

$$\frac{d\bar{x}_1}{dP_1} \approx \frac{\lambda}{u''\cdot(1-\alpha)^2}$$

$$\text{where } u'' = \frac{d^2u_1}{d^2\bar{x}_1{}^2} < 0 \tag{8.12}$$

As α increases, the effect of a permanent price change increases. Larger values of α are associated with greater levels of addiction.

Replacing the certain description of individual behavior with one that considers a person attaching a subjective probability $\pi(S_t)$ to the full-time stream of consumption yields Eq. (8.13) as an alternative description of the effects of risk on demand responsiveness to price. Here the strength of the addiction (α) and risk perceptions also play a role in influencing how steady state quality demanded responds to price.[15] If $\alpha > 1$ (Becker's definition of addiction), then the second term in the denominator of Eq. (8.13) is positive, reducing the size of the denominator and thus potentially reducing the price effect on demand. For less addictive behavior, the price effect will be larger.

$$\frac{d\bar{x}_1}{dP_1} \approx \frac{\lambda}{u''\cdot(1-\alpha)^2 + 2\left(\frac{\pi'}{\delta}\right)\cdot u'(1-\alpha)} \tag{8.13}$$

$$\text{where } u'' = \frac{du}{d\bar{x}_1} > 0$$

$$\pi' = \frac{d\pi}{dS_t}$$

To derive Eq. (8.13), we assumed $\pi'' = 0$.[16] If $\pi' < 0$, reflecting smokers' understanding that smoking does have an effect on mortality, then the demand response to a permanent increase in price depends on both risk and the perceived strength of adjacent complementarity.[17]

In sum, when people exhibit some form of foresight with future price expectations and recognize the future consequences of current choices, then we can expect that the current effects of adjacent complementarity and price on current demand will be influenced in comparable ways by risk perceptions, time horizons, and departures from time-consistent discounting.

Under these circumstances, we must rely on empirical evidence to allow us to distinguish among specific hypotheses about how smoking behavior will respond to policy. We have selected the link to longevity expectations and risk to argue that information that motivates smokers to realign their longevity expectations with what experts anticipate in both life span and quality of life at the end of one's life should lead to reductions in demand. This follows because smokers' current longevity expectations are not consistent with what experts judge will be their experience. This is especially true for quality-of-life effects. The link between any revisions in life expectancy, reductions in smoking, and decisions to quit will depend on the actual nature of adjustment effects experienced by each person. Suranovic, Goldfarb, and Leonard (1999) offered alternative descriptions that are consistent with observed behaviors. We do not attempt to reconcile those alternatives here because our primary focus is on the responses to the new information in terms of the quantity demanded, given that the individual has been a long-term smoker.

Hypotheses for an Empirical Cigarette Demand Model

The preceding capsule description of key elements in economic models of cigarette demand suggests several classes of hypotheses that underlie development of a plausible demand model. They include a test of individual foresight and consistency in choice over time. Conditional on the outcome of that test, we should expect to observe some forms of adjacent complementarity and ultimately, given our focus on risk, a link between longevity expectations and smoking choices.

We estimated demand models with explanatory variables designed to reflect the individual's longevity expectations, addictive stock, future price expectations, demographic characteristics, and, of course, current cigarette price and family income. As noted in earlier chapters, the panel structure of the HRS provides information to represent intertemporal consumption effects as well as the evolution of longevity expectations for each individual. Although the panel structure and the rich detail on individual and household characteristics offer substantial advantages over data available for research on this topic in the past, the panel is short, spanning six years (four separate interviews). Before turning to the specifics of our results, we first highlight a few aspects of the literature on demand for cigarettes that are relevant to our results.

Past Literature on Demand for Cigarettes

Chaloupka and Warner (2000) divided the literature on cigarette demand into conventional studies of cigarette demand based on a traditional model of demand and studies based on the Becker-Murphy (1988) rational addiction model.

Conventional Studies

Conventional studies have used aggregate time series, time series composed of state cross sections, and individual data. Most of the price elasticities of demand reported in these studies fall in the −0.3 to −0.5 range.

Particularly in aggregate time series analysis, estimates of the price and other factors are sensitive to specifications used for each demand function. Studies conducted with the state and year as the observational unit have generally used sales data. With sales data, there is the added difficulty that persons may purchase cigarettes in low cigarette price states for use or resale in the higher price states where they live. While conventional studies have addressed these issues in various ways, the overall results are fairly comparable, with reported price elasticities of demand in a narrower range, centered around −0.4. The more sophisticated of these efforts, based on aggregate time series data, have been published since 1990.

An alternative approach for assessing cigarette demand has been to rely on natural experiments. An example of a natural experiment would be an excise tax increase in one state that did not occur in a comparison state. Such studies have reported price elasticities of cigarette demand in the −0.017 to −0.56 range. Some studies have separated the effect of price on the decision to smoke from smoking quantities conditional on smoking. For example, Harris (1994) estimated a participation (smoking versus nonsmoking) elasticity of −0.24 while finding an overall (unconditional) elasticity to be comparable to those reported by others (in his study, −0.47).

The use of data on individuals (as opposed to data with aggregate consumption or per capita consumption by state and year as the observational units) to study the demand for cigarettes has been much more unusual. Surveys of individuals have an advantage in providing a direct measure of cigarette consumption. Use of micro data from household surveys also mitigates, but does not eliminate, two other problems with the aggregate studies: simultaneous equations bias and multicollinearity.

Of course, individual-level data are not without their own limitations. Among these are underreporting of smoking and failure to capture all demand determinants, some of which may be correlated with variables as price. For example, antismoking sentiment, which is not captured in household surveys, may be correlated with cigarette taxes and, hence, price.

The studies using individual data have made several important contributions. First, they have allowed more detailed analysis of determinants of smoking versus not smoking and amounts of smoking conditional on smoking at all. Lewit and Coate (1982), for example, found the price elasticity of demand (overall effect including participation) to be −0.42 and the participation elasticity to be −0.26. A more recent study by Hu, Sung, and Keeler (1995a, 1995b), limited to California, reported an overall price elasticity of −0.46, with the effects about equally divided between smoking participation and demand. For very young individuals, the participation decision is more likely to be whether or not to initiate the smoking habit. For older persons, the participation decision is almost without exception whether or not to quit.

Second, availability of large micro data sets has permitted researchers to stratify samples by various personal characteristics, such as age. In general, the evidence indicates that youth cigarette demand is more price elastic than is demand among older persons.

Third, use of micro data has permitted analysis of qualitative as well as quantitative responses to price. Particularly noteworthy is the Evans and Farrelly (1998) analysis of compensating behavior of smokers facing increased excise taxes for cigarettes. Using data from the 1979 and 1987 National Health Interview Survey, the authors found that the total number of cigarettes consumed per day fell in response to tax increases, but total daily tar and nicotine intake were unaffected. Smokers in high-tax states consumed longer cigarettes.

Empirical Analysis Based on the Rational Addiction Model

Economic models of cigarette demand with addiction can be grouped into three categories: (1) imperfectly rational behavior; (2) models of myopic addictive behavior; (3) and models of rational addictive behavior. The first type is typified by the work of Jon Elster, Gordon Winston, and Thomas Schelling and was described in Chapter 2. In myopic models, current consumption depends in part on past consumption. By contrast, with rational addiction, individuals consider the future implications of current consumption decisions. This does not preclude individuals' exhibiting behavior that would be consistent with a fairly high discount rate, an important feature that distinguishes them from myopic models, which assume the discount rate is infinite.

Chaloupka (1991) and Becker, Grossman, and Murphy (1994) are the most widely cited empirical applications of the rational addiction model. Chaloupka (1991) found that in estimates using micro data from the Second National Health and Nutrition Examination Survey, the long-run price elasticity of demand ranges from -0.27 to -0.48. These measures are larger in absolute value than most estimates based on conventional demand models. He also estimated separate demand equations by age and educational attainment. In general, his estimates were consistent with the view that younger and less educated persons are more myopic. Less educated smokers were more responsive to price (long-run elasticities in the range of −0.57 to −0.62).

The Becker, Grossman, and Murphy (1994) empirical models were based on a time series of state cross sections in the United States for the years 1955 to 1985. During this period, there was substantial intertemporal as well as cross-sectional variation in the price of cigarettes. The authors obtained a negative coefficient for current cigarette price from their reduced-form equation for cigarettes. They estimated positive coefficients for past and future consumption, a pattern consistent with forward-looking rational behavior.[18] The long-run price elasticity of demand was approximately −0.75, nearly twice the short-run elasticity of −0.40. As Chaloupka and Warner (2000) reported, empirical evidence on the rational addiction models from other studies has been mixed. However, the authors did introduce an important caveat to their summary, noting that the studies failing to support the rational addiction framework tended to be based on small samples with highly correlated independent variables.

Measuring Cigarette Price

One of the most important aspects of the modeling of the demand for any product is the measure used for the price of the commodity. Despite the long-standing interest in cigarette demand, there has been little direct attention given to the effects of the price measure used in the demand models. As Gruber and Köszegi noted, the price measure is a key ingredient in tests of smokers' foresight and in recognizing the effects of addiction on demand responsiveness to price.

Our empirical research on cigarette demand used a measure of the price of cigarettes that, to our knowledge, has not been used previously in analyses of cigarette demand studies. Past research at both the level of the individual and at the aggregate level has generally relied on either the Tobacco Institute's weighted average price by state and year or a measure of cigarette taxes.[19] While there are recognized problems with this measure, the publicly available alternatives usually have been judged to be inferior.[20]

To test the foresight and addiction properties of our smoking model, we sought an improved price measure. We requested and obtained unpublished price information, the Price Indexes for Tobacco and Smoking Products, from the U.S. Bureau of Labor Statistics (BLS). The data had sufficient geographic detail to permit us to merge the price measure with confidential geographic codes obtained from the HRS.[21] The merge was done at the level of the HRS primary sampling unit (PSU). We obtained these data from January 1991 to December 1999 as a monthly index of values for all urban consumers.[22] Access to the monthly data for each area allowed us to construct price expectation measures for each smoker.

Three aspects of these price data merit detailed discussion: the potential for within-state variation in prices across smokers; the relationship between the BLS index and a more conventional price measure; and our approach for using the BLS index to measure price expectations.

There is substantial within-state variation in price. The HRS smokers were assigned using the BLS's primary sampling units matched to the relevant PSUs of the Health and Retirement Study. Smokers in twenty-eight of the forty-four states included in our sample were assigned different prices than would have occurred with the assumption of constant statewide prices, based on variation in their locations.

Table 8.1 reports a regression with the BLS index regressed on our version of the conventional price index.[23] While the two price measures were correlated, there were also substantial differences—as reflected in the very low R^2 statistics for the regression for each of the two waves. These regres-

Table 8.1 A comparison of Bureau of Labor Statistics and conventional price indexes

Explanatory variable	Wave 2	Wave 3
Conventional price index^2	0.42	0.20
	(5.86)	(2.74)
Number of observations	1,551	1,549
R^2	0.02	0.01
Intercept	2.78	3.31
	(23.12)	(23.55)

Note: Numbers in parentheses are *t*-values. See text for description of the conventional price index.

sions were based on the average of the monthly BLS price indexes for the PSUs defined for each year corresponding to a wave of the HRS (1994 for wave 2, 1996 for wave 3, and so on). Our assignment of prices accounted for mobility of HRS respondents between waves. Between waves 1 and 2, 5.6 percent of HRS households moved. Between waves 2 and 3, 1.7 percent did.

We used monthly price values for each of two years following waves 2 and 3 to construct a simple measure of price expectations. Rather than expecting a high level of resolution in the ability of consumers to formulate price expectations, we followed the logic of Gruber and Köszegi (2001) and asked instead if they reacted to consistent future price movements. In our analysis we fitted time trends for each smoker. The first time trend considered the movements in the price index for the twelve months in the year after the survey was completed. The second trend considers the twelve months two years after the HRS interview was completed or two years ahead of the reported consumption. Each trend analysis was considered separately. For each smoker, we coded a price-expectations measure based on whether the parameter estimate on the one-year-ahead time trend was positive or negative. If the trend coefficient was positive, this implied an expectation that prices were to increase. If it was not positive, the price expectations variable was coded as zero. Based on this criterion, about 27 percent of the respondents in wave 2 might have expected stable or declining prices in 1995 (Table 8.2). For longer time periods than a year, the fraction who could anticipate stable or declining prices fell, thus limiting our ability to use this gauge to test for forward-looking behavior. Also, because wave 3 respondents were observed only for two additional years, we were limited in this respect as well. With these qualifications, our method did offer the potential for a general test of adjacent complementarity.

Table 8.2 Testing for forward-looking behavior: Future price expectations

Wave	One year ahead: Percentage with increases	Two years ahead: Percentage with increases
2	72.60	93.50
3	93.80	100.00

Estimates of Cigarette Demand of Older Adults

We will present our estimates of the features of the demand in three subsections. After briefly discussing the sample constructed from the HRS to consider smoking demand, we begin our analysis by describing the results of our nonparametric test of forward-looking behavior and the potential for adjacent complementarity. These results focus on cross tabulations of our sample price-expectation measures with a categorical variable describing the level of current smoking. By progressively subsampling smokers in the HRS panel, we isolated the demographic characteristics of HRS respondents that are important to estimates of the response of current demand to future price signals. We next discuss our demand model. The specification takes account of price foresight, simple forms of addictive behavior, longevity expectations, demographics, and complementary behaviors (such as drinking). Finally, we use the model together with the results from Chapter 7 to evaluate the effects of the information treatment.

Health and Retirement Study Sample

For purposes of the demand analysis, we limited the HRS sample to persons who said that they were current smokers in waves 2 and 3. The percentage of HRS respondents who reported smoking at least one cigarette per day fell from 27 percent at wave 1 in 1992 to 21.5 percent at wave 4 in 1998 (Table 8.3). While there are variations in this group's smoking decisions, more persons quit smoking than restarted. People begin smoking for the first time in this age range only very rarely. Independent evidence con-

Table 8.3 Smoking status by wave (percent)

Smoking status	Wave 1	Wave 2	Wave 3	Wave 4
Current smoker	27.10	24.51	23.44	21.47
Former smoker	36.85	39.64	40.72	42.75
Never smoker	36.05	35.85	35.84	35.78

Note: This sample was composed of respondents participating in all four waves (n = 10,462).

firms that smokers in this age group had been smoking for more than twenty-five years.[24]

Although four waves of the HRS were available to test the rational addiction model, measures of lagged and future consumption were needed. Smoking data from waves 1 and 4 were used for this purpose. To achieve consistency with the smoker survey we conducted in Raleigh (see Chapter 7), we limited the sample of current smokers from the HRS to persons between the ages of fifty-one and sixty-four.

Table 8.4 describes characteristics of persons in our demand analysis

Table 8.4 Descriptive statistics for cigarette demand sample

Explanatory variables	Wave 2	Wave 3
Amount smoked (per day)		
Current	19.4 (13.3)	18.3 (12.6)
Previous wave	20.4 (12.8)	19.4 (13.3)
Future wave	18.3 (12.6)	15.8 (13.1)
Household income ($ 000s)[a]	38.71 (47.7)	36.4 (41.9)
Proportion who currently drink alcoholic beverages	0.91 (1.00)	0.81 (0.95)
Age (at wave 1)	55.8 (3.4)	
Gender (male = 1)	0.50 (0.50)	
Race (African American = 1)	0.17 (0.38)	
High school graduate	0.36 (0.48)	
Health described as excellent	0.15 (0.36)	0.13 (0.34)
Health described as fair or poor (= 1)	0.26 (0.44)	0.29 (0.45)
Proportion with one parent currently living	0.21 (0.41)	0.11 (0.32)
Longevity expectation to 75 or more years of age	0.59 (0.31)	0.57 (0.33)

Note: Numbers in parentheses are standard deviations.

[a] Expressed in thousands here.

sample. They were nearly fifty-six years of age at wave 1, on average. About half were men. Our measure of cigarette consumption was based on the HRS question asking how many cigarettes or packs a respondent usually smoked each day (at the time of the interview). The responses were converted into a count of cigarettes using information they provided in response to this question. The averages reflect a gradual decline in average consumption from about a pack a day to about three-fourth's of a pack by wave 4. The proportion reporting that they currently drank alcoholic beverages also declined form 92 percent to 82 percent between 1994 and 1996. By wave 4, this proportion was 76 percent.

Three features of our data allowed us to avoid some of the problems encountered in past research on cigarette demand. First, we had better data at the individual level for smokers' behavior. With information at the individual level we avoid aggregation bias. Second, we had a geographic and time-specific measure of cigarette prices, and thus avoided measurement errors in prices. Finally, with monthly values of this location-specific price index, we could implement a test of forward-looking behavior based on the price expectation measure defined earlier.

Unfortunately, the HRS did not obtain data on consumption before wave 1; thus, we knew the number of years before that a former smoker had quit but not the years of consumption for current smokers. As a result, we relied on the HRS panel structure for information on two-year lagged and two-year lead consumption to test for stock effects. The resulting multicollinearity and sensitivity of our estimates to the assumptions made about the functional form for the demand model are also limitations that we discuss below.

Nonparametric Tests of Foresight and Addiction

Our nonparametric test is a simultaneous test of respondents' ability to forecast future prices and adjacent complementarity. As noted earlier, a monthly tobacco price trend model was estimated for each respondent, using price movements one year ahead of the current wave (1995 for wave 2 and 1997 for wave 3). Following the implicit logic in Gruber and Köszegi (2001), we formulated a simple hypothesis to describe consumers' forecasting abilities.[25] Our test maintained that smokers can recognize and anticipate upward price trends and respond to them differently from constant or downward movements. We would expect (from adjacent complementarity and a conventional demand response to price) that anticipated future price increases would reduce current demand, which is what Gruber and Köszegi found for one of the samples considered in their study.[26]

The results in the first panel in Table 8.5 are based on our binary variable identifying a positive future price trend. Our test considers whether increased future prices lead to differences in current smoking levels. Current smoking levels decline with these future price increases. That is, the test rejects the null hypothesis of no change for increases in future prices using the one-period-ahead prices at the 10 percent level of statistical significance. The results presented in the second panel are based on repeating the test using monthly price trends for the second year (that is, two periods ahead). Here we cannot reject the null hypothesis. However, the test results are limited by the observed price movements—that is, there were too few cases of stable or declining prices.

In Table 8.6, we report the cross tabulations underlying the chi-square

Table 8.5 Nonparametric test of the effects of risk, foresight, and addiction

Hypothesis test	Reject (R), not reject (NR) null hypothesis	Chi-square	Degrees of freedom	*p*-value
I. Current smoking level and one-period ahead price expectations				
Waves = 1994–1996	R	5.66	2	0.06
Men	NR	1.32	2	0.52
Women	R	5.88	2	0.05
Without high school	NR	1.38	2	0.50
With high school	R	5.99	2	0.05
II. Current smoking level and two-period ahead price expectations				
Waves = 1994–1996	NR	0.41	2	0.82
Men	NR	1.73	2	0.42
Women	NR	1.58	2	0.45

Note: We tested a null hypothesis of equal distribution between those respondents with increasing prices and those without, and the distribution of amounts smoked in the current wave.

Table 8.6 Cross tabulation of price expectations and current cigarette consumption

	Level of usual current daily consumption (percent)			
	Total	Less than a pack	One pack	More than a pack
One-year-ahead monthly trend in prices				
Stable or declining	16.90	15.08	17.37	19.29
Increasing	83.10	84.92	82.63	80.71
Two-year-ahead monthly trend in prices				
Stable or declining	3.04	2.91	2.95	3.41
Increasing	96.96	97.09	97.05	96.59

tests. With the one-period-ahead test, 17 percent of the observations experienced stable or declining prices in the year following their reported cigarette consumption. By contrast, with the two periods ahead, only 3 percent experienced stable or declining trends.

In our sample, women smoked about 20 percent less than men (16.7 versus 20.9 cigarettes as the usual daily consumption). Using the, Goldfarb, and Leonard (1999) analysis, we would expect that individuals' responses to anticipated price increases would be affected by how adjustment costs change when cigarette consumption is reduced. Given that women smoke less, we can use gender to evaluate whether, as a group, the response to anticipated future prices is different for those smoking less. We tested for differences in response by gender. This disaggregation suggests that support for adjacent complementarity with one-year-ahead price trends comes from women's, not men's responses. There are no pronounced differences in the patterns of price movements (17.7 percent stable or declining prices for men and 16.1 percent for women). Yet women respond to the anticipated price increases and men do not. We pursued these differences further by considering whether completion of college and high school could serve as indicators of greater ability to form price expectations.

Although a college degree was not an informative factor in discriminating among responses, high school was. Moreover, this was also true only for women. Thus, we have the strongest support (despite a smaller sample size) for adjacent complementarity using a sample of female smokers with at least a high school degree. The limited number of cases with stable or declining prices two years ahead precluded our gaining further insights into the role of gender and education in formation of longer time-horizon price expectations.

Overall, then, we have found consistent evidence supporting a role for anticipated future cigarette prices and an effect for adjacent complementarity attributed to the addictive nature of cigarettes. These findings arise primarily with groups that smoke less (women). Heavier smokers may experience larger adjustment costs and follow the "cold turkey" strategy discussed by Suranovic and colleagues (1999).

Basic Demand Results

Table 8.7 reports our primary demand models. The demand models use a double log specification with the current consumption of cigarettes, specified as a function of the lagged consumption, the BLS tobacco price index, and household income. With this functional form, parameters on explanatory variables in logs are estimates of the respective elasticities. Age, binary variables for the direction of future price movements, gender, a binary variable for whether a smoker consumes alcoholic beverages, and the longevity-expectations measure enter linearly.

The first three columns report ordinary least squares (OLS) estimates of cigarette demand pooling responses to waves 2 and 3. The specification given in the first equation is our preferred model. Price, longevity expectations, the binary variable indicating a positive trend in future price movements, gender, and an indicator for whether a respondent currently consumes alcohol are all statistically significant determinants of demand. The estimated price elasticity of -0.18 is at the low end of the range of elasticity estimates and comparable to Wasserman et al. (1991) and other estimates for the price elasticity of those who smoke in studies that distinguish the consumption and participation decision. Income has a positive effect but is statistically insignificant, also consistent with recent studies based on individual data.

Our results for the price expectations variable confirm the nonparametric results. The expectation of price increases is a negative and significant determinant of cigarette demand. This equation also includes the smoker's current longevity expectations. This term is intended to reflect each individual's perceived risks from their smoking behavior. Higher longevity expectations, all else equal, are consistent with lower levels of cig-

Table 8.7 Demand for cigarettes by older adults

	OLS estimates			IV estimates	
Explanatory variables	1	2	3	4	5
Price	−0.18	−0.07	−0.18	−0.18	−0.05
	(−2.87)	(−1.43)	(−3.20)	(−2.87)	(−0.84)
Income	0.01	0.01	0.02	0.03	0.02
	(0.61)	(0.94)	(1.14)	(2.00)	(1.74)
Prices one year ahead up (= 1)	−0.09	−0.04		−0.09	−0.04
	(−2.16)	(−1.28)		(−2.08)	(−1.00)
Longevity expectations	−0.22	−0.10		−0.55	−0.10
	(−3.77)	(−2.30)		(−4.85)	(−1.92)
Respondent drinks alcoholic beverages (= 1)	0.08	0.06		0.08	0.05
	(3.98)	(4.22)		(4.28)	(3.43)
Gender (male = 1)	0.16	0.03	0.20	0.15	0.02
	(3.98)	(0.89)	(5.58)	(4.21)	(0.40)
Age (of wave 1)	−0.01	0.00		−0.01	0.00
	(−1.21)	(−0.35)		(−1.82)	(−0.61)
Cigarette consumption in previous wave		0.62			0.70
		(16.52)			(4.17)
Intercept	3.32	1.09	2.70	3.48	0.84
	(8.57)	(3.72)	(17.28)	(9.63)	(1.33)
Number of observations	2540	2414	2956	2252	2342
R^2	0.03	0.35	0.02	0.03	0.35

Note: Numbers in parentheses are *t*-values.

arette demand. Moreover, the sign and statistical significance of this effect is not influenced by treating longevity expectations as a variable that is jointly determined with the quantity of cigarettes demanded. The fifth column in the table reports the two-stage least-squares estimates, labeled as instrumental variable (IV) estimates. The estimated effect for the longevity expectations remains negative and statistically significant, but the absolute magnitude of the parameter is substantially larger with the adjustment for simultaneity.

Table 8.8 reports the first-stage equation for longevity expectations. As seen in the table, our primary instrumental variables are past serious health effects, an indicator variable for whether or not the respondent's

Table 8.8 First-stage models for instrumental variable estimates

Explanatory variables	Cigarette consumption in previous wave	Longevity expectation in current wave
Price in same wave	−0.26	—
	(−3.89)	—
At least one parent living	−0.11	0.04
	(−3.24)	(2.83)
Experienced cancer in same wave (= 1)	−0.06	−0.04
	(−0.83)	(1.26)
Experienced lung disease in same wave (= 1)	0.24	−0.05
	(4.44)	(−2.45)
Experienced heart attack in same wave (= 1)	0.03	−0.05
	(0.36)	(−1.51)
Experienced congestive heart failure (CHF) in same wave (= 1)	−0.13	−0.06
	(−0.82)	(−1.06)
Longevity expectations in previous wave	—	0.48
	—	(25.57)
Intercept	3.15	0.30
	(37.26)	(22.52)
Number of observations	2,735	2,383
R^2	0.02	0.04

Note: Numbers in parenthesis are *t*-values.

parents were alive at the interview date, and the past wave's longevity expectation.

A Hausman (1978) likelihood ratio test for the null hypothesis that the longevity expectation variable can be treated as exogenous fails to reject the null hypothesis (= 1.72, degrees of freedom = 7, p-value = 0.15). Nonetheless, in terms of signs on coefficients and their consistency with a priori expectations and the precision of our estimates (and especially the income term), the IV estimates of the basic model would seem to be the preferred set (Table 8.7). The primary difference in the results is the magnitude of the effect attributed to longevity expectations, the variable treated as jointly determined with cigarette consumption. For this variable, the IV estimate is nearly twice as large in absolute value as its OLS counterpart. With the other coefficients in the same order of magnitude, a choice between the two models will make a major difference in the effect we attribute to the information treatment. As a result, both sets of results are presented, but to be conservative, we rely on the smaller OLS estimates for our policy analysis.

One of the remaining models in the table compares our model with a simple, sparsely parameterized demand specification in the third column to evaluate the sensitivity of the price elasticity to these other variables. The estimate remains virtually identical to the OLS estimate with a more complete specification.

The second and fifth columns in Table 8.7 report OLS and IV estimates for specifications that include lagged consumption. This additional term substantially reduces the estimated price elasticity; the coefficient on price indicates a negative but statistically insignificant influence of price on demand. The parameter estimate for longevity expectations remains negative and is marginally significant. Support for adjacent complementarity is now split between this new term and the binary variable for the trend in future price movements. The latter remains negative but is no longer statistically significant. The IV estimates for this model specification are not improvements. Of the primary hypothesized determinants, only longevity expectations remain significant at the 10 percent level. The Hausman statistic for a test of exogeneity of the past consumption level is not well defined for this case.

Two alternative issues were considered as part of our evaluation of different models. The first involved an adapted version of the Becker-Murphy rational addiction specification including both lagged and future consumption, in addition to our simple one-period price-expectation measure to test for complementarity. Table 8.9 reports the OLS and IV estimates using the instrumental variables given in Table 8.8 in combination with our qualitative variable for the direction of future price movements. The second set of models distinguishes demand by gender, motivated in part by the results of our nonparametric tests of the price expectations measure.

The OLS results support inclusion of lagged and future consumption measures. Both are positive and significant determinants of demand, but the price and price expectation measures do not have statistically significant impacts when they are included. The longevity expectations measure remains a negative and statistically significant influence (at the 5 percent level). The estimated parameters for the lagged future consumption agree with prior expectations and reflect the effect of discounting. A Hausman test indicates that adjustment for endogeneity of the longevity expectations variable is not warranted.

Given the impact of this specification on the estimates for the effects of the current price, as well as our price expectations measure, we selected the simpler model as our final demand specification. By using a discrete indicator of forward-looking behavior, we avoid the effects of multicollinearity and can also accommodate partial depreciation of the addictive stock, foresight, and take into account the effect of adjacent complementarity.

Our nonparametric tests suggest that there are differences in the temporal complementarity for men and women. These could be due to different smoking histories or a greater propensity to take price behavior into account.[27] Whatever the cause, the gender-based differences in price responsiveness reinforce the importance of allowing for differences in the impact of the addictive stock on individual demand.

The last two columns in Table 8.9 provide parametric demand estimates supporting the results of these cross tabulations. Here we compare the estimates for gender-differentiated demand functions. The estimates suggest that women seem to be more responsive to price, with the price elasticity twice as large in absolute magnitude as the former estimates.[28] For both men and women, the results suggest demand responses to anticipated price that are consistent with adjacent complementarity, but the estimated parameters are not statistically significant.

There is another interesting distinction in the demand functions estimated for men and women. Nearly all of our demand specifications confirm complementarity between drinking alcoholic beverages and cigarette

Table 8.9 Further test of rational addiction and gender-based demand effects

	Rational addiction		Gender-based demand	
Explanatory variables	OLS	IV	Male	Female
Price	−0.04	−0.04	−0.11	−0.25
	(−0.99)	(−0.57)	(−1.17)	(−2.94)
Income	0.02	0.03	0.03	0.04
	(1.36)	(1.75)	(1.11)	(1.76)
Price one year ahead up (=1)	−0.03	0.05	−0.09	−0.10
	(−1.00)	(0.52)	(−1.30)	(−1.60)
Longevity expectations	−0.09	−0.03	−0.38	−0.71
	(−2.13)	(−0.30)	(−2.25)	(−4.69)
Respondent drinks alcoholic beverages (= 1)	0.05	0.02	0.06	0.12
	(3.73)	(0.62)	(2.32)	(3.99)
Gender	0.03	0.02		
	(1.48)	(0.33)		
Age (at wave 1)	0.00	0.01	−0.01	−0.01
	(0.59)	(0.66)	(−1.10)	(−1.72)
Cigarette consumption in previous wave	0.51	0.01		
	(17.24)	(0.01)		
Cigarette consumption in current wave	0.20	0.91		
	(7.65)	(1.09)		
Intercept	0.60	0.20	3.45	3.77
	(2.53)	(−0.17)	(6.34)	(7.62)
Number of observations	2,206	2,047	1,018	1,234
R^2	0.39		0.02	0.00
Chi-square (*p*-value)		2.00		
		(0.99)		

Note: Unless otherwise indicated, numbers in parentheses are *t*-values.

demand. Smokers who said at the interview that they consume alcoholic beverages also smoked more. This result holds for both men and women, but it is about twice as large for women than for men. This finding contrasts with the results from Decker and Schwartz (2000) suggesting comparable but only marginally significant complementarity relationships for men and women's cigarette demand with alcohol when the effect was measured with a price effect for beer.

A Chow test (Chow 1960) rejects the hypothesis of equality of all the demand parameters between the models for men and women at the 1 percent level, $F(9,2526) = 3.69$. This result is consistent with evidence from our nonparametric tests of price expectations; that is, women exhibit a different response pattern to future price movement than men. If we consider the differences in the two groups, then their different demand responses are consistent with the hypothesis that higher levels of smoking, and the associated higher adjustment costs of stopping, lead to different patterns of adjustment. Gradual reduction is more consistent with lower adjustment costs (and less pronounced addiction). This pattern is consistent with the behavior found for women in the HRS sample, and lower adjustment costs may well be the reason. A failure to observe a response on the part of men may simply reflect the all-or-nothing behavior attributed to the high adjustment cost group. In analysis reported below, we present a model that includes a binary variable distinguishing the level of demand of men and women, but we do not allow other parameters to differ. The main reason for relying on this restrictive form is the small sample available for our test of information treatments.[29]

Evaluating the Effect of the COPD Information Treatment for Cigarette Demand

Our research has argued that a more complete understanding of smokers' behavior requires integrating models of their perception of the risks of premature death with models that capture the addictive effects of smoking. Our theoretical analysis implies that when this is done we find that the effects of pricing policy on demand also depend on those risk perceptions.

Most observers' personal experience (including our own) suggests that the American consumer receives a large number of messages from reliable sources about the risks of smoking. Nonetheless, as discussed in Chapter 5, our analysis of longevity expectations for the HRS sample indicates that smokers respond differently to risk information and that heavy smokers may understate the health consequences of their behavior.

In Chapter 7, we described two new approaches to presenting smoking risk messages. One was based on more detailed information about the relative risks of smoking related diseases and attempted to personalize the risks messages to each respondent's experience. The message using an individual's own experience was labeled the relative risk treatment. The second was based on describing the "quality of life" effects associated with diseases linked to long-term smoking. It focused on limitations in carrying out personal activities toward the end of life that are common to virtually all of the smoking-related diseases. This was labeled the COPD information treatment. We found that this information message and not the one associated with relative risks had a significant impact in reducing smokers' longevity expectations. The magnitude of response varied among smokers and was related in part to cognitive ability and to the amount they smoked. To gauge the potential importance of this effect, we developed a simple computation to mimic what might be the impact of a policy experiment.

Table 8.10 provides the results of a simple exercise that combines results from Chapter 7 with our preferred demand model and the actual characteristics of the older smokers in the HRS sample. We classified responses by gender and amount smoked. The analysis is intended to provide a quantitative gauge of the effect that the COPD information treatment might have.

Based on our estimates, the COPD information treatment reduced the usual daily consumption of cigarettes by 11 to 15 percent, depending on the smoker's gender and amount smoked. We found the largest response for women who were heavy smokers (using the composite demand model) and the smallest for men. Before turning to the specifics and considering the size of the required price change to realize an equivalent reduction, we provide a brief overview of the process used to develop these estimates.

Our analysis of the demographically matched sample receiving the COPD information and HRS subsample implied that longevity expectations would be reduced from the baseline levels when smokers were aware of these end-of-life health consequences. We assumed that when smokers form their subjective beliefs about how long they will live, these expectations include their personal recognition of the links between their individual behavior and the risks they face. That is, there is consistency between their steady-state behavior and the voluntary risks they believe they face.

Table 8.10 Effects of the COPD information treatment on cigarette demand

Policy outcome	Current level of smoking (no. cigarettes)		
	Less than one pack	One Pack	More than One Pack
Usual daily smoking levels (cigarettes)—Women			
Longevity expectations: exogenous			
Actual behavior (average)	9.05	20	38.05
Baseline prediction	13.80	14.15	14.58
With COPD information	12.12	12.18	12.25
Difference	−1.68	−1.97	−2.25
Longevity expectations: endogenous			
Actual behavior (average)	9.03	20	37.99
Baseline prediction	13.87	14.37	15.13
With COPD information	9.98	9.88	9.92
Difference	−3.88	−4.50	−5.21
Usual daily smoking level (cigarettes)—Men			
Longevity expectations: exogenous			
Actual behavior (average)	8.96	20	38.79
Baseline prediction	16.9	17.18	17.74
With COPD information	14.95	14.96	15.09
Difference	−1.91	−2.19	−2.61
Longevity expectations: endogenous			
Actual behavior (average)	9.04	20	38.81
Baseline prediction	17.33	17.73	18.52
With COPD information	12.78	12.53	12.32
Difference	−4.52	−5.14	−6.11

Note: COPD = chronic obstructive pulmonary disease.

Any change in the information they have will lead to a change in behavior that aligns their behavior with new risk beliefs. Our smoking demand models support this view of the expectations formation process. Smokers with high assessments of their prospects of living to seventy-five tend to smoke *less,* while those who have lower assessments have heavier typical consumption patterns.

An information policy that disturbs this equilibrium, suggesting to the smoker that his or her longevity perception is inconsistent with their current beliefs and behavior, should lead to adjustment in cigarette consumption behavior. We hypothesize that this adjustment leads to a drop in the amount smoked and corresponding adjustments in the longevity expectation to achieve consistency between decisions and risk perceptions. By reducing cigarette consumption, the adjustment has the effect of realigning the original longevity expectation. The information policy leads to the update, and the hypothesized reduction in cigarette use is the way we assume smokers adapt to make their behavior consistent with their longevity beliefs. Under this view of the adjustment process, the modified smoking level brings longevity expectations into alignment with the longevity expectation that is associated with the new information. Thus, the consumer is more realistic about the effect of his or her smoking habit.

Our follow-up interviews of the Raleigh matched sample several months after the information treatment was administered suggested that after several months respondents had a sustained acceptance of the new information and had begun to reduce their usual cigarette consumption. Although the sample was small, we found a statistically significant response, even six months after the COPD information treatment was administered. Of course, we cannot know whether the effect of the information treatment was permanent.

Using the maintained assumption that smokers seek to modify behavior to realize the consistent longevity expectations at their baseline level, we can compute how the new information affects cigarette demand. The quantity demand must adjust to compensate for the reduced longevity expectations associated with the new information.

We first computed the COPD information treatment's effect on updating of longevity expectations, using estimates from the first column of Table 7.2 (Chapter 7). The numerical effects of the cognitive variable and smoking levels are approximately the same, irrespective of the criteria used to select respondents from the HRS sample.

To provide an example of how our information policy would be evaluated, we limited our computation to this first matched sample. Computing differences for our sample of smokers based on their demographic characteristics, prices faced, and existing longevity expectations in each of the two waves provided the results we present in Table 8.10.

The reductions in usual smoking vary, depending on the estimate used from the demand model. Using the OLS estimates of demand including men and women in the same model (with an intercept shift based on gender), the smoking reductions range from 1.68 to 2.61 cigarettes per day, depending on gender and the initial level of usual daily consumption. For example, a woman smoking about a pack a day is estimated to experience about a 14 percent decline, while a man with the same level of consumption is estimated to experience a 13 percent decline. Using estimates from the model in which longevity expectations were treated as endogenous implies a 31 percent decline for women and 29 percent for men.

Based on the respective estimates of the price elasticity of demand, these reductions would require quite large increases in price—more than 70 percent based on the OLS demand elasticity. With the IV estimates, price increases would exceed 150 percent. These differences in the estimated response are due to the larger estimated effect for the longevity expectations as an influence on cigarette demand. When we tested for the simultaneity in these specifications using a Hausman test, we could not reject the null hypothesis of exogeneity. Thus, while the IV parameter estimates appear to be numerically different, the variation in the estimates is large enough that we cannot conclude cigarette demand and longevity expectations are jointly determined.[30] Thus, we used the smaller estimated price effect to develop our simple policy scenario.

The COPD information message offers a clear prospect for reducing usual cigarette consumption. Using the most conservative demand estimates, estimates of impact from this information intervention suggest that a 40 to 50 percent increase in the price of cigarettes would be needed to achieve a steady-state reduction in demand equivalent to the information intervention. Of course, these results rely on the presumption that, in response to the intervention, smokers adjust their behavior to align their longevity expectations with what they infer from the COPD information.

We found that the demand model overpredicts low levels of smoking and underpredicts the high levels. There is no reason to expect that this would cause the model to overestimate the effect of the information treatment. If anything, the double log specification would likely understate the impact at intermediate levels of consumption. Our computations ignore any impact working through the rational addiction framework, and consider only the one-time impact of the price policy. The estimated effect for recognizing future price increases translate[31] into about an 8 percent decline in current demand when future prices are expected to increase. Thus, a smaller permanent price increase may well accomplish the same reduction in the amount of smoking as the information treatment.

Conclusions

This chapter has covered a lot of ground. We began with economic concepts for modeling addictive goods, presenting and extending the rational addiction framework. We explained the framework and provided a link between longevity expectations and smoking decisions within the context of the rational addiction model.

We began our empirical analysis by using a new cigarette price series to study forward-looking behavior, based on an approach proposed by Gruber and Köszegi (2001). While there are limitations in our ability to track anticipated price changes far into the future, our evidence nonetheless suggests on balance that female smokers in this age cohort are forward looking in the sense that price changes anticipated to occur in the future are reflected in current cigarette consumption. In this sense, our results support those of Gruber and Köszegi.

Following tests for forward-looking behavior, we turned to our empirical analysis of cigarette demand. Our key finding is that smokers in this age cohort respond to both information and price interventions. We computed the equivalent demand response from an information intervention and from a policy of increasing cigarette prices, presumably by increases in state excise taxes on cigarettes. Calculating the tax increase that would be required to accomplish the same reduction as information provides a direct gauge of the scale of the impact. The result is quite supportive of a new approach to providing information about the long-term health effects of smoking.

However, before expecting those charged with the responsibility of tobacco control policy to "dance in the streets," some caveats are in order. First, the effect applies to smokers in late middle age. A message that smoking may lead to the inability to care for oneself may not be effective for younger individuals, who may take "caring for themselves" (and their parents) for granted. Second, our result is based on one information message, which though probably generalizable beyond chronic obstructive pulmonary disease, may not be typical of all adverse health effects attributable to smoking. The fact that our other information message did not reduce longevity expectations gives us some pause. Third, as seen in Chapter 7, we found residual effects of the message within six months of the time it was administered; We do not know about longer-term effects. Fourth, we have pieced together our estimates of effects of the information message from

Chapter 7 with the effect of longevity expectations on demand estimated in this chapter. Although we may be viewed as congratulating ourselves for milking the data we had available to us, this limitation is worth noting nevertheless.

Fifth, our simple variation on the Becker-Murphy (1988) theoretical structure, including both risk and adjacent complementarity into their framework, and some common sense suggest that there may be even greater effects on smokers' longevity expectations and hence on cigarette demand from strategies that combine price increases with information policies. In fact, this is what California has done, with some favorable results from a public health vantage point (Fichtenberg and Glantz 2000). Price increases may be a relatively more effective policy than information more younger persons. However, worldwide, hundreds of millions of persons are mature smokers. Even if the success of the information intervention is localized to mature adults, this does not mean that it is has a small social benefit—quite the contrary.

Finally, in an ideal world, we would seek to vary information messages on the adverse health effects of smoking and cigarette prices, to evaluate their composite effect. This was not possible given the resources available for our study. At best we could have considered stated preference models that included price variation as one of the potential hypothetical treatments. Overall, our results point in the direction of a redesign of smoking information materials. They identify the areas where further research is needed to confirm whether our simple estimates of their potential impact are likely to be realized with a broad-based modification of the information used to describe the health consequences of smoking.

CHAPTER

9

Conclusions and Policy Implications

Cigarettes are a product of the twentieth century. The growth of this industry over the century created enormous wealth, gave rise to the only major new U.S. research university to be established in the twentieth century (Duke University), and got more people addicted worldwide than have all the illegal drugs to date.

Smoking cigarettes must be close to the top of nearly every adult's list of bad choices. Yet after four decades of sustained public warnings on the hazards of smoking, many adults continue to smoke.

An inquiry into the factors influencing smokers' choices, their beliefs about the risks they incur from smoking, and their responses to information about its full health consequences offers an opportunity to consider more general questions about how personal decisions are made. Are people rational? Why do some people engage in behaviors that are potentially harmful to their own health while others do not? How do people interpret and use information about risks to their health? How do people handle uncertainty, especially about events that are more likely to occur in the distant future? What factors precipitate changes in health behavior?

We have summarized the literature and presented new empirical evidence on information, risk perception, and smoking behavior. There are numerous studies on risk taking and risk bearing in many spheres of human activity. We have chosen to focus on a single decision involving risk and to investigate this decision from several perspectives.

Although social scientists have studied choices made under uncertainty for many years, consensus is lacking. Two prominent economists who have spent much of their careers studying consumer choices have quite different views. Daniel McFadden (1999) has argued that evidence from psychologists is sufficiently compelling to warrant questioning the narrow view of rational choice—what he terms "Chicago man." This Chicago approach is reflected in the rational addiction model described in Chapter 8. Mark Machina (1999), by contrast, describes his own research perspective as one that treats the classical model of rationality as fundamentally correct, but with some modifications to incorporate factors not accounted for by the classical model. He has remained confident of his strategy even in light of McFadden's detailed appraisal and differing judgment.

Psychologists tend to paint the future even more starkly than economist McFadden by stressing people's propensity to make mistakes. They tend to stress the limits individuals face in making personal decisions. Economists such as Machina tend to stress individuals' ability to make decisions that enhance their personal welfare.

Our discussion of findings and implications in this chapter is organized according to the implicit goal expressed in the title of this book, to break down the smoking puzzle into its constituent elements—information, risk perception, and smoking behavior. After discussing findings under these headings, we will discuss public policy implications, several overarching issues to which our research applies, and, finally, unresolved issues and an agenda for future research.

Information

Information about the dangers of smoking has been an important aspect of public health policy in the United States since the mid-1960s (Chapters 1 and 3). Public information strategies have taken the form of publications, such as surgeon generals' reports, public antismoking messages (such as those displayed on billboards), restrictions on advertising, and requirements that specific messages be displayed on cigarette packs. In addition, smoking is now banned in many public places, places of employment, and in other areas subject to government regulation, such as on airplanes. These bans not only impose additional costs on smokers by making it more inconvenient to smoke but also signal of public attitudes and thereby convey information, at least indirectly, about the hazards of smoking.

One view in the argument over the proper role of policy is that people ought to have access to information about the probabilities of harm associated with various personal choices they make, and that any disregard of relevant information is a private matter, not a public one. In general, policy should be designed to respect the sovereignty of people's (at least adults') consumption decisions. Government intervention is seen as appropriate only when consumption decisions have clear external effects; requiring vaccination against communicable diseases would be one example.

Probably most economists, but not all, share this view. A leading advocate of the position in the context of smoking is W. Kip Viscusi. Viscusi (1992) argued that the main objective of information programs should be to inform a sovereign consumer about the underlying incremental risks of smoking and then to let the individual decide. By simply stating that "smoking is bad for you," such information programs have not fulfilled their welfare-enhancing role (Chapter 5). Viscusi has criticized public information programs in the context of smoking, noting that the messages ask people to change their tastes rather than offering objective data on the probabilities of suffering a smoking-related illness. Quantitative evidence of smoking's harms has been provided in large amounts in the scholarly literature for decades (Chapter 1), but it has not made it to health messages about the adverse effects of smoking.

Our findings suggest that more detailed and personalized risk messages focusing on the probabilities of dying from a smoking-related disease, an approach Viscusi appears to advocate, are ineffective. The notion that smoking kills apparently is not news to most people (Chapter 7). But information about the impact on quality of life of a smoking-related disease *is* news and does cause smokers to change their perceptions of the risk associated with smoking.

In our focus groups and the empirical analysis based on our survey of current smokers, we found that smokers were more likely to respond to new information about smoking-induced disability than to further information about the risks of premature death from smoking. Respondents' subjective beliefs about their longevity were affected when they were told how smoking led to restrictions in daily activities and the ability to function on one's own, as a result of chronic obstructive pulmonary disease. Our results suggest that smokers would act to avert those types of health effects that would make them more reliant on others, especially relatives and friends. The prospect of losing their ability to manage everyday activities and of requiring extensive care is one that definitely gets their attention; it is among their most dreaded risks. Developing messages that believably describe the prospects for these types of outcomes is a strategy our research suggests is likely to be effective.

We have interpreted these results as indicating that smokers think about both probabilities and the outcomes of risk. When they conceive of premature death as an "easy passage," the trade-off between a little more or less risk due to their smoking choice is apparently resolved with the decision to continue smoking. When smokers realized that the transition would be to a lower quality of life—not the easy passage they anticipated—they seemed to focus more on the risk they were taking by smoking. Thus, all risk messages are not created equal. In sum, providing probabilities to the smoker, what McFadden (1999) describes as the "Chicago man's" approach, does not work. We do not overturn consumer sovereignty or rationality, but rather conclude that *risk and context* need to be presented together.

An alternative to the Chicago view is a more activist public policy. Proponents cite two premises in their call for active engagement of the public sector. One, government intervention is needed to correct smoking's serious externalities (see Chapter 1). Two, people are essentially incapable of processing, or at least unwilling to process, the information as presented, and cognitive limits might pose a fundamental barrier to the effectiveness of quantitative information. Unwillingness to process information stems in part from a perceived lack of salience of the message. In either case, the policy implication is the same: Merely providing quantitative information about the probabilities of harms associated with personal choices will be ineffective. A more activist policy involves, among other things, various bans on dissemination of the product and direct bans on the activity—not only enactment but active enforcement of laws and regulations.

Based on our research, we take an intermediate view. Our results imply that an information policy *can* work, but not just any information policy. Clearly, not all messages are salient, even those that seem to make logical sense. Indeed, some people seem to require experiencing a major health shock, such as a heart attack, to get the message that smoking is harmful to *their own* health. Further, some messages evidently have been misinterpreted. For example, in our focus group sessions we learned that some smokers reason that "if it's never too late to quit," why not postpone quitting? The intent of the message was to give older smokers (truthful) information and encourage them to realize some benefit in terms of increased survival if they quit. For information programs to succeed, a considerable amount of sophistication in message development and delivery is necessary.

In none of our focus groups did we hear a comment from current or former smokers echoing the line of the tobacco companies for almost all of the twentieth century, that deleterious effects of smoking had not been proven. Everyone acknowledged that smoking is harmful. This impression is reinforced with data from other sources.[1]

Some of the current smokers in our focus groups believed that smoking was harmful in general but less harmful to them personally because of their "good" genes. Many current smokers in these groups had been convinced by the public service antismoking messages that they have time. For them, the effects of smoking are reversible. With their "good genes," they can "enjoy" their habit a bit longer, stop later, and be none the worse off.

Although heavy smokers were more likely to be optimistic about their chances of living to age seventy-five than were others (Chapters 5 and 7), they were not *that* optimistic. They gave themselves too much credit in terms of increased life expectancy when they quit, but this finding indicates that smokers are well aware of the risks associated with smoking, not that they are unaware.

Much of the information people acquire about smoking and its effects comes from peers, friends, and relatives.[2] Because susceptibility to smoking-related diseases is inherited—certainly the belief of current and former smokers in our focus groups—people pay particular attention to the smoking-related experiences of their close blood relatives as well as to experiences with their own health.

Many smokers in their fifties and sixties receive highly personalized health messages in the form of adverse health events more likely to occur among smokers (Chapter 4). A finding that the health of persons in late middle age is adversely affected by smoking can hardly be considered news. In particular, mortality effects are well documented. However, disability impacts arising from to smoking are less well documented. Using a panel spanning a six-year period that measured health and functional status as well as risk perception, smoking behavior, and many other factors, we found appreciable rates of onset of smoking-related disease and disability for persons in the sixth and seventh decades of life.

Although the risk of adverse outcomes in late middle age is elevated among smokers, the amount of variation in susceptibility to smoking-related diseases is appreciable. Mean values indeed do not typify most persons' future prospects, giving comfort to those who think that they have inherited good genes. Perhaps with the advances in gene technology, health professionals will be able to provide much more precise, patient-specific advice about the health risks of smoking. Such advice may be viewed by smokers as much more credible.

The variation in the historical record of public policy reflects the lack of social consensus about the appropriate role of government involvement in this sphere. At one level of stringency, the role of the regulatory authority is merely to see that claims made by manufacturers are accurate. In this role, governments rely on data provided by private enterprises, challenging the blatantly false claims. Alternately, the public sector can take a more active role as an independent monitor of claims by conducting independent assessments of pertinent product characteristics. In the context of smoking, claims about tar and nicotine content have been subject to Federal Trade Commission review, with the FTC conducting its own independent assessments (Chapters 1 and 3). The FTC has not required provision of probabilities of harm from smoking.

At a more stringent level of regulation are entry controls, such as those enforced by the Food and Drug Administration for pharmaceutical products and medical devices. FDA regulation entails a combination of activities, including oversight to guard against misleading claims by manufacturers and protection from unsafe products. The FDA is empowered, for example, to ban a product outright if it concludes that the product is too dangerous to the public relative to its potential benefit.

During the late 1990s there were efforts to make nicotine subject to FDA regulation as a drug. Cigarettes would then have to be considered drug delivery systems. The FDA argued that tobacco products have druglike properties. Cigarette manufacturers vigorously opposed such regulation, and they have succeeded to date. In 2000, the U.S. Supreme Court ruled by a vote of five to four that the FDA did not have jurisdiction over cigarettes (Chapter 3). While recognizing tobacco's harms to health, the majority on the court argued that Congress had not given the FDA jurisdiction over tobacco products. We have not heard the last word on FDA oversight of tobacco products. Depending on the balance of power between the opposing legislative forces and the composition of the U.S. Supreme Court, the issue seems likely to be revisited in the near future.

However, even the FDA does not require provision of probabilities of good and bad outcomes from the pharmaceutical products and devices under its scrutiny. Nor are probabilities provided in other contexts.[3]

Private enterprises either release or fail to release pertinent information about their products, which in turn affects consumption decisions. From a public perspective, it seems straightforward that companies should always release information on the risks of consuming their products. But from a *private* perspective, is it advisable for companies to release such information as soon as they know it? Would this not expose them unduly to tort claims and adverse publicity? In the initial stages of research, knowledge of adverse effects is likely to be tentative, especially for long-run effects. At what point in the information-gathering process is the underlying knowledge sufficiently certain to justify public release? What is the appropriate role of such enterprises in an environment in which the underlying parameters are first known only with considerable uncertainty, as was the case for the health effects of smoking during the first half of the twentieth century?

Of course, to ask tobacco manufacturers to publicize the adverse effects of their products may be asking more of them than we ask of others. After all, even the pharmaceutical industry does not boast of the adverse effects of its products. It simply complies with regulations requiring that potential adverse effects be acknowledged. As a rule, this type of information is conveyed to consumers in small print or in a spokesperson's monotone, as unobtrusively as possible.

The public health community in general and the tobacco control community in particular have been quite willing to heap blame on the cigarette manufacturers for withholding pertinent evidence on the harmful effects of smoking, a position with which we have sympathy. However, critics of the conduct of tobacco companies have been much less willing to blame government agencies on this score. One speculation is that many of the critics do not know the history of the public sector role in tobacco policy in the twentieth century.

We now know that public health officials were unwilling to take a public stance on the harmful effects of smoking even after they had accumulated fairly strong epidemiological evidence of this relationship, in part because these officials feared the loss of political support from the tobacco growing states (Chapter 1). Such a loss of support, it was feared, could have taken the concrete form of reductions in congressional appropriations. Publication of the first surgeon general's report in 1964 changed all that. In fact, with hindsight the significance of the report was more as an indicator of a change in public policy than in its release of new scientific evidence. The same criticism can be levied against the media, who feared loss of advertising revenue from tobacco manufacturers if they publicized the health harms from smoking. The decline in cigarette and tobacco consumption during the second half of the twentieth century (Chapter 1) might have occurred faster if the manufacturers had been more honest about the harmful effects of their product or had both engaged in research on adverse health effects from smoking *and* publicized such results.

Since the new empirical research presented in this book was based on data drawn from the 1990s and samples of persons in late middle age, we are limited in what we can say about the allegations against the cigarette manufacturers. We did not assess youth smoking. The smokers in our samples were teenagers in the 1940s and 1950s, before or at the time that information about smoking's harms was just becoming known, even to health scientists (Chapter 1). Even if these smokers were duped many decades ago, they had had quite a bit of time to assimilate truthful information from many sources, including the media, their physicians, and others.

Risk Perception

Many economists, and even more noneconomists, are convinced that when individuals are asked to formulate probabilities, they are unlikely to do so correctly (see, for example, Machina 1990). However, many of the same analysts would probably add that people do have a reasonably articulated—if biased—internal scale of risk perception. Some psychologists argue that preferences, especially for goods not typically consumed, are so ill-formed that eliciting choices to infer consumers' values and preferences requires that special attention be paid to the process. In effect, there is a "building code" that helps people construct their preferences in new situations (see Payne, Bettman, and Schkade 1999).

Among economists and psychologists there is no consensus on the extent of bias in risk perception or whether risk perceptions are a well-formed construct at the individual level. For the most part, available evidence on risk perception stems from simple laboratory experiments and comparisons of subjective and expert risk assessments for a diverse array of activities (Fischhoff et al. 1993). Current public policy associated with many different sources of risk implicitly trusts that these biases are not substantial. With few exceptions, there has been no opportunity to gauge biases in risk perceptions outside the setting of laboratory experiments.

Using longitudinal data from the Health and Retirement Study, we studied the reliability of the most important subjective risk assessment a person can make—an expectation of personal longevity. Our approach was to

(1) study risk perceptions about personal longevity as a predictor of actual longevity, (2) determine how subjective longevity expectations are updated, and (3) study the link between subjective longevity expectations and behavior.

Until now, it has been largely impossible to evaluate how subjective perceptions of mortality predict actual deaths at the individual level. The HRS has changed the landscape for evaluations of risk perception. In our analysis, we took the most complete version of the HRS available and evaluated the relationship between subjective beliefs about mortality and actual deaths at the individual level. We found remarkable, but not complete, consistency.

Three distinct conclusions emerged from our analysis of perceptions about personal longevity as a predictor of actual longevity (Chapter 5). First, subjective beliefs about longevity are consistent with observed survival patterns for these same individuals. After accounting for the selected nature of the sample of surviving respondents for each wave of the HRS, we found that observed deaths were "signaled" through the lower longevity expectations those same respondents reported in earlier interviews. Second, over time the evolution of subjective beliefs of those who died during the panel displayed a consistent decline. In contrast, survivors' longevity expectations, on average, were higher and approximately constant over the six-year time span observed in the panel. Third, longevity expectations fell following the occurrence of serious new health shocks and the onset of new functional limitations. Although an individual's longevity expectation was a predictor of actual survival, the subjective probability did not reflect all the private information individuals have about their survival prospects.

We found that for the sample as a whole, HRS respondents were amazingly good at assessing the probability of living to age seventy-five, although the accuracy of subjective assessments varied considerably about the mean value (Chapter 7). Of course, in the cases in which a person gave a subjective assessment that was very different from the corresponding objective one, it is possible that the respondent knew more about his health than we did and he was actually more correct than we thought.

In our analysis of longevity expectation updating, we classified our sample by smoking status, distinguishing between current and former smokers and those who never smoked (Chapter 5). The panel structure of HRS allowed us to investigate how individuals' subjective health beliefs are updated in response to new information. With information on individuals over time, we could know that the health shocks that occurred took place prior to the person's response to the longevity question.

Current smokers reacted differently to health shocks than those who had quit smoking or never smoked. The link between health shocks and subjective assessments of longevity is more complex than previously anticipated. Heavy smokers were more optimistic about their likely survival prospects than their smoking behavior would warrant. When current smokers experienced a smoking-related health shock, such as lung cancer, a heart attack, or a stroke, they interpreted this information as reducing their chances of living to seventy-five or more. In fact, our estimated models imply that current smokers update their longevity expectations more dramatically than either former smokers or those who never smoked; current smokers assigned a larger risk to these shocks. But current smokers did not react comparably to general health shocks that are not considered to be smoking related (such as the onset of diabetes), implying that specific information about smoking-related health events is most likely to cause them to update their beliefs.

We can only speculate why this is so. Perhaps smokers are generally less responsive to health messages. Over time, they have heard repeatedly that cigarette smoking is bad for one's health. They are optimistic that these messages do not apply to them, given their own beliefs about their genetic makeup. They might, as our focus group suggested, believe they still have time to change their behavior. When they receive a health signal that can be attributed to smoking, they realize that the time is up.

We assessed the ability of HRS respondents to give reliable answers to the longevity probability questions. This aspect of our research specifically addressed the issue of cognitive limits (Chapter 2). We gauged a person's ability to give accurate answers to questions about their probability of living to old age, based on whether the respondent gave the same value (0.0, 0.5, or 1.0) to the live-to-seventy-five subjective probability question as to the identically worded live-to-eighty-five question. If the probabilities were the same, we considered this to be a "focal" response.

Two findings were particularly noteworthy. First, persons who had lower cognitive skills, based on the word-recall test administered by the HRS, were more likely to give focal responses, implying that there are bounds on cognitive ability to assess probabilities, but such bounds vary among individuals in predictable ways, such as by the person's education level. Second, we found clear differences between the former or never smokers and current smokers regarding the role of cognitive ability scores in determining the ability to provide plausible longevity responses. The relationship between cognitive ability and focal response was less pronounced for smokers than for the other two groups.

Two implications follow from this result. First, there are indeed cognitive limits on some persons' ability to think about probabilities of future events, including events with a personal impact. Although this may seem obvious, to our knowledge the empirical link between cognitive ability and subjective probability setting had not been established previously. Second, again we found differences in the cognitive processes of smokers versus others. Unfortunately, we could only document the fact that differences exist. We could not determine *why* the differences exist. This should be an important priority for future research on smoking.

In past research it has been hypothesized that smokers are unduly optimistic about their health and the possible adverse health effects of their behavior (Chapters 2 and 5). Using data from a cross section of smokers, Viscusi (1992) found contradictory evidence, namely that people in general, including smokers, overestimated the probability of getting lung cancer. By contrast, we found that heavy smokers tend to be overly optimistic about their longevity prospects and to assign too high a value of life extension from quitting (Chapters 5 and 6). Clearly, survey responses depend on how questions are framed (Chapter 2), and we did not analyze the same question that Viscusi assessed. His question dealt with lung cancer and expressed it as a "third-party" judgment. We focused on longevity expectations in general, where death could be from any cause, and the longevity in question was the respondent's, not some other group's.

A general risk question is really the more relevant one. Although lung cancer is one disease from which smokers die in disproportionate numbers, there are many others (Chapter 4). In particular, smoking has been linked to other lung diseases and to various cardiovascular diseases. Also, if the person has a higher probability of dying prematurely from a smoking-related disease, he is less likely to die from a disease not linked to smoking. Thus, an individual's assessment should be based on a much broader measure than the chances of getting lung cancer alone. Equally important, a person's behavior is more plausibly based on risk expectations that are personal, not what easily could be perceived as a factual question about a detached group.

We asked participants in our focus groups to tell us what they thought was their probability of living to age seventy-five, and we asked them why they gave the value they did (Chapter 7). The HRS has asked the question in each wave, but has not probed into the motivations for specific answers. Many focus group participants who were smokers referred to robust parents who had smoked and lived to an old age. The former smokers on the whole seemed to be more pessimistic about their longevity. They told negative stories about parents or close relatives.

In the experimental component of the survey of smokers we conducted in summer 1999, we sought to evaluate how smoking information affected longevity expectations, so we included two information treatments. Only one succeeded in changing these expectations. That treatment involved information about smoking and the link to chronic obstructive pulmonary disease. Not only is COPD smoking-related and a killer, but it also leads to appreciable disability before death. We found not only that the COPD information treatment affected risk perceptions immediately after the treatment was administered, but also that these risk perceptions seemed unchanged six months later when the respondents were reinterviewed (Chapter 6).

However, when we considered only their preinformation longevity expectations (elicited in the baseline recruiting interview) and the expectations reported six months after the information was presented, we were less able to detect the effect of the information treatment. Signs of the parameter estimates measuring the direction of the effects were comparable to the immediate responses, but the parameter estimates were not statistically significant at conventional levels, reflecting lack of statistical power, at least in part.

Two lessons were learned from this experiment. First, one of the messages, a relatively complex message relating to relative risks of harm from smoking, was not effective. This speaks to the inherent complexity of designing messages that affect risk perceptions and behavior—the bad news. Second—the good news—one of the messages was effective, implying that information programs can succeed if proper attention is given to message design.

Smoking Behavior

The third leg of our analytic stool concerns the effect of information, through risk perception, on smoking behavior. After all, reducing still-high rates of smoking is ultimately the public health goal (see, for example, U.S. Department of Health and Human Services 1991, 2000).

By the sixth and seventh decades of life, the age group on which our analysis is focused, rates of smoking are on the decline by any measure. Smoking rates decrease in part due to premature deaths of smokers and, to a lesser extent, former smokers. But cessation rates also are high.

There appears to be one magic bullet for smoking reduction: experiencing a major adverse health event (Chapter 6). When smokers' lungs and cardiovascular systems are hit, they listen. Our analysis of cessation determinants revealed that people in late middle age do quit after they experience a major health shock. Less serious messages, such as the onset of difficulty walking several blocks or climbing stairs, did not induce people in this age cohort to quit smoking.

Such health shocks constitute highly personalized information. They affect both risk perception *and* behavior. But waiting until such health shocks occur is an unsatisfying solution. Many of these adverse events could be averted if people would act earlier. One would hope that we could develop information messages that operate on behavior through modified risk perception before serious health events occur, thus mitigating smoking's harm.

We examined the influence of risk perception on the decision to smoke (Chapter 6) and on the intensity of smoking (Chapter 8). On the decision to smoke, current smokers were more optimistic about their longevity relative to objective measures of longevity than were other individuals. Overly optimistic persons are likely to believe that if they stop smoking, they will not increase their life expectancy by much, because they are not as prone as others to suffer from smoking-related health shocks.

Of course, as already noted, individuals might know more about their health than they reported to the HRS. But for our finding that on average smokers are overly optimistic about their survival chances to be wrong, such "omitted heterogeneity" in health measurement by the HRS would have to have been systematically biased. In other words, smokers would truly have to be in better health than the many HRS health measures suggested. Although one cannot rule out this explanation, it seems unlikely.

Given the conclusion about smokers' optimism, is there any evidence that the less optimistic among the smokers are more likely to quit? If so, it would be worthwhile to develop interventions that address smokers' undue optimism. We would have preferred to find that optimism matters to smoking behavior, but for cessation, we could not find a statistically significant result for the variable measuring the difference between subjective and objective longevity expectations (Chapter 6).

An alternative, or perhaps complementary, strategy to information interventions is raising the price of cigarettes by excise taxes. We found a substantial impact of price on the probability of cessation. A one-dollar increase in the price of a pack of cigarettes would lower the relative risk of continuing to smoke by 14 percent. However, the underlying parameter estimate was statistically significant at only the 11 percent level, which is slightly below conventional levels of statistical significance.

Smoking intensity was clearly associated with the likelihood of quitting. People who smoked a pack or more a day were about twice as likely to continue to smoke two years hence as those who smoked less than a pack a day. For many individuals, we observed a transition over time from higher levels of daily cigarette consumption to lower levels and finally to cessation. Many smokers quit by gradually reducing the amount of smoking rather than quitting cold turkey, suggesting a strategy for encouraging cessation. If the individual can cut down on smoking frequency, he might more easily quit.

In Chapter 8, we integrated findings on longevity expectations of smokers and their responses to different types of information about the health risks of smoking with new estimates of the demand for cigarettes. Our key finding here is that demand for cigarettes among smokers in late middle age is responsive to both information and price interventions. Holding a number of other variables constant, we found that higher subjective probabilities of living to at least age seventy-five (that is, an increase in the individual's time horizon) reduced cigarette demand. This result held up in specifications estimated with ordinary least squares as well as with instrumental variables.

We found that an information message linking smoking to developing COPD caused cigarette consumption to decline by 11 to 15 percent. This was the same information treatment described above that caused the smokers' longevity expectations to decline. To realize the same reduction in cigarette demand through cigarette price increases would require at least a 40 to 50 percent increase in the price of cigarettes for this group of individuals. Thus, information messages *can* have the desired impact of reducing demand for this harmful product, but, as we learned in our study, not just any message will accomplish this objective.

Since reductions in amounts smoked per day lead to cessation, information programs logically can play an important role in smoking cessation. One issue is the extent to which such reductions in demand are permanent. The reduction in the probability of continuing to smoke six months after the COPD information treatment (Chapter 6) suggests that there is some continuing effect, but it would be unwise to extrapolate from our limited six-month experience to conclude that message reinforcement is not needed. Indeed such reinforcement is probably needed, although our study did not yield information on the desired frequency of such reminders.

The Bottom Line and Public Policy

In sum, a causal chain exists from information to risk perception to smoking behavior. However, we need to know more about the details of effective messages that may change risk perceptions. We need to monitor the permanence of such risk perception changes, as well as of the behavioral changes they induce.

The harm from smoking is substantial and, if anything, has not elicited sufficient public attention. The probability of harm from smoking greatly exceeds the vast majority of other well-publicized risks to which individuals are exposed, such as silicone breast implants, asbestos, or Firestone tires on Ford Explorers, to name a few. This is not a new finding but one well worth emphasizing.

Public intervention against smoking has two important target populations: youths making the decision to start smoking—the key target group for a smoking prevention strategy—and smokers, for whom the goal of public policy is to encourage cessation. To emphasize the first group over the second is to condemn a billion smokers worldwide to premature death and disability (Peto and Lopez 2001). Our research admittedly has much to say about the second group and little to say about the first.

Information provision is one of several forms of public intervention. Others involve cigarette prices and outright bans on smoking. Dissemination of information about the probability of harm from smoking and the adverse health effects is not really new, but the fundamental message of our research is that people, at least in the age cohort we studied, do have the cognitive ability to understand probabilities involving their own future health. They can understand life years gained from quitting and the effect of smoking on quality of life. Harms from years of smoking are not low probability events. Thus, the difficulty people have in dealing with very low-probability events is not an issue in this context. Moreover, messages *can be* framed in ways that are salient to people, for example, by characterizing disability that arises with a higher probability when a person smokes.

One obstacle to effective messages about the probability that harm will result from smoking is heterogeneity among individuals. Although we have by no means perfected the process, empirical evidence in this book and elsewhere demonstrates the possibility of formulating messages that recognize at least some of this heterogeneity. Our empirical analysis clearly shows that people who have suffered health harms are more likely to respond to advice to stop smoking. This suggests that information-provision strategies aimed at persons who have already encountered such wake-up calls might be relatively productive. Perhaps relative productivity should be the basis for targeting in the short run, with broader strategies being implemented over time.

An important implementation issue is how to target smokers who are likely to be receptive. Physicians probably are in the best position to make this distinction, but they need practical and effective tools for conveying information messages.

Our research does not offer any new evidence on the design of information messages for youths, except possibly to include the new evidence on smoking's harms in late middle age. But we have no basis for being optimistic that young people will place much weight on events likely to occur four decades hence.

By emphasizing the role of information provision, we do not intend to downplay the importance of price. As did previous researchers, we found that price has an important effect on the quantity of cigarettes demanded. And unlike information provision, price is something to which youth smoking is particularly sensitive. Also, smoking bans might be particularly useful for their effect in delegitimizing smoking.

Other Questions

Rationality

Viscusi (1992) distinguished between three models. In one, "the rational smoker," smoking decisions are perfectly rational in terms of both risk perceptions and smoking decisions, given those risk perceptions. Given knowledge of the underlying probabilities, the rational person bases the choice of whether to smoke on whether the benefits of smoking outweigh the costs. In a second model, "the stylized smoker," individuals are unaware of the hazards they face, or if they are aware of them, they ignore considerations of risk in making the smoking decision. It is this framework, Viscusi maintained, that is typically used in public policy discussions about smoking. A third model is the smoker with cognitive limitations. This model is somewhere between the other (polar) models. He acknowledged that all three types are likely to exist in the population. The important question concerns their relative proportions.

Based on his empirical evidence, Viscusi rejected the stylized smoker model. He said, "There is much stronger support for the rational smoker framework and the model of smokers with cognitive limitations" (p. 141). He found that knowledge about the health impacts of smoking was widespread. As a consequence of antismoking campaigns, it is the smoker with cognitive limitations, who might have the most difficulty processing risk information, and who might thus be prone to overestimate the risks from smoking. Viscusi had no measure of such limitations; rather, this was inferred from some persons' overestimation of the lung cancer risk from smoking by a factor of four to eight (see our Chapter 5). He took as evidence for rationality the finding that people who believed the risk of contracting lung cancer was comparatively high were less likely to smoke.

Our results go a step further. Not all risk messages are the same. Informing smokers is not simply a matter of telling them the probabilities. Rational consumers, even McFadden's description of the extreme "Chicago man," consider both the probabilities and consequences. The event at risk from smoking is not simply a little more or less of a "normal life" with full discretion over one's activities. Instead, the event at risk is more aptly described as a shorter life in which some part of one's final months (or years) is severely constrained, causing one to have little discretion over daily activities and creating a substantial need for assistance.

This presentation of the consequences appears to have an impact, and so it should. The consequences of disability is the relevant object of choice. It should not, therefore, be surprising that communicating a more accurate description of smoking's consequences seems to be effective in changing beliefs.

Realistically, it is unlikely that anyone, economist or psychologist, will prove or disprove rationality to the satisfaction of the other group. The intellectual tussle will no doubt continue. However, from it we can expect further insights into how to communicate with lay people about risk and which dimensions of the context of choices are important.

Our study suggests both pluses and minuses for the notion that people are rational. We make four points supporting rationality, although not unambiguously. First, participants in our research were able to form judgments about the probability of living to age seventy-five strikingly well on average (Chapter 5), although there was some variation in the accuracy of the prediction relative to a more objective standard (Chapter 7). People are able to predict their own demise. From focus groups, we found that people gave reasoned explanations for subjective longevity expectations. Some underestimated their survival prospects, but in no way to the extent that Viscusi (1990, 1991, 1992) found for lung cancer deaths.

Second, people updated subjective longevity expectations in systematic ways based on life events, in a manner originally suggested by Bayes. But smokers' updates of beliefs about longevity differed from those of nonsmokers (Chapter 5). We have documented this difference, but we are unable to explain it.

Third, some but not all of our empirical evidence on smoking supports the rational addiction model, as formulated by Becker and Murphy (1988). Early approaches typically attributed addictive behavior to myopic behavior. Articles by Stigler and Becker (1977) and Becker and Murphy (1988) formulated the addiction process as the outcome of rational behavior of forward-looking individuals with stable preferences. Key to this model is the notion that current behavior is guided by expectations of future values, particularly price, as well as current values.

In aggregate time-series analysis of cigarette demand presented elsewhere (Sloan, Smith, and Taylor 2002), we obtained coefficients on the future consumption consistent with the rational addiction hypothesis. We would have expected that cessation and relapsing would respond to future as well as current prices, but we did not find this (Chapter 6). However, for those persons who smoked, the expected direction of future price as well as current price had negative impacts on current demand (Chapter 8). The latter result implies that smokers can recognize and anticipate upward trends and that they respond to them differently from constant or downward movements in price.

Fourth, if answers to the direct questions on time preferences are to be believed, most people in this age cohort are not very myopic. Only about a fifth of people reported having a time horizon of less than a year (Chapter 6). We are less persuaded by this type of evidence, because respondents might have given "correct" responses rather than ones reflecting what they believe, but it adds support to the above evidence.

Other evidence, although not clear-cut, detracts from the rationality theory. First, the link of expectations to behavior change in our analysis was not uniformly strong (see Chapter 6).

Second, we did find that smokers (especially heavy smokers) are more optimistic about their life expectancy relative to their objective life probabilities than nonsmokers. Such optimism may be a device people use to justify the risks they undertake (Chapters 2 and 5). Of course, this might also mean only that people are heterogeneous in the way they make decisions.

Third, we found variation among respondents in their ability to answer the longevity expectation questions. In particular, persons who performed less well on a word recall test had more difficulty providing plausible answers to the probability questions. To our knowledge, ours is the first study to present direct evidence on the relationship between cognitive ability and the ability to provide plausible responses to questions involving probabilities.

Fourth, more of a caveat than a minus, almost all of our evidence is for persons in the near-elderly age cohort. As emphasized in Chapter 2, people begin to smoke at an early age. It is entirely possible that people are irrational about smoking initiation but more nearly rational at a later stage of life. Also, our results might not apply to a later birth cohort. Persons in the HRS cohort began to smoke before adverse health effects of smoking were well documented. They lived through the era in which the social stigma against women's smoking evaporated. Both genders lived through the emergence of the filter tip and low-tar cigarettes.[4]

Mass Torts

During the late twentieth century, mass torts were increasingly used as a method of achieving particular public policy objectives. They were employed in the context of asbestos, breast implants, and oil spills, as well as smoking. As in the other applications, tort litigation against cigarette manufacturers appears to serve several public purposes. In a narrow sense, it should deter certain types of undesirable behavior and compensate injury victims. In some contexts, such as asbestos, product liability has served to make products safer.

If we were to grade mass tort cases against cigarette companies in terms of deterrence and compensation, such litigation to date would deserve no more than a C+. Deterrence appears to have been limited to a few effects, such as limits on billboard advertising. Development and marketing of filter-tipped and low-tar and low-nicotine cigarettes predated successful tort litigation by decades, so it is not possible to attribute the diffusion of allegedly safer cigarettes to the threat of tort. On compensation, the most one can say is that tort liability to date has been a very inefficient method for meting out compensation to persons who suffered from smoking-related illnesses.

Plaintiffs in tobacco litigation have alleged that cigarette manufacturers engaged in outright deception and fraud by: (1) not revealing what they knew about the addictive nature and generally harmful effects of their products, (2) claiming that they were engaging in research on any harmful effects when their main objective was to portray a favorable image, and (3) discrediting research findings not directly under their control (Chapter 3). Further, they have been negligent in marketing products they knew to be unsafe and failing to warn consumers about their products' deleterious effects, about which they knew. Much of the cigarette marketing effort has been directed toward youths, who are both not yet addicted to tobacco products and plausibly more receptive to the companies' self-serving arguments. Attached to plaintiffs' claims of liability have been claims of damages, including compensation for medical expenditures that resulted from smoking.[5]

The suits against tobacco manufacturers contained many documents demonstrating what the companies knew and said. However, documentation of a direct link between companies' policies and a corresponding decline in smokers' perception of smoking's risk or an unambiguous increase in smoking behavior has been lacking. The best and only evidence is indirect—for example, studies demonstrating the effect of antismoking campaigns (see Chapter 3).

Such litigation, as some commentators have argued, serves broader roles, however.[6] For one, it seems to have delegitimized the industry. Cigarette company executives have been forced to take absurd public positions, such as claiming that cigarette consumption is not addictive. In defending these claims, companies have been forced to take the position that people are stupid to consume their products. This message seems unlikely to be lost on consumers. Once such positions have been taken by those in the know, top executives of tobacco companies, it is difficult to accept the concept that public interference in their business practices is un-American.

Telling smokers, in a message cast in terms of statistical lives lost, that cigarettes are harmful is one thing. It is another for the cigarette manufacturer to tell smokers they are stupid for consuming its product. Finally, litigation has led to price increases, and demand for cigarettes is inversely related to their price (Chapter 8).

The defense in such cases, admittedly inconsistent with the statement that it is not smart to smoke, is that smokers know the underlying risk of smoking. Also, variables correlated with smoking, such as risk taking, have been excluded from many of the studies that conclude that smoking adversely affects health. Thus, even if there is an effect on health, it is smaller than is commonly alleged.

Historically, the tobacco companies have also argued that associations do not prove causation. However, adverse effects of smoking have been shown in experimental settings with animals, and it is difficult to explain away a very high relative risk of smoking, such as for the probability of contracting lung cancer, on the basis of some third omitted factor that might cause both smoking and lung cancer. It would also seem difficult to conclude that some third factor explains the relationship observed between smoking and disability in our research (Chapter 4). We, like others (see in particular Thun, Apicilla, and Henley 2000) included a number of other potential confounders in our empirical analysis.

Whether people know the risk of smoking is an empirical question. From our research, we conclude that, at least in the 1990s, middle-aged and near-elderly people who had smoked for decades were fairly good assessors of the effect of smoking on survival. Smokers appeared to give themselves too much credit in terms of increased longevity expectations when they quit (Chapter 5), and they were somewhat overly optimistic, but on average they were informed, at least in the age cohort we studied.

Tort rules should be constructed to give tobacco manufacturers an incentive to develop and market a safer cigarette (see discussion in Hanson and Logue 1998). In fact, the industry responded to concerns about safety of cigarettes (but not the threat of tort) by developing and marketing lower tar, lower nicotine, and filtered products, but the empirical evidence that such products are indeed safer is meager (Chapters 1 and 3). Unfortunately, it takes decades for the harmful effects of smoking to become manifest.[7] The smokers in the HRS probably switched away from high-tar, high-nicotine, and nonfiltered cigarettes at least two decades before they were interviewed, yet their serious health effects still could be attributed to smoking. Smokers change their smoking patterns to compensate for the reduced levels of harmful substances. In much the same way, it is not clear that availability of low-fat and no-fat foods has reduced obesity levels in this country, for simply eat more of those foods.

Thus, relying on the incentives of tort to induce manufacturers to develop and market safer cigarettes—while an interesting conceptual proposition—does not seem very fruitful. Perhaps the combination of price increases and possible bankruptcies from tort will help to downsize the industry. Of course, once tobacco consumption is controlled, demand may be channeled into other harmful substances.

Use of Longitudinal Data in Social Science Research

Most research on smoking and on other health behaviors has been based on single cross sections, with which discerning cause from effect often is exceedingly difficult, although econometric techniques have been developed to address this problem. By establishing time sequencing, panel data make it somewhat easier to determine causal influences. For example, in our research, we examined the impact of different types of health shocks on longevity expectation updating and on smoking cessation.

Panel data are not a panacea. In our example, there remains the underlying assumption that the health shock represents new personal information—that is, the shock was not anticipated. But even with this caveat, the availability of panel data renders single cross-sectional analysis out of date.

Unresolved Issues and Suggestions for Future Research

Several issues are unresolved and merit further investigation. We will mention a few here.

Additional Outcome Measures

This study has focused on subjective and objective longevity expectations, specifically the probability of surviving to age seventy-five and beyond. Many other dimensions of risk are pertinent to smokers—in particular, smoking-related morbidity and disability outcomes. Not only would analysis of these other outcomes reveal more about individual decision making in this context, but also the results could be used for designing information messages. It is quite possible that people are less knowledgeable about the underlying probabilities of getting certain diseases, as Viscusi's analysis of lung cancer probabilities suggests (Viscusi 1990, 1991, 1992). Information messages should tell people if they are overestimating the probabilities of some undesirable outcomes. Individuals may give high probabilities to some risks, such as the probability of contracting lung cancer, but they may not give such beliefs much weight ("credibility" in Bayesian jargon) in their own decision-making calculus.

It is not clear that a nationally representative sample is needed for this research. Some samples of the types we used in Chapters 7 and 8 could suffice. It would be useful, however, to adopt questions from nationally representative samples, as we did in the surveys conducted for our research. Such linking permits one to assess the representativeness of a localized sample and aids in interpreting responses to questions in the national surveys.

Interrelationships among Various Health Behaviors

Many health behaviors affect longevity and quality of life: smoking, heavy use of alcohol, obesity, lack of exercise, stress, and other behaviors. While we have controlled for some of these behaviors in our analysis of tobacco use, more realistically all of these are jointly determined. Also, various behaviors might be complements to smoking (heavy drinking) or substitutes for it (overeating). The complementary relationship implies that policies aimed at reducing heavy drinking, such as raising the excise tax on alcoholic beverages or imposing dramshop liability on commercial alcohol servers, would reduce smoking. Bans on cigarette advertisements and promotions in bars also might decrease smoking prevalence. Likewise, smoking cessation efforts may reduce heavy drinking. If smoking and overeating are substitutes, concerns about weight gain may be a barrier to smoking cessation. To the extent that such concerns are quantitatively important, it may be fruitful to incorporate weight gain avoidance in interventions designed to promote smoking cessation. We need quantitative evidence on the probability of weight gain following smoking cessation. Also, the relative impact of being overweight on survival and disability seems to be far lower than the relative impact of smoking on those outcomes. Although being overweight has its own drawbacks, both emotional and physical, having quantitative information should better inform the smoking cessation decision.

Genetics and the Probability of Harm from Smoking

Many smokers apparently believe that they are immune from harm because they have inherited "good" genes. But we are not far from the point at which it will be possible to determine whether one's genetic makeup predisposes one to specific smoking-related diseases. The concern has often been expressed that availability of genetic information will injure individuals by making it more difficult, for example, for them to obtain employment or individual health insurance. But provision of such would be extremely useful for developing messages for individual smokers. Even after receiving such personalized information, some people still will not quit, but at least their decision will be a much more informed one. Research on this topic will require advances in genetic science.

Research on Younger Age Groups

Our research has focused on persons over age fifty. The same analytic approach plausibly could be applied to younger persons. A major difference, however, is that health shocks would be much less frequent motivators for behavior change than in the age cohort we studied. But it is possible to study risk perceptions, risk perception change, and development of effective antismoking information messages. Having a national sample would be desirable, but having a panel would be even more desirable. Therefore, given cost constraints, compromising should be done in favor of the latter.

Private and Social Costs of Smoking

We have documented effects of smoking on individuals and their risk perceptions and behavioral decisions. Each decision involves costs and benefits. Although several previous efforts have been made to quantify the costs of smoking, such calculations have not been based on panel data. Also, they have focused on external costs. Many of the costs of smoking are borne internally by households. Knowledge of such costs would be useful for the design of health information messages.

Final Word

We remain optimistic (perhaps overly optimistic, like average smokers about their longevity prospects) that information about the underlying risks of smoking can be used to better inform smokers about the health consequences of their actions. Admittedly, however, the needed research is its infancy. We believe we have moved the topic forward by assessing the risks of smoking, perceptions of those risks, and the influence of risk perceptions on smoking behavior. We recognize that much remains to be done. Many millions of lives are at stake.

Notes

1. Linking Information, Risk Perception, and Choice

1. The quantitative importance of this second group of externalities remains controversial. See, e.g., Glantz and Parmley (1991), U.S. Environmental Protection Agency (1992), and Moore and Zhu (2000).
2. Citation taken from Sobel (1978).
3. See the list of references in Ochsner (1954), pp. 83–84. The earliest references are for 1912 and 1924, but these were not in journals.
4. A mortality study of graduates in the Dartmouth College class of 1868, conducted in the 1920s, showed that nonsmokers could expect to live on average about seven years longer than smokers (cited in Tate 1999, p. 143). Interestingly, this is close to longevity calculations based on recent data (see, e.g., Taylor et al. 2002).
5. We constructed Table 1.2 from published data. For this reason, the age categories in it are different from those in Table 1.1.
6. As Desvousges and Smith (1988) suggest, focus groups offer a window on conversations. The key dimension in running them is to minimize direct questions and probe according to the on-going discussion of the participants.

2. Cognition, Perception, and Behavior

1. This does not mean people would not prefer a clear recommendation about how to assure themselves of safety. Smith, Devousges, and Payne (1995) and Smith et al. (1990) evaluated different methods of explaining radon risks to different homeowners. A framework describing what experts recommended (as opposed to one encouraging private evaluation) was found to be more effective in promoting mitigation of risk and reducing demand for supplementary information.
2. Arcidiacono, Sieg, and Sloan (2001) tested whether middle-aged male smokers

were myopic in their behavior or not. They obtained a mixed result in their analysis of decision making about heavy drinking and smoking, with results suggesting behavior that was somewhere in between completely myopic or completely forward-looking.

3. Of course, most of the present company is excluded. One of the three of us privately acknowledged (to the rest) at least one traffic ticket linked to such a motivation. Safety in numbers prevents our revealing who among us this might be.
4. Endogeneity and the problems it poses for identifying and measuring peer effects is a clear challenge. See Brock and Durlauf (2001).
5. There might be a resurgence of smoking in new movies, but it has been accompanied by criticism of the images presented. Therefore, it is not clear if it will continue.

3. Government Policy and Advertising as Sources of Information

1. The Illinois supreme court declared its statute illegal, so there were effectively twelve such laws on the books in 1909.
2. According to LaFrance (2000), from 1954 to 1994 about 813 claims were filed by private citizens in tort actions in state courts against tobacco companies. Only twice did courts find in favor of plaintiffs, and both decisions were substantially reversed on appeal. One of the two cases was *Cipollone vs. Liggett Group, Inc.*
3. These documents, from the tobacco company Brown and Williamson, were allegedly stolen and revealed by a paralegal who was working at the Kentucky law firm that represents the company. The paralegal, after reviewing the documents in preparation for trial, began to believe that his own heart disease had been caused by his addiction to cigarettes.
4. The other objectives include: developing, disseminating, and testing the effectiveness of counteradvertising campaigns; commissioning studies on factors influencing youth smoking and smoking abuse; and studying reasons why youth smoking and drug use rates fail to decline (if in fact rates increase).
5. Other restrictions: the use of cartoon characters in tobacco advertising was banned; cigarette promotions were limited but not totally banned; distribution of free samples was banned, except in a facility or enclosed area where the operator ensures no underage person is present; and gifts of products were banned without proof of the recipient's age.
6. Specifically, tobacco companies are prohibited from opposing proposed state or local laws or administrative rules intended to limit youth access to and consumption of tobacco products.
7. We thank Richard Daynard, Northeastern University Law School, for this insight.

8. His article contains several references to earlier literature on effects of cigarette advertising, but antismoking campaigns were either nonexistent or too new to be included in those earlier studies.
9. Ippolito, Murphy, and Sant (1979) linked effects of qualitative variables for information policies to time trends with interaction terms. This maintains an increasing effect over time. Hamilton (1972) assumed a constant intercept shift for the information events, and Warner (1989) assumed declining effects with time for the effects of the 1950s health scare. We discuss the issue of lags in effect below.
10. See Chaloupka and Warner (2000) for a critique of this work.
11. One important innovation was the reconstituting of waste products—stems, scraps, tobacco dust—into sheets used in the cigarette manufacturing process. The tobacco leaf stem has substantially lower nicotine content than the leaf. Once consumers began to demand filtered cigarettes because they thought they were safer, manufacturers could use parts of the leaf previously discarded (Goodman 1993, p. 111).
12. See, for example, Duffy (1996). Duffy discussed several articles not included in this section's review.

4. Can Smokers Expect Personal Health Signals?

1. See Chapter 1 for a brief overview of the HRS. Evidence on effects of secondary smoke on health is an important topic in its own right. Readers who wish to learn about this issue should consult the comprehensive review of the literature in Watson and Witten (2001).
2. A past drinking problem at wave 1 was indicated by one or more affirmative answers to the four CAGE questions: Have you ever felt you should *Cut down* on your drinking? Have people *Annoyed* you by criticizing your drinking? Have you ever felt bad or *Guilty* about your drinking? Have you ever had a drink first thing in the morning *(Eye-opener)* to steady your nerves or to get rid of a hangover?

5. Determinants of Risk Perception

1. The same member in each household was interviewed both times. (The original analysis is reported in Desvousges, Smith, and Rink 1992.)
2. In our study, we were able to take advantage of the panel feature of the HRS, which facilitates making causal interpretations but does not totally rule out endogenity.
3. Interestingly, some psychological research has found that optimistic bias reflects people's overestimation of the average person's risk. See Rothman, Klein, and Weinstein (1996).

4. Viscusi's updating model was estimated with a single cross section. As a result, the roles he discussed for these demographic characteristics in the models for risk perception are conjectures that rely on accepting the updating framework as a maintained hypothesis. Moreover, they require fairly specific roles for the independent variables in influencing unobserved elements in that framework.
5. Ippolito (1981) suggested that, after some point in the life cycle, concerns about health risks would be dominated by the consumption benefits from smoking. That is, the gains in life extension are superceded by the increased satisfaction.
6. It is interesting that Nichols and Zeckhauser (1986) made this same point in criticizing "conservatism" (e.g., overstatement of risk) in public risk assessments. Rather than providing greater safety, overstating risk misallocates resources and could well lead to higher, not lower, risks imposed on consumers. The same conclusion (misallocating resources) could be reached for private decisions with differences in the conservatism of risk perception.
7. In fact, there is some evidence that survival is actually worse in the short run for quitters, probably because an adverse health events led to the decision to quit (U.S. Department of Health and Human Services 1990, p. 78). In this sense, smokers who quit were overly optimistic as well.

6. Do Health Shocks Influence Smoking Behavior?

1. Of course, it would also be possible to model these decisions within a formal hazard framework. However, that approach would require a more detailed behavior model of the choice process and would be quite sensitive to the distributional assumptions made in characterizing unobserved heterogeneity in individual responses. As a result, we selected a strategy that partitions the various choices into separate groups and considers the factors associated with each as reduced form models.

7. Personalized Health Messages and the Perceived Risks of Smoking

1. Data from the conjoint survey are being analyzed separately. Results will be presented in a forthcoming paper.
2. We used the foundational logic of Heckman's (2001) methodological research program. His approach seeks to evaluate the effect of an intervention or the availability of a specific program on participants. The counterfactual of interest is what would have happened to those individuals had they not participated. Addressing this issue involves separating the characteristics of the individuals that are relevant to the participation decision from those relevant to the training program. One of the strategies Heckman uses to address this ques-

tion involves matching samples of individuals with comparable observable characteristics to that of the program participants, to evaluate outcome measures for the two groups (see Heckman, Ichimura, and Todd 1997). A challenge in developing these evaluations stems from finding comparable groups to those involved in the program.

In our study, we used a comparable group, participants in the HRS study, to design a more limited experiment. In this case the prior existence of the large-scale, long-term panel allowed a more modest (and economical) approach to evaluating the information programs. For us, the roles of the treatment group and the matched control group were reversed. Because the control already existed, we could match the experimental group to it as part of the evaluation. In Heckman's work, the experimental group exists first, and the evaluation requires the analyst to identify controls.

3. One of us volunteered to participate as a pretest subject for the HRS, in wave 4. The interview took two hours and nine minutes, which was probably longer than it took for the average subject but not totally atypical.
4. See Heckman, Ichimura, and Todd (1997) and Smith and Todd (2000) for discussion of the use of matching in evaluating job training programs.
5. The response pattern for the longevity expectations from HRS wave 2 (control sample) has more resolution. Wave 2 used a continuous 0–100 response for longevity expectations rather than wave 1's 0–10 range.
6. Columns 3 and 4 refer to the second information treatment, discussed below.
7. Here we assumed that the dummy variable for the treatment simply reflected the baseline effect and was offset by the no-show variable.
8. Past studies of risk perception due to radon (an indoor air pollutant believed to be associated with lung cancer) are consistent with this maintained hypothesis (see Smith, Desvousges, and Payne 1995). That is, the new information was retained in that case. Nonetheless, there are some important differences between this study and that research. For example, the information messages included in the radon risk communication project were repeated during the course of the study. At the time, radon was also a newly recognized source of risk from the perspective of the public. By contrast, our research design allowed the information messages to be administered only once. For the revised longevity expectations to be maintained, it might well be necessary to reinforce the messages periodically.

8. Risk, Longevity Expectations, and Demand for Cigarettes

1. Our test does not require the assumption of full depreciation of the addictive stock.
2. See Chapter 7 for a description of this information treatment.

3. Temporal separability in this context refers to the effect of consumption in a period *j* on the marginal utility of consumption of the same good in another period. Under additive separability, consumption in *j* does not affect the person's marginal utility in it. This is a strong assumption, especially for an addictive good like cigarettes.
4. We return to this issue below in the context of geometric discounting.
5. Two goods are complements if they tend to be consumed together so that consumption of both goods tends to rise or fall simultaneously in response to a rise or fall in one of the goods. Examples of complements to VCRs are television sets, videotapes, and snacks. In the context of the discussion in the text, the two goods are cigarettes consumed in two periods. If they are complements temporally, consumption of cigarettes in the two different time periods rise or fall together.
6. Becker and Murphy (1988) also allowed for a term reflecting endogenous depreciation or appreciation to the stock, but eliminated this term in discussing their model's dynamic features and implications for empirical testing.
7. The stock evolution equation can be written as follows (with L = log operator): $(1 - (1 - \delta)\,\mathrm{L})S_t = x_{1t}$. Solving for S_t using $\alpha = (1 - \delta)$, we have $S_t = x_{1t}/(1 - \alpha \mathrm{L}) = x_{1t} + \alpha x_{1t-1} + \alpha^2 x_{1t-2} + \ldots + \alpha^k x_{1t-k} + \ldots$
8. The marginal rate of substitution gives the maximum amount of one good a consumer is willing to give up to obtain additional units of another good.
9. In their discussion of dynamics.
10. Becker and Murphy use a slightly different form of the stock equation that leads to a comparable power series, but does allow $S_t = x_{1t-1}$ when $\delta = 1$. This is readily established. In their model it evolves as: $\Delta S_t = x_{1t} - \delta S_t$ with $\Delta S_t = S_{t+1} - S_t$. This can be rewritten as: $S_{t+1} = S_t + x_{1t} - \delta S_t$, so when $\delta = 1$ we have $S_{t+1} = x_{1t}$ or $S_t = x_{1t-1}$ and thus preferences are given by: $U(x_{1t}, x_{2t}, x_{1t-1})$.
11. By time consistent, we mean that the individual considers costs and benefits from consumption in future and current periods in making current consumption decisions.
12. To some degree, any separation of time horizon, foresight, and discounting is artificial. The formal models incorporating these factors indicate that they have comparable effects on optimal choices. As we described earlier, a simple modification to conventional discounting could also be interpreted as one way a person might incorporate perceptions about longevity and their effects. Our objective is to distinguish these issues conceptually. As a result, when we formulate the hypotheses implied by each attribute of our behavioral model, we will also discuss our ability to separate their individual influences on observed behavior.
13. These adjustment or quitting costs are discussed in Chapter 2.
14. This is the strategy Suranovic and colleagues used in the appendix to their pa-

per (p. 23). They defined a survival function in terms of an integrated empirical death rate, $\mu(t, S_A)$ function as: exp. $(-f^t{}_A\mu(\tau, S_A))d\tau$ with S_A equalling stock of smoking to age, A, and t, the time horizon or life span associated with the probability.

15. When risk is introduced we redefine the instantaneous contribution of consumption to expected utility, designed here as v_t.
    $\pi(S_t)$ is the smoker's subjective belief about being alive in each period, expressed as a function of the stock of past smoking to reflect the fact that smokers recognize that smoking influences their likelihood of survival, as our results suggest. This simplifies Becker and Murphy's (1988) result in their Eq. (18). The same analysis and assumptions that Becker used to derive the cigarette demand response to price as given in Eq. (8.12) in the text can be used to describe the subjective link between past smoking and survival probabilities. We report these results in Eq. (8.13) in the text.
16. This means that people consider only first-order effects of steady-state smoking levels on survival probabilities.
17. If we relax our assumption about risk perceptions (i.e., assume $\pi'' \neq 0$), we could describe cases that parallel the outline given by Suranovic and coauthors for different adjustment cost and time horizon specifications. As noted above, because the form we used to introduce risk limits its impact to a composite effect, the results also parallel those derived by Gruber and Köszegi for the case of hyperbolic discounting.
18. This pattern was somewhat sensitive to the set of instruments used in their two-stage least-squares analysis. When future price measures were excluded, lagged consumption of cigarettes had a negative effect on demand. Moreover, we would expect (with the maintained assumption that consumers have a finite discount rate) that future consumption would have a smaller impact on demand than lagged consumption. Becker and colleagues' (1994) "final" demand estimates with lagged and future price as instruments displayed this pattern. Those that dropped these variables from the instruments along with the tax measures did not.
19. See Chaloupka and Warner (2000).
20. See Gruber and Köszegi (2001) for discussion of some of their limitations. In addition, the Tobacco Institute does not provide details about how its price index treats per-package and carton prices or the sampling procedure used to collect the price information. The American Chamber of Commerce Research Association price measure is the price of a carton of Winston cigarettes and is based on a convenience sample.
21. The confidential codes were made available to us on a restricted basis by the University of Michigan's Survey Research Center, the organization that conducts the HRS.

22. The BLS does not consider these price indexes to be appropriate for analysis at the area (or PSU) level. Their various properties are unknown and therefore they are not official price statistics.
23. The alternative measure combined data from the American Chamber of Commerce Researchers Association (ACCRA) and the Tobacco Institute. If ACCRA provided price information for the HRS primary sampling unit, we used ACCRA information. If the HRS PSU did not overlap with a city for which we had ACCRA price information, we used the mean price for the state and year from ACCRA. If the respondent lived in a state in which ACCRA does not collect data (such as New Jersey), then we used information on the mean price per pack in that year from the Tobacco Institute. We experimented with alternative measures of price. The results were quite similar to those we report.
24. See Chapter 2 for a discussion of smoking initiation. Cessation patterns are described in Chapter 6.
25. Gruber and Köszegi's test used announced (but not yet implemented) increases in the taxes on cigarettes. They found the effective tax rate reduced aggregate sales of cigarettes (in the context of a time series of state cross sections) and the announced rate increases actually resulted in increases in the current demand. They attributed the former effect to ordinary demand responses and the latter to a hoarding response resulting from forward-looking behavior.
26. Gruber and Köszegi used a sample that provided women's smoking rates based on the Vital Statistics Natality Survey. Their results confirmed forward-looking behavior and the demand responses anticipated based on the rational addiction framework. That is, using these rates to measure monthly average smoking levels by state in a specific month from 1989 to 1996, they tested for the same effect and found evidence supporting adjacent complementarity. Announced future tax increases *reduced* current levels of cigarette consumption.
27. In an unpublished study, Smith and Desvousges (1994) found that women were more likely to take account of information related to food purchasing choices. Because tobacco products were included with food, this may indicate that women are more observant of changes in tobacco prices as well.
28. Decker and Schwartz (2000) also estimated separate cigarette demand functions for men and women. They found women less sensitive to price than were the men. Their F test rejected pooling of the two samples.
29. See Chapter 7 for a discussion of the information treatments.
30. This result might seem to contradict the argument we used to motivate the process by which we developed our policy analysis. It does not. We argued that, in a steady state, there would be alignment. Adjustment of behavior with subjective risk beliefs takes time, especially in situations where the adjustment costs are significant.

31. Converting the coefficients on the binary variable for anticipated price change in a percentage change, using the method in Halvorsen and Palmquist (1980).

9. Conclusions and Policy Implications

1. According to Hall, Tunstall, and Rugg (1984, p. 173), "Eighty to ninety percent of adults surveyed in recent years agree that smoking is harmful to one's health." The authors added, however, "Again, whether the smoker perceives smoking as harmful to his own health cannot be determined by such data. However, as one ages, the relevance of the health-related consequences of cigarettes may become greater."
2. Desvousges, Smith, and Rink (1992) found that for public information campaigns about radon, a focus on friends and family as information sources was important to understanding the full effect of these programs on home testing.
3. This may be so for two reasons. First, the companies want to say as little as possible about adverse effects of their products. They typically disclose no more information than the minimum required. Second, the prevailing conventional wisdom seems to be that people have difficulty dealing with probabilities.
4. On cohort effects related to smoking, see Bosse and Rose (1984a and 1984b).
5. Interestingly, an important byproduct of the litigation of the 1990s against tobacco companies involved state Medicaid program claims. Because the Medicaid programs themselves were not smokers and did not contribute to patients' smoking, the assumption of risk defense (smokers "knew" of the harms) did not apply. Thus, in those cases, issues of consumer information and risk perceptions were not applicable.

   This insight was made in an analysis of class action suits by managed care organizations. See Epstein and Sykes (2001).
6. We thank Richard Daynard for the ideas in this paragraph.
7. This is not unique to tobacco. Clinical trials of drugs cover only a relatively short time period. Long-run effects of drugs are not known at the time they are marketed. Tracking long-term effects is the responsibility of post-marketing surveillance.

References

Akerlof, George A. 1970. "The Market for 'Lemons': Quality, Uncertainty, and the Market Mechanism," *Quarterly Journal of Economics* 84 (3): 488–500.

Almirall, Jordi, et al. 1999. "Proportion of Community-Acquired Pneumonia Cases Attributable to Tobacco Smoking," *Chest* 116 (2): 375–379.

Antoñanzas, Fernando, et al. 2000. "Smoking Risks in Spain, Part 1: Perceptions of Risks to the Smoker," *Journal of Risk and Uncertainty* 21 (2/3): 161–186.

Arcidiacono, Peter, Holger Sieg, and Frank A. Sloan. 2001. "Living Rationally under the Volcano? An Empirical Analysis of Heavy Drinking and Smoking," unpublished paper, Duke University.

Arnett, Jeffrey Jensen. 2000. "Optimistic Bias in Adolescent and Adult Smokers and Nonsmokers," *Addictive Behaviors* 28 (4): 625–632.

Ayanian, John Z., and Paul D. Cleary. 1999. "Perceived Risks of Heart Disease and Cancer among Cigarette Smokers," *Journal of the American Medical Association* 281 (11): 1019–1021.

Baltagi, Badi H., and Dan Levin. 1986. "Estimating Dynamic Demand for Cigarettes Using Panel Data: The Effects of Bootlegging, Taxation and Advertising Reconsidered," *Review of Economics and Statistics* 68 (1): 148–155.

Barsky, R. B., et al. 1997. "Preferences, Parameters, and Behavioral Heterogeneity: An Experimental Approach in the Health and Retirement Study," *Quarterly Journal of Economics* 112 (3): 537–579.

Bartecchi, Carl E., et al. 1994. "The Human Costs of Tobacco Use" (first of two parts), *New England Journal of Medicine* 33 (13): 907–912.

Becker, Gary S. 1992. "Habits, Addictions, and Traditions," *Kyklos* 45 (3): 327–345.

———. 1993. "The Economic Way of Looking at Life," *Journal of Political Economy* 101 (June): 385–409.

———. 1996. *Accounting for Tastes.* Cambridge, Mass.: Harvard University Press.

Becker, Gary S., Michael Grossman, and Kevin M. Murphy. 1994. "An Empirical Analysis of Cigarette Addiction," *American Economic Review* 84 (June): 396–418.

Becker, Gary S., and Casey Mulligan. 1997. "The Endogenous Determination of Time Preference," *Quarterly Journal of Economics* 112 (3): 729–758.

Becker, Gary S., and Kevin M. Murphy. 1988. "A Theory of Rational Addiction," *Journal of Political Economy* 96 (4): 675–700.

———. 2000. *Social Economics: Market Behavior in a Social Environment.* Cambridge, Mass.: Belknap Press of Harvard University Press.

Becona, Elisardo, and Fernando L. Vazquez. 1998. "Smoking Cessation and Weight Gain in Smokers Participating in a Behavioral Treatment at 3-Year Follow-Up," *Psychological Reports* 82 (3): 999–1006.

Benjamin, Daniel K., and William R. Dougan. 1997. "Individuals' Estimates of the Risks of Death, Part I: A Reassessment of the Previous Evidence," *Journal of Risk and Uncertainty* 15 (2): 115–123.

Benowitz, Neal L. 1997. "The Role of Nicotine in Smoking-Related Cardiovascular Disease," *Preventive Medicine* 26: 412–417.

Bjornson, Wendy, et al. 1995. "Gender Differences in Smoking Cessation after 3 Years in the Lung Health Study," *American Journal of Public Health* 85 (2): 233–230.

Bosse, Raymond, and Charles L. Rose. 1984a. "Age, Health Status, and Other Factors in Smoking Cessation," in Raymond Bosse and Charles L. Rose, eds., *Smoking and Aging.* Lexington, Mass.: D. C. Health/Lexington Books, 187–202.

———. 1984b. "Conceptual and Methodological Aspects of Smoking and Aging," in Raymond Bosse and Charles L. Rose, eds., *Smoking and Aging.* Lexington, Mass.: D. C. Health/Lexington Books, 1–24.

Boyle, Peter. 1997. "Cancer, Cigarette Smoking and Premature Death in Europe: A Review Including the Recommendations of European Cancer Experts Consensus Meeting, Helsinki, October 1996," *Lung Cancer* 17: 1–60.

Brigham, Janet. 1998. *Dying to Quit: Why We Smoke and How We Stop,* Washington, D.C.: John Henry Press.

Brock, William A., and Steven N. Durlauf. 2001. "Discrete Choice with Social Interaction," *Review of Economics and Statistics* 68 (2): 235–260.

Browning, Martin. 1987. "Eating, Drinking, Smoking, and Testing the Lifecycle Hypothesis," *Quarterly Journal of Economics* 70 (2): 329–347.

Burnham, John C. 1993. *Bad Habits: Drinking, Smoking, Taking Drugs, Gambling, Sexual Misbehavior, and Swearing in American History.* New York: New York University Press.

Burt, A., et al. 1974. "Stopping Smoking after Myocardial Infarction," *Lancet* 1: 304–306.

Byrne, D. G., A. E. Byrne, and M. I. Reinhart. 1995. "Personality, Stress and the Decision to Commence Cigarette Smoking in Adolescence," *Journal of Psychosomatic Research* 39 (1): 53–62.

Califf, Robert M. 2000. "Cigarette Smoking: How Much Worse Can It Get?" *Circulation* 102: 1340–1341.

Chaloupka, Frank. 1991. "Rational Addictive Behavior and Cigarette Smoking," *Journal of Political Economy* 99 (4): 722–742.

Chaloupka, Frank J., and Kenneth E. Warner. 2000. "The Economics of Smoking," in Antony J. Culyer and Joseph P. Newhouse, eds., *Handbook of Health Economics.* Amsterdam: Elsevier, 1539–1627.

Chaloupka, Frank J., and Henry Wechsler. 1997. "Price, Tobacco Control Policies, and Smoking among Young Adults," *Journal of Health Economics* 16 (3): 359–373.

Chetwynd, Jane, et al. 1988. "Impact of Cigarette Advertising on Aggregate Demand for Cigarettes in New Zealand," *British Journal of Addiction* 83: 409–414.

Chow, Gregory. 1960. "Tests of Equality between Sets of Coefficients in Two Linear Regressions," *Econometrica* 28: 591–605.

Cohen, Sheldon, and Edward Lichtenstein. 1990. "Partner Behaviors That Support Quitting Smoking," *Journal of Consulting and Clinical Psychology* 38 (3): 304–309.

Cohen, Sheldon, et al. 1993. "Smoking, Alcohol Consumption, and Susceptibility to the Common Cold," *American Journal of Public Health* 83 (9): 1277–1283.

Combs, B., and P. Slovic. 1979. "Newspaper Coverage of Causes of Death," *Journalism Quarterly* 56: 837–849.

Croog, S. H., and N. P. Richards. 1977. "Health Benefits and Smoking Patterns in Heart Patients and Their Wives: A Longitudinal Study," *American Journal of Public Health* 67: 921–930.

Daughton, D. M., et al. 1980. "Smoking Cessation among Patients with Chronic Obstructive Pulmonary Disease (COPD)," *Addictive Behavior* 5: 125–128.

Davidson, D. Kirk. 1996. *Selling Sin: The Marketing of Socially Unacceptable Products.* Westport, Conn.: Quorum Books.

Daviglus, M. L., et al. 1998. "Benefit of a Favorable Cardiovascular Risk-Factor Profile in Middle Age with Respect to Medicare Costs," *New England Journal of Medicine* 339: 1122–1129.

Decker, Sandra L., and Amy E. Schwartz. 2000. "Cigarettes and Alcohol: Substitutes or Complements?" National Bureau of Economic Research, Working Paper W7535, February.

Desvousges, William H., and V. Kerry Smith. 1996. "Focus Groups and Risk Communication: The 'Science' of Listening to Data," in V. Kerry Smith, ed., *Estimating Economic Values for Nature: Methods for Non-market Valuation,* New Horizons in Environmental Economics. Cheltenham, U.K.: Elgar, 441–446.

Desvousges, William H., V. Kerry Smith, and Hillary H. Rink III. 1992. "Communicating Radon Risks Effectively: The Maryland Experience," *Journal of Public Policy and Marketing* 2: 68–78.

Doll, Richard, and A. B. Hill. 1952. "A Study of the Aetiology of Carcinoma of the Lung," *British Medical Journal* 2: 1271–1286.

Doll, R., et al. 1994. "Mortality in Relation to Smoking: 40 Years' Observations on Male British Doctors," *British Medical Journal* 309: 901–911.

Douglas, Stratford. 1998. "The Duration of the Smoking Habit," *Economic Inquiry* 36 (1): 49–64.

Dow, William H., Tomas J. Philipson, and Xavier Sala-I-Martin. 1999. "Longevity Complementarities under Competing Risks," *American Economic Review* 89 (5): 1358–1371.

Duffy, Martyn. 1991. "Advertising and the Consumption of Tobacco and Alcoholic Drink: A System-Wide Analysis," *Scottish Journal of Political Economy* 38 (4): 369–385.

———. 1996. "Econometric Studies of Advertising, Advertising Restrictions, and Cigarette Demands: A Survey," *International Journal of Advertising* 15: 1–23.

Edell, Mark Z. 1986. "Cigarette Litigation: The Second Wave," 22 *Tort and Insurance Law Journal* 90 (Fall).

Elster, Jon. 1997. "More than Enough: Review of *Accounting for Tastes* by Gary S. Becker," *University of Chicago Law Review* 64: 749–764.

———. 1999. *Alchemies of the Mind: Rationality and Emotion,* New York: Cambridge University Press.

Epple, Dennis, and Richard E. Romano. 1998. "Competition between Private and Public Schools, Vouchers, and Peer-Group Effects," *American Economic Review* 8 (1): 33–62.

Epstein, Richard A., and Alan O. Sykes. 2001. "The Assault on Managed Care: Vicarious Liability, ERISA Preemption, and Class Actions," *Journal of Legal Studies* 30 (2) (Pt. 2): 625–659.

Ernster, Virginia L. 1998. "Female Lung Cancer," *Annual Review of Public Health* 17: 97–114.

Escobedo, L. G., and J. P. Peddicord. 1996. "Smoking Prevalence in U.S. Birth Cohorts: The Influences of Gender and Education," *American Journal of Public Health* 86 (2): 231–236.

Evans, William, and Matthew C. Farrelly. 1998. "The Compensating Behavior of Smokers: Taxes, Tar, and Nicotine," *Rand Journal of Economics* 29 (3): 578–595.

Farrell, Phillip, and Victor R. Fuchs. 1982. "Schooling and Health: The Cigarette Connection," *Journal of Health Economics* 1 (December): 217–230.

Ferrucci, Luigi, et al. 1999. "Smoking, Physical Activity, and Active Life Expectancy," *American Journal of Epidemiology* 49 (7): 645–653.

Fichtenburg, Caroline M., and Stanton Glantz. 2000. "Association of the California Tobacco Control Program with Declines in Cigarette Consumption and Mortality from Heart Disease," *New England Journal of Medicine* 343 (24): 1772–1777.

Fiore, Michael C., et al. 1990. "Methods Used to Quit Smoking in the United

States: Do Cessation Programs Help?" *Journal of American Medical Association* 263 (20): 2760–2765.

Fishbein, Martin, and Icek Ajzen. 1975. *Belief, Attitude, Intention, and Behavior: An Introduction to Theory and Research.* Reading, Mass.: Addison-Wesley.

Fischhoff, Baruch. 1989. "Appendix C: Risk: A Guide to Controversy," in National Research Council, *Improving Risk Communication.* Washington, D.C.: National Academy Press, 211–308.

Fischhoff, B., and D. MacGregor. 1983. "Judged Lethality: How Much People Seem to Know Depends upon How They Are Asked," *Risk Analysis* 3: 229–235.

Fischhoff, Baruch, et al. 1993. "Embedding Effects: Stimulus Representation and Response Mode," *Journal of Risk and Uncertainty* 6 (3): 211–234.

Freedman, David S., et al. 1998. "Relation of Cigarette Smoking to Non-Hodgkin's Lymphoma among Middle-Aged Men," *American Journal of Epidemiology* 148 (9): 833–841.

Gaffney, M., and B. Altshuler. 1988. "Examination of the Role of Cigarette Smoke in Lung Carcinogenesis Using Multistage Models," *Journal of the National Cancer Institute* 80: 146–149.

Gans, Joshua S., and George B. Shephard. 2000. "How Are the Mighty Fallen: Rejected Classic Articles by Leading Economists," in Joshua Gans, ed., *Publishing Economics: Analysis of the Academic Journal of Medicine in Economics.* Cheltenham, U.K.: Elgar, 26–42.

Garvey, Arthur J. 1984. "Age, Health Status, and Other Factors in Smoking Cessation," in Raymond Bosse and Charles L. Rose, eds., *Smoking and Aging.* Lexington, Mass.: D. C. Health/Lexington Books, 187–202.

Gerace, Terance A. 1999. "Perceptions of Health Risks by Cigarette Smokers," letter to editor, *Journal of American Medical Association* 282 (18): 1722.

Ginsberg, Dorothy, Sharon M. Hall, and Marishka Rosinski. 1991. "Partner Interaction and Smoking Cessation: A Pilot Study," *Addictive Behaviors* 16: 195–202.

Glantz, S. A., and W. W. Parmley. 1991. "Passive Smoking and Heart Disease: Epidemiology, Physiology, and Biochemistry," *Circulation* 83 (1): 1–12.

Glantz, Stanton A., et al. 1996. *The Cigarette Papers.* Berkeley: University of California Press.

Goodman, Jordan. 1993. *Tobacco in History: The Culture of Dependence.* London: Routledge.

Gottsegen, Jack. 1940. *Tobacco: A Study of Its Consumption in the United States.* New York: Pitman.

Greenhouse, Linda. 2001. "Supreme Court Roundup; Justices to Hear Challenge to Cigarette Ad Restrictions," *New York Times,* Jan. 9, 2001.

Grossman, Michael. 1975. "The Correlation between Health and Schooling," in

Nester E. Terleckyj, ed., *Household Production and Consumption*. New York: Columbia University Press for the National Bureau of Economic Research, 147–211.

———. 1995. "The Economic Approach to Addictive Behavior," in Mariano Tommasi and Kathryn Ierulli, eds., *The New Economics of Human Behavior*. Cambridge: Cambridge University Press, 157–170.

Grossman, Michael, Frank J. Chaloupka, and Richard Anderson. 1998. "A Survey of Economic Models of Addictive Behavior," *Journal of Drug Issues* 28 (3): 631–643.

Gruber, Jonathan, and Botond Köszegi. 2001. "Is Addiction 'Rational'? Theory and Evidence," *Quarterly Journal of Economics* 116 (4): 1261–1303.

Gruber, Jonathan, and Jonathan Zinman. 2000. "Youth Smoking in the U.S.: Evidence and Implications," National Bureau of Economic Research Working Paper 7780, July.

Hall, Sharon M., Chrysal D. Tunstall, and Deborah L. Rugg. 1984. "Psychological Aspects of Smoking Behavior throughout the Life Cycle," in Raymond Bosse and Charles L. Rose, eds., *Smoking and Aging*. Lexington, Mass.: D. C. Health/ Lexington Books, 157–85.

Halvorsen, Robert, and Raymond Palmquist. 1980. "Interpretations of Dummy Variables in Semilogarithmic Equations," *American Economic Review* 70 (3): 471–75.

Hamermesh, Daniel S. 1985. "Expectations, Life Expectancy, and Economic Behavior," *Quarterly Journal of Economics* 100 (May): 389–408.

Hamilton, James L. 1972. "The Demand for Cigarettes: Advertising, The Health Scare, and the Cigarette Advertising Ban," *Review of Economics and Statistics* 54 (4): 401–411.

Hanson, Jon D., and Kyle D. Logue. 1998. "The Costs of Cigarettes: The Economic Case for Ex Post Incentive-Based Regulation,." *Yale Law Journal* 107 (5): 1163–1361.

Harris, Jeffrey E. 1994. "A Working Model for Predicting the Consumption and Revenue Impacts of Large Increases in the U.S. Federal Cigarette Excise Tax," National Bureau of Economic Research Working Paper 4803, Cambridge, Mass.

Hausman, Jerry A. 1978. "Specification Tests in Econometrics," *Econometrica* 46 (6): 1251–1271.

Heckman, James J. 1979. "Sample Bias as a Specification Error," *Econometrica* 47 (1): 153–162.

———. 2001. Micro Data, Heterogeneity, and the Evaluation of Public Policy: Nobel Lecture," *Journal of Political Economy* 109 (4): 673–748.

Heckman, James J., Hidehiko Ichimura, and Petra E. Todd. 1997. "Matching as an Econometric Evaluation Estimator: Evidence from Evaluating a Job Training Programme," *Review of Economic Studies* 64: 605–654.

Heckman, James J., and Burton Singer. 1986. "Econometric Analysis of Longitundinal Data," in *Handbook of Econometrics*, vol. 3, ed. Zvi Greleches and Michael D. Intrilligatar (Amsterdam: North Holland Press).

Hersch, Joni, and W. Kip Viscusi. 1998. "Smoking and Other Risky Behaviors," *Journal of Drug Issues* 28 (3): 645–661.

Herzog, A. Regula, and Robert B. Wallace. 1997. "Measures of Cognitive Functioning in the AHEAD Study," *Journals of Gerontology*, Series B, 52B (Special Issue): 37–48.

Hsieh, Chee-Ruey, et al. 1996. "Smoking, Health Knowledge, and Anti-Smoking Campaigns: An Empirical Study in Taiwan," *Journal of Health Economics* 15 (1): 87–104.

Hu, Teh-wei, Han-Yen Sung, and Theodore E. Keeler. 1995a. "Reducing Cigarette Consumption in California: Tobacco Taxes vs. an Anti-Smoking Media Campaign," *American Journal of Public Health* 85 (9): 1218–1222.

———. 1995b. "The State Antismoking Campaign and the Industry Response: The Effects of Advertising on Cigarette Consumption in California," *American Economic Review* 85 (2): 85–90.

Hughes, J. R., et al. 1992. "Smoking Cessation among Self-Quitters," *Health Psychology* 11: 1331–1334.

Hurd, Michael D., Daniel McFadden, and Li Gan. 1998. "Subjective Survival Curves and Life Cycle Behavior," in Daniel A Wise, ed., *Inquiries in the Economics of Aging*. Chicago: University of Chicago Press, 259–305.

Hurd, Michael D., and Kathleen McGarry. 1995. "Evaluation of the Subjective Probabilities of Survival in the Health and Retirement Study," *Journal of Human Resources* 30 (Supplement): S268–S292.

Ippolito, Pauline M. 1981. "Information and the Life Cycle Consumption of Hazardous Goods," *Economic Inquiry* 19: 529–558.

Ippolito, Richard A., R. Dennis Murphy, and Donald Sant. 1979. *Staff Report on Consumer Responses to Cigarette Health Information*, Bureau of Economics, Federal Trade Commission, August.

Jacobson, Peter D., and Kenneth E. Warner. 1999. "Litigation and Public Health Policy Making: The Case of Tobacco Control," *Journal of Health Politics, Policy and Law* 24 (4): 769–804.

Jacobson, Peter D., and Jeffrey Wasserman. 1997. "Tobacco Control Laws: Implementation and Enforcement." Santa Monica, Calif.: Rand Corporation.

Jette, A. M., and L. G. Branch. 1981. "The Framingham Disability Study, II: Physical Disability among the Aged," *American Journal of Public Health* 71: 211–216.

Johnson, E. J., and A. Tversky. 1983. "Affect, Generalization, and the Perception of Risk," *Journal of Personality and Social Psychology* 45: 20–31.

Jones, Andrew M. 1994. "Health, Addiction, Social Interaction and the Decision to Quit Smoking," *Journal of Health Economics* 13: 93–110.

Jones, Raymond M. 1997. "Strategic Management in a Hostile Environment," *Lessons from the Tobacco Industry.* Westport, Conn.: Quorum Books.

Juster, F. Thomas, and R. Suzman. 1995. "An Overview of the Health and Retirement Study," *Journal of Human Resources* 30: S6–S56.

Kabat, Geoffrey C., and Ernst L. Wynder. 1987. "Determinants of Quitting Smoking," *American Journal of Public Health* 77 (10): 1301–1305.

Kagan, Robert A., and David Vogel. 1993. "The Politics of Smoking Regulation: Canada, France, and the United States," in Robert L. Rabin and Stephen D. Sugarman, eds., *Smoking Policy, Law, Politics and Culture.* New York: Oxford University Press, 22–48.

Kahneman, Daniel, and Amos Tversky. 1981. "The Framing of Decisions and the Psychology of Choice." *Science* 211: 453–458.

———. 1982. *Judgment under Uncertainty: Heurstics and Biases.* Cambridge: Cambridge University Press.

Kaplan, R. M., J. P. Anderson, and T. G. Ganiats. 1993. "The Quality of Well-Being Scale: Rationale for a Single Quality of Life Index," in S. M. Walker and R. M. Rosser, eds., *Quality of Life Assessment: Key Issues in the 1990s.* Boston: Kluwer Academic Publishers, 65–94.

Katz, S., et al. 1970. "Progression in the Development of an Index of ADL," *Gerontologist* 10: 20–30.

Keeler, Theodore E., et al. 1993. "Taxation, Regulation, and Addiction: A Demand Function for Cigarettes Based on Time-Series Evidence," *Journal of Health Economics* 12 (1):1–18.

Kenkel, Donald S. 1991a. "Health Behavior, Health Knowledge, and Schooling," *Journal of Political Economy* 99 (2): 287–305.

———. 1991b. "What You Don't Know Really Won't Hurt You." *Journal of Political Analysis and Management* 10 (2): 304–309.

Klesges, Robert C., et al. 1998. "The Relationship between Smoking and Body Weight in a Population of Young Military Personnel," *Health Psychology* 17 (5): 454–458.

Kluger, Richard. 1996. *Ashes to Ashes: America's Hundred– Year Cigarette War, the Public Health, and the Unabashed Triumph of Philip Morris.* New York: Alfred A. Knopf.

Krosnick, Jon A. 2001. "Americans' Perceptions of the Health Risks of Cigarette Smoking: Important New Findings," unpublished paper, Ohio State University.

Krosnick, Jon A., and C. M. Judd. 1982. "Transitions in Social Influence at Adolescence: Who Induces Cigarette Smoking," *Developmental Psychology* 18: 359–368.

LaFrance, A. B. 2000. "Tobacco Litigation: Smoke, Mirrors and Public Policy," *American Journal of Law and Medicine* 26 (2–3): 187–203.

Lancet. 1857. "What Are the Effects of Smoking upon the Human Frame?" March 14: 270–271.

Lawton, M. P., and E. M. Brody. 1969. "Assessment of Older People: Self-Maintaining and Instrumental Activities of Daily Living," *Gerontologist* 9 (3): 179–186.

Lewit, Eugene M., and Douglas Coate. 1982. "The Potential for Using Excise Taxes to Reduce Smoking," *Journal of Health Economics* 1 (2): 121–145.

Lewit, E. M., D. Coate, M. Grossman. 1981. "The Effects of Government Regulation on Teenage Smoking," *Journal of Law and Economics* 24 (3): 545–569.

Lichtenstein, S., et al. 1978. "Judged Frequency of Lethal Events," *Journal of Experimental Psychology: Human Learning and Memory* 4: 551–579.

Liu, Jin-Tan, and Chee-Ruey Hsieh. 1995. "Risk Perception and Smoking Behavior: Empirical Evidence from Taiwan," *Journal of Risk and Uncertainty* 11 (2): 139–157.

Lucas, Robert E., Jr. 1986. "Adaptive Behavior and Economic Theory," *Journal of Business* 59(Supp.): S401–S426.

Machina, Mark J. 1990. "Choice under Uncertainty, Volume 1: Risk, Elgar Conference Collection," in Karen Schweers-Cook and Margaret Levi, eds., *The Limits of Rationality.* Chicago: University of Chicago Press, 90–132.

Machina, Mark J. 1999. "A Challenge to the 'Econoclasts': A Commentary on 'Rationality for Economists?'" *Journal of Risk and Uncertainty* 19 (1–3): 107–108.

Manning, W. G., et al. 1991. *The Costs of Poor Health Habits.* Cambridge, Mass.: Harvard University Press.

Mausner, J. S. 1970. "Cigarette Smoking among Patients with Respiratory Disease," *American Review of Respiratory Disease* 102 (5): 704–713.

McFadden, Daniel. 1999. "Rationality for Economists?" *Journal of Risk and Uncertainty* 19 (1–3): 73–105.

Mermelstein, Robin, et al. 1986. "Social Support and Smoking Cessation and Maintenance," *Journal of Consulting and Clinical Psychology* 54 (4): 447–453.

Moolgavkar, S. H., A. Dewanji, and G. Luebeck. 1989. "Cigarette Smoking and Lung Cancer: Reanalysis of the British Doctor's Study," *Journal of the National Cancer Institute* 81: 415–420.

Moore, Michael J., and Carolyn W. Zhu. 2000. "Passive Smoking and Health Care: Health Perceptions Myth as Health Care Reality," *Journal of Risk and Uncertainty* 21 (November): 283–310.

Nagi, S. Z. 1976. "An Epidemiology of Disability among Adults in the United States," *Milbank Memorial Fund Quarterly* 54: 439–468.

National Cancer Institute. 1997. *Changes in Cigarette-Related Disease Risks and Their Implication for Prevention and Control,* Monograph 8, NIH Publication No. 97–4213.

New York Times. 2000. "Justices to Air Dispute over Limiting Cigarette Ads," Jan. 8, p. 1.

Ney, Tara, and Anthony Gale. 1989. *Smoking and Human Behavior.* New York: John Wiley.

Nichols, Albert L., and Richard J. Zeckhauser. 1986. "The Dangers of Caution: Conservatism in Assessment and the Mismanagement of Risk," in V. Kerry Smith, ed., *Advances in Applied Micro-Economics,* vol. 4. Greenwich, Conn.: JAI Press, 55–82.

Novotny, T. E., et al. 1988. "Smoking by Blacks and Whites: Socioeconomic and Demographic Differences," *American Journal of Public Health* 78 (9): 1187–1189.

Ochsner, Alton. 1954. *Smoking and Cancer: A Doctor's Report.* New York: Julian Messner.

O'Reilly, James T. 1997. "Tobacco and the Regulatory Earthquake: Why the FDA Will Prevail after the Smoke Clears," *Northern Kentucky Law Review* 24: 509–533.

Orleans, C. T., et al. 1992. *Smoking among Older Adults: Findings from Three Surveys.* Washington, D.C.: American Association of Retired Persons.

———. 1994a. "Quitting Motives and Barriers among Older Smokers: The 1986 Adult Use of Tobacco Survey Revisited," *Cancer* 74 (7): 2055–2061.

———. 1994b. "Use of Transdermal Nicotine in a State-Level Prescription Plan for the Elderly: A First Look at 'Real-World' Patch Users," *Journal of the American Medical Association* 271 (8): 601–607.

Orphanides, A., and D. Zervos. 1995. "Rational Addiction with Learning and Regret," *Journal of Political Economy* 103: 739–758.

Osler, Merete, et al. 1999. "Gender and Determinants of Smoking Cessation: A Longitudinal Study," *Preventive Medicine* 29: 57–62.

Patton, G. C., et al. 1998. "Depression, Anxiety, and Smoking Initiation: A Prospective Study over 3 Years," *American Journal of Public Health* 88 (10): 1518–1522.

Payne, John W., James R. Bettman, and David R. Schkade. 1999. "Measuring Constructed Preferences: Towards a Building Code," *Journal of Risk and Uncertainty* 19 (1–3): 243–270.

Pearl, Raymond. 1938. "Tobacco Smoking and Longevity," *Science* 87 (March 4): 216–217.

Pearson, David C., et al. 1987. "Smokers and Drinkers in a Health Maintenance Organization Population: Lifestyle and Health Status," *Preventive Medicine* 16: 783–795.

Pertschuk, Michael. 1986. *Giant Killers.* New York: W. W. Norton.

Peto, Richard, and Alan D. Lopez. 2001. "The Future Worldwide Health Effects of Current Smoking Patterns," in C. Everett Koop, Clarence Pearson, and M. Roy Schwarz, eds., *Critical Issues in Global Health.* San Francisco: Jossey-Bass.

Peto, R., et al. 1994. "Mortality from Tobacco in Developed Countries: Indirect Estimation from National Vital Statistics," *Lancet* 339:1268–1278.

———. 1996. "Mortality from Smoking World-wide," *British Medical Bulletin* 52: 12–21.

———. 2000. "Smoking, Smoking Cessation, and Lung Cancer in the U. K. since 1950: Combinatiion of National Statistics with Two Case-Control Studies," *British Medical Journal,* 321 (7257): 323–329.

Pierce, John, et al. 1989. "National Age and Sex Differences in Quitting Smoking," *Journal of Psychoactive Drugs* 21 (3): 293–298.

Rabin, Robert L. 1993. "Institutional and Historical Perspectives on Tobacco Tort Liability," in Robert L. Rabin and Stephen D. Sugarman, eds., *Smoking Policy: Law, Politics, and Culture.* New York: Oxford University Press, 110–130.

Rabin, Robert L., and Stephen D. Sugarman, eds. 1993. *Smoking Policy: Law, Politics, and Culture.* New York: Oxford University Press.

Raffel, Marshall, and Norma Raffel. 1989. *The U.S. Public Health System.* Toronto: John Wiley and Sons, 1989.

Reed, Dwayne M., et al. 1998. "Predictors to Healthy Aging in Men with High Life Expectancies," *American Journal of Public Health* 88 (10): 1463–1468.

Rosow, Il, and N. Breslau. 1966. "A Guttman Health Scale for the Aged," *Journal of Gerontology* 21: 556–559.

Rothman, Alexander J., William Klein, and Neil D. Weinstein. 1996. "Absolute and Relative Biases in Estimations of Personal Risk," *Journal of Applied Social Psychology* 26 (14): 1213–1237.

Royce, J. M., et al. 1993. "Smoking Cessation Factors among African-Americans and Whites: COMMIT Research Group," *American Journal of Public Health* 83 (2): 220–226.

Schelling, Thomas C. 1984. "Self-Command in Practice, in Policy, and in a Theory of Rational Choice," *American Economic Review* 74 (2): 1–11.

———. 1991. "Cigarette Smoking: A Study of Change in Behavior," in Martin Shubik, ed., *Risk, Organizations, and Society.* Boston: Kluwer Academic Publishers, 129–141.

Schmalensee, Richard L. 1972. *On the Economics of Advertising.* Amsterdam: North Holland Press.

Schneider, Lynne, Benjamin Klein, and Kevin M. Murphy. 1981. "Governmental Regulation of Cigarette Health Information," *Journal of Law and Economics* 24 (December): 575–612.

Schoenbaum, Michael. 1997. "Do Smokers Understand the Mortality Effects of Smoking? Evidence from the Health and Retirement Survey," *American Journal of Public Health* 87 (5): 755–764.

Schoenberg, E. H. 1933. "The Demand Curve for Cigarettes," *Journal of Business* 6: 15–35.

Schuessler, Alexander A. 2000. *A Logic of Expressive Choice.* Princeton: Princeton University Press.

Schwartz, John. 1995. "1973 Cigarette Company Memo Proposed New Brands for Teens; RJR Official Cited Need for 'Share of Youth Market,'" *Washington Post,* October 4, p. A2.

Seeman, T. E., et al. 1994. "Predicting Changes in Physical Performance in a High-Functioning Elderly Cohort: MacArthur Studies of Successful Aging," *Journal of Gerontology Medical Sciences* 49: M97–M108.

———. 1995. "Behavioral and Psychosocial Predictors of Physical Performance: MacArthur Studies of Successful Aging," *Journal of Gerontology Medical Sciences* 50A: M177–M183.

Shavell, Stephen. 1987. *Analysis of Accident Law.* Cambridge, Mass.: Harvard University Press.

Shiffman, S., et al. 1997. "A Day at a Time: Predicting Smoking Lapse from Daily Usage," *Journal of Abnormal Psychology* 106: 104–116.

———. 2000. "Dynamic Effects of Self-Efficacy on Smoking Lapse and Relapse" *Health Psychology* 19 (4): 315–323.

Siegel, Michael. 1993. "Smoking and Leukemia: Evaluation of a Causal Hypothesis," *American Journal of Epidemiology* 138 (1): 1–9.

Simon, Julian. 1967. "The Effect of the Competitive Structure upon Expenditures for Advertising," *Quarterly Journal of Economics* 81: 610–627.

Slade, J., et al. 1998. "Nicotine and Addiction: The Brown & Williamson Documents," *Journal of American Medical Association* 274: 225.

Sloan, F. A., V. K. Smith, and D. H. Taylor, Jr. 2001. "Are Smokers Too Optimistic?" in Michael Grossman and Chee-Ruey Hsieh, eds., *The Economic Analysis of Substance Use and Abuse: The Experience of Developed Countries and Lessons for Developing Countries,* Cheltenham, U.K.: Elgar, 103–133.

———. 2002. "Information, Addiction, and 'Bad Choices': Lessons from a Century of Cigarettes," *Economics Letters* 77 (2): 147–155.

Sloan, Frank A., et al. 1998. "Alternative Approaches to Valuing Intangible Health Losses: The Evidence for Multiple Sclerosis," *Journal of Health Economics* 17 (14): 475–497.

———. 2000. *Drinkers, Drivers and Bartenders: Balancing Private Choices and Public Accountability.* Chicago: University of Chicago Press.

———. 2002. "Is Rehabilitation Following an Acute Hospital Stay Productive? Evidence from Elderly Patients in the United States," in Tei Weh Hu and Chee Ruey Hsieh, eds., *The Economics of Health Care in Asia-Pacific Countries.* Cheltenham, U.K.: Elgar, 85–110.

Slovic, Paul. 1987. "Perception of Risk," *Science* 236: 280–285.

———. 1998. "Do Adolescent Smokers Know the Risks?" *Duke Law Journal* 47: 1133–1141.

Slovic, Paul, Baruch Fischhoff, and Sarah Lichtenstein. 1977. "Behavioral Decision Theory," *Annual Review of Psychology* 28:1–39.

———. 1980. "Facts and Fears: Understanding Perceived Risk," in R. C. Schwing and W. A. Albers, ed., *Social Risk Assessment: How Safe Is Safe Enough?* New York: Plenum Press.

Smith, Jeffrey, and Petra Todd. 2000. "Does Matching Overcome Lalonde's Critique of Non-experimental Estimator?" unpublished paper, University of Pennsylvania, October 6.

Smith, V. Kerry. 1997. "Feedback Effects and Environmental Resources," in J. R. Behrman and N. Stacey, eds., *The Sound Benefits of Education.* Ann Arbor: University of Michigan, 175–218.

Smith, V. Kerry, and William H. Desvousges. 1994. "Information and Risk Perceptions—Cholesterol, Radon, and Breast Cancer: A Report on a Pilot Test of 'Bright Lines,'" unpublished notes, North Carolina State University.

Smith, V. Kerry, William H. Desvousges, and John Payne. 1995. "Do Risk Information Programs Promote Mitigating Behavior?" *Journal of Risk and Uncertainty* 10 (May): 203–221.

Smith, V. K., Donald H. Taylor, Jr., and Frank A. Sloan. 2001. "Longevity Expectations and Death: Can People Predict Their Own Demise?" *American Economic Review* 91 (4): 1126–1134.

Smith, V. Kerry, et al. 1987. "Communicating Radon Risk Effectively: A Mid-Course Evaluation." *Report of the U.S. Environmental Protection Agency,* EPA-230–07–87–029.

———. 1989. "Do Smokers Respond to Health Shocks?" unpublished manuscript.

———. 1990. "Can Public Information Programs Affect Risk Perceptions?" *Journal of Policy Analysis and Management* 9 (1): 41–59.

———. 2001. "Do Smokers Respond to Health Shocks?" *Review of Economics and Statistics* 83 (4): 675–687.

———. 2002. "Do Meaningful Smoking Messages Exist?" unpublished paper, North Carolina State University.

Sobel, Robert. 1978. *They Satisfy: The Cigarette in American Life.* New York: Doubleday, 50–51.

Sparrow, David W. 1984. "The Influence of Aging and Smoking on Pulmonary Function," in Raymond Bosse and Charles L. Rose, eds., *Smoking and Aging.* Lexington, Mass.: D. C. Health/Lexington Books, 49–72.

Starr, Paul. 1982. *The Social Transformation of American Medicine.* New York: Basic Books.

Stata Corp. 2001. *Stata Statistical Software,* Release 7.0. College Station, Tex.: Stata Corporation.

Stigler, George, and Gary Becker. 1977. "De Gustibus Non Est Disputandum," *American Economic Review* 67: 76–90.

Suranovic, S. M., R. S. Goldfarb, and T. C. Leonard. 1999. "An Economic Theory of Cigarette Addiction," *Journal of Health Economics* 18 (1): 1–29.

Tate, Cassandra. 1999. *Cigarette Wars: The Triumph of "The Little White Slaver."* New York: Oxford University Press.

Taurus, John A. 1999. "The Transition to Smoking Cessation: Evidence from Multiple Failure Duration Analysis," Working Paper Series. Cambridge, Mass.: National Bureau of Economic Research.

Taylor, Donald H., Jr., et al. 2002. "The Benefits of Smoking Cessation for Longevity," *American Journal of Public Health* 92 (6): 990–996.

Telser, Lester G. 1962. "Advertising and Cigarettes," *Journal of Political Economy* 70: 471–499.

Tennant, R. B. 1950. *The American Cigarette Industry.* New Haven: Yale University Press.

Thaler, Richard H., and H. M. Shefrin. 1981. "An Economic Theory of Self-Control," *Journal of Political Economy* 16 (3): 392–406.

Thun, Michael J., Louis Apicilla, and S. Jane Henley. 2000. "Smoking vs. Other Risk Factors as the Cause of Smoking-Attributable Deaths: Confounding the Courtroom," *Journal of the American Medical Association* 284 (6): 706–712.

Thun, Michael J., and Clark W. Heath, Jr. 1997. "Changes in Mortality from Smoking in Two American Cancer Society Prospective Studies since 1959," *Preventive Medicine* 26: 422–426.

Tiara, Deborah A., et al. 2000. "Impact on Smoking on Health-Related Quality of Life after Percutaneous Coronary Revascularization," *Circulation* 102 (September 19): 1369–1374.

Tversky, Amos, and Daniel Kahneman. 1974. "Judgment under Uncertainty: Heuristics and Biases," *Science* 185: 1124–1131.

U.S. Centers for Disease Control and Prevention. 1999. "Selected Actions of the U.S. Government regarding the Regulation of Tobacco Sales, Marketing, and Use." *www. cdc.gov/tobacco/overview/regulate.htm.*

U.S. Department of Commerce. 1999. *Statistical Abstract of U.S.* Washington, D.C.: U.S. Government Printing Office.

———. 2000. *Statistical Abstract of U.S.* Washington, D.C.: U.S. Government Printing Office.

U.S. Department of Health, Education, and Welfare. 1964. *Smoking and Health: Report of the Advisory Committee to the Surgeon General of the Public Health Service.* Washington, D.C.: U.S. Government Printing Office.

U.S. Department of Health and Human Services. 1989. *Reducing the Health Consequences of Smoking: 25 Years of Progress: A Report of the Surgeon General.* U.S. Department of Health and Human Services.

———. 1990. *The Health Benefits of Smoking Cessation: A Report of the Surgeon General.* Rockville, Md.: Centers for Disease Control, DHHS Pub. No. (CDC) 90–8416.

———. 1991. *Strategies to Control Tobacco Use in the United States: A Blueprint for Public Health Action in the 1990s,* NIH Publication No. 92–3316, National Cancer Institute.

———. 1994. *Preventing Tobacco Use among Young People: A Report of the Surgeon General.* Atlanta: U.S. Dept. of Health and Human Services.

———. 2000. "*Reducing Tobacco Use: A Report of the Surgeon General.* Atlanta: U.S. Department of Health and Human Services.

U.S. Environmental Protection Agency. 1992. *Respiratory Health Effects of Passive Smoking: Lung Cancer and Other Disorders,* EPA 600/6–90/00F. Washington, D.C.: U.S. Environmental Protection Agency, Office of Research and Development (December).

U.S. Food and Drug Administration. 1995. *Nicotine in Cigarettes and Smokeless Tobacco Products Is a Drug and These Products Are Nicotine Delivery Devices under the Federal Food, Drug, and Cosmetic Act (August 1995),* 60 Fed. Reg. 41, 454–41, 787 (August 11).

U.S. National Cancer Institute. *SEER Cancer Statistics Review 1973–1998, http://seer.cancer.gov/Publications/CSR1973_1998/lung.pdf.*

Ussher, Michael H., et al. 2000. "Does Exercise Aid Smoking Cessation? A Systematic Review," *Addiction* 95 (2): 199–208.

Van de Ven, Wynand P. M. M., and Bernard van Praag. 1981. "The Demand for Deductibles in Private Health Insurance: A Probit Model with Sample Selection," *Journal of Econometrics* 17 (2): 229–252.

Viscusi, W. Kip. 1990. "Do Smokers Underestimate Risks?" *Journal of Political Economy* 98 (6): 1253–1268.

———. 1991. "Age Variations in Risk Perceptions and Smoking Decisions," *The Review of Economics and Statistics* 73 (4): 577–588.

———. 1992. *Smoking: Making the Risky Decision.* New York: Oxford University Press.

Viscusi, W. Kip, and Jahn K. Hakes. 1998. "Why the Health and Retirement Study Survival Probability Is Not a Probability," unpublished paper, Harvard University.

Viscusi, W. Kip, Jahn K. Hakes, and Alan Carlin. 1997. "Measures of Mortality Risks," *Journal of Risk and Uncertainty* 14 (3): 213–233.

Vita, Antony J., et al. 1998. "Aging, Health Risks, and Cumulative Disability," *New England Journal of Medicine* 338 (15): 1035–1041.

Wagenknecht, L. E., et al. 1993. "Environmental Tobacco Smoke Exposure as Determined by Cotinine in Black and White Young Adults: The CARDIA Study," *Environmental Research* 63 (1): 39–46.

Warner, Kenneth E. 1981. "Cigarette Smoking in the 1970s: The Impact of the Advertising Campaign on Consumption," *Science* 24 (February 13): 729–731.

———. 1985. "Cigarette Advertising and Media Coverage of Smoking and Health," *Journal of the American Medical Association* 312 (6): 384–388.

———. 1989. "Effects of the Antismoking Campaign: An Update," *American Journal of Public Health* 79 (February): 144–151.

Warner, Kenneth E., et al. 1986. "Promotion of Tobacco Products: Issues and Policy Options," *Journal of Health Politics, Policy and Law* 11: 367–392.

Wasserman, J., et al. 1991. "The Effects of Excise Taxes and Regulations on Cigarette Smoking," *Journal of Health Economics* 10 (1): 43–64.

Watson, Ronald R., and Mart Witten, eds. 2001. *Environmental Tobacco Smoke.* Boca Raton: CRC Press.

Waxman, Henry. 1994. "Regulation of Tobacco Products," Hearings before the Subcommittee on Health and the Environment of the House Committee on Commerce and Energy, 103rd Congress, 2nd sess., pt. 2, pp. 418–522.

Weinblatt E., S. Shapiro, and C. W. Frank. 1971. "Changes in Personal Characteristics of Men, over Five Years, Following First Diagnosis of Coronary Heart Disease," *American Journal of Public Health* 61 (4): 831–842.

Weinstein, Neil D. 1989. "Optimistic Biases about Personal Risks," *Science* 246 (4935): 1232–1233.

Weiss, Scott T. 1984. "Chronic Bronchitis, Asthma, and Obstructive Airways Disease: Age, Smoking, and Other Risk Factors," in Raymond Bosse and Charles L. Rose, eds., *Smoking and Aging.* Lexington, Mass.: D. C. Health/Lexington Books, 73–94.

White, Larry C. 1988. *Merchants of Death: The American Tobacco Industry.* New York: Beech Tree Books.

Winston, Gordon C. 1980. "Addiction and Backsliding: A Theory of Compulsive Consumption," *Journal of Economic Behavior and Organization* 1: 295–324.

Wray, Linda A., A. Regula Herzog, and Robert J. Willis. 1998. "The Impact of Education and Heart Attack on Smoking Cessation among Middle-Aged Adults," *Journal of Health and Social Behavior* 39: 271–294.

Wynder, Ernst L., and M. Orlandi. 1991. "Smoking and Health Promotion: Obstacles and Opportunities," in Martin Shubik, ed., *Risk, Organizations, and Society.* Boston: Kluwer Academic Publishers, 105–128.

Zhang, Zuo-Feng, et al. 1996. "Adenocarcinomas of the Esophagus and Gastric Cardia: Medical Conditions, Tobacco, Alcohol, and Socioeconomic Factors," *Cancer Epidemiology, Biomarkers and Prevention* 5: 761–768.

Index